DAYLIGHT IN THE SWAMP

Robert W. Wells

NORTHWORD
PRESS, INC

Box 1360 • Minocqua, WI 54548

To Edith

Library of Congress Cataloging in Publication Data
Wells, Robert W.
Daylight in the swamp.
1. Lumbering—Lake States—History.
2. Lumber trade—Lake States—History.
I. Title. HD9757.A14W44 338.4'7'6740977
Library of Congress Catalog Card Number 77-77666
ISBN 0-942802-07-1

Cover illustration by Gryphon Studio.
Cover design by Moonlit Ink.
Printed in the United States of America by George Banta Company, Inc.

For a free catalog describing NorthWord's line of nature books and gifts,
call 1-800-336-5666

Contents

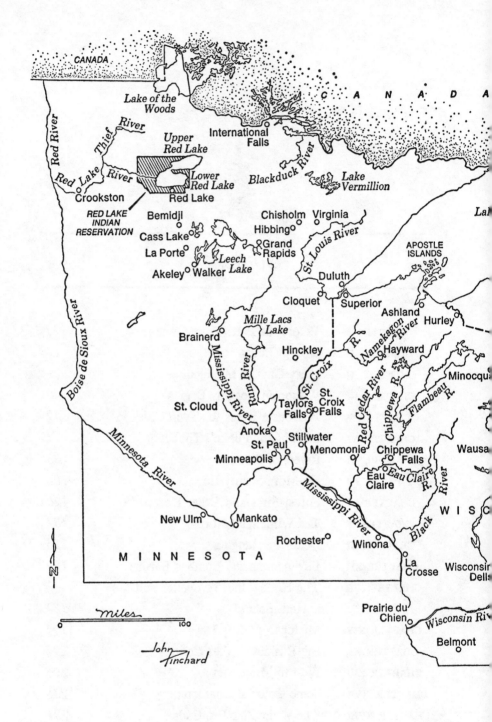

DAYLIGHT IN THE SWAMP!

ISLE ROYALE

Superior

Houghton

Lake Superior

CANADA

Ontonagon

Ontonagon River

Ewen

Michigamme River

Seney

Sault St. Marie

MICHIGAN

Manistique

Escanaba

Florence

Menominee River

Rhinelander

Cheboygan

Lake Huron

Peshtigo River

Oconto River

Menominee

Thunder Bay River

Alpena

Thunder Bay

Wolf River

Peshtigo

Marinette

Au Sable River

Stevens Point

Traverse City

Oscoda

Green Bay

Manistee

Cadillac

Titabawassee River

N S I N

Oshkosh

Muskegon River

Tobacco River

Bay City

Saginaw River

Cass River

Sheboygan

Averill

Fond du Lac

Saginaw

Portage

Muskegon

Ionia

Shiawassee River

Flint River

Port Huron

Madison

Milwaukee

Lansing

CANADA

Lake Geneva

Holland

Detroit

Lake Michigan

MICHIGAN

Acknowledgments

IN RESEARCHING THIS BOOK, I have searched for nuggets of information in several hundred articles, most notably in *The Wisconsin Magazine of History* and in files of the Milwaukee *Journal,* and delved into dozens of books. Among the latter are these:

Stewart H. Holbrook's *Burning an Empire* (Macmillan, New York, 1943), *Holy Old Mackinaw* (Macmillan, New York, 1938) and *Yankee Loggers* (International Paper Company, New York, 1961); George Forester's *History of the Chippewa Valley* (A. Warner, Chicago, 1892); L. G. Sorden's *Loggers Words of Yesteryears* (Wm. C. Brown, Dubuque, 1956) and *Lumberjack Lingo* (Wisconsin House, Madison, 1969); Walker D. Wyman's *The Lumberjack Frontier* (University of Nebraska Press, 1969); Clint Dunathan's *The Century Book: Escanaba* (Photo Offset Printing Company, Escanaba, 1963); James K. Jamison's *This Ontonagon Country* (Ontonagon Herald Company, Ontonagon, 1939); James I. Clark's *The Wisconsin Pineries* (State Historical Society of Wisconsin, Madison, 1956); John E. Nelligan's *A White Pine Empire* (North Star Press, St. Cloud, 1969) and *The Life of a Lumberman,* as told to Charles M. Sheridan (Wisconsin State Historical Society, Madison, 1929); Robert C. Nesbit's *Wisconsin* (University of Wisconsin Press, Madison, 1973); Robert F. Fries' *Empire in Pine* (State Historical Society of Wisconsin, Madison, 1951); Walter Havighurst's *Upper Mississippi* (Farrar & Rinehart, New York, 1937) and *The Long Ships Passing* (Macmillan, New York, 1942); Grace Lee Nute's *Lake Superior* (Bobbs-Merrill, Indianapolis, 1944); James Stevens' *The Saginaw Paul Bunyan*

(Knopf, New York, 1932); Irene Hargreaves and Harold M. Foehl's *The Story of Logging the White Pine in the Saginaw Valley* (Red Keg Press, Bay City, 1964); E. C. Beck's *They Knew Paul Bunyan* (University of Michigan Press, Ann Arbor, 1956); Gerard Schultz's *Walls of Flame* (privately printed, 1968); William H. Ellis' *Pick-ups and a Horse* (privately printed, Oscoda, Michigan, 1975); Walter L. Blair's *A Raft Pilot's Log* (Arthur H. Clark, Cleveland, 1930); Euclid J. Bourgeois, John G. Morrison, Jr., and Charles L. Wight's *Mainly Logging* (Minneota Clinic, Minneota, Minnesota, 1974); David C. Smith's *A History of Lumbering in Maine* (University of Maine Press, Orono, 1972); Paul Wallace Gates' *The Wisconsin Pine Lands of Cornell University* (Cornell University Press, Ithaca, 1943); Richard N. Current's *Wisconsin in the Civil War Era* (State Historical Society of Wisconsin, Madison, 1976); *Menominee Illustrated* (Art Gravure & Etching Company, Milwaukee, 1891); John Bartlow Martin's *Call It North Country* (Knopf, New York, 1944); Lewis C. Reimann's *When Pine Was King* (Edwards Brothers, Ann Arbor, 1952); Reuben Gold Thwaites' *Wisconsin in Three Centuries* (Century History Company, Madison, 1906); Isaac Stephenson's *Recollections of a Long Life* (R. R. Donnelly, Chicago, 1915); John D. Guthrie's *Great Forest Fires in America* (U. S. Government Printing Office, Washington, D.C.); James I. Clark's *Farming the Cutover, Cutover Problems* and *The Wisconsin Pineries* (State Historical Society of Wisconsin, Madison, 1956) and the Reverend E. J. Goodspeed's *History of the Great Fires in Chicago and the West* (privately printed, Chicago, 1871).

Foreword

I'VE BEEN PLANNING to write this book for more than ten years, ever since I spent time in and around the old lumber town of Hayward, Wisconsin. My visit was under the expert guidance of Eldon Marple, who worked in logging camps as a lad and never quite escaped from the fascination of that experience. The lumberjacks I met were old men then. But their recollections of life in the big woods before the white pine was gone convinced me that this story of one of the most colorful periods of American history would be worth the telling.

I've been squirreling away material on lumberjack life ever since. Some came from conversations with men who were present during the tag end of an era when the North was as wild as the West used to be. Some came from written recollections of logging's pioneer days. Other sources ranged from scholarly books and articles to newspaper accounts printed before events in the pinery had congealed into history.

To tell about that time in Michigan, Wisconsin and Minnesota, I have had to go back farther in time and move eastward geographically to Maine and New Brunswick, where the pattern for the three Lake States was established. I also found that the era was more complex than it had seemed at first glance, necessitating discussions not only of logging, rafting and lumbering but of lynchings, barroom brawls, gamblers, madams, preachers, timber thieves; of natural and man-made disasters; of men who became rich through hard work or shady dealing, and of men who stayed poor and didn't much care.

It was a time like no other. The legacy it left was mixed—rotting stumps in useless fields on the one hand, boards to build a nation on the other.

Robert W. Wells
Delafield, Wisconsin, 1977

CHAPTER I

Before the Pines Were Gone

"THE FIRST DAYS," Thomas Pederson recalled when he was an old man looking back on his youth in a Wisconsin lumber camp, "the backbreaking work made me so stiff and sore that I could barely walk when night came. That, however, soon wore off. Our foreman was a peppery little Frenchman . . . He would rouse us very early in the morning and it was into the cook shanty for breakfast. Then, when we were back in the sleeping shanty, he would throw the door open and yell, 'Daylight in the swamp!'

"That was the signal for us to file out of the shanty, collect our tools and march out to the choppings. Nearly always it was so dark that we couldn't see to work, but he was bound to have us out there . . . There was competition in everything. The sawyers had to count the logs they sawed each day and report to the foreman every evening. So also the skidders, who followed the sawyers with an ox team and hauled the logs out to the road where they were rolled up on a rollway ready for the teamsters to load on their sleds and take to the river."

Pederson remembered what it had been like to work in a forest where the white pines grew so thick that no underbrush sprouted and the sky could not be seen overhead. Some of the trees were more than a hundred feet tall. The biggest one he sawed that winter measured six feet across at the butt. The crosscut saw was only eighteen inches longer than that, so it took the young man and his partner the better part of a forenoon to bring the giant crashing to earth. This tree stood out among its fellows, but the others were impressive enough. A tree less than three feet in diameter at the stump was considered too small in those days to be worth the cutting.

Pederson's first logging camp was a small one, with only twenty men. The facilities were primitive—a log sleeping shanty, a log cook shanty that also served as dining room, a log barn for the horses and oxen. The buildings had been put up in the fall by the logging crew, and the cook's hut stocked with such staples as dried beans, prunes and salt meat. Rude bunks were built, with the men cutting evergreen boughs to serve in place of mattresses. Legs were attached to a split log to form a bench called the deacon seat, where the men could perch in the evening and relax before their early bedtime.

Aside from such tools as axes and saws, most of the things needed in camp were fashioned on the spot from logs, wire or whatever else came to hand. Such preliminaries were hurried through. The goal was to get such chores finished and start on the work the men had been hired for—cutting down tall pines, sawing them into logs and getting them to the bank of a stream which would carry them to the mill when the ice melted in the spring. Until railroads snaked into the wilderness, loggers depended on high water created by melting snow to move their product to the snarling saws that waited downstream. The pattern was to cut the trees in the winter, when the timber could be moved on sleds, use the rivers to transport the pine in spring, and operate the sawmills in the summer as long as the supply of logs held out.

Even in a small camp, the work was divided. Under the foreman's direction, some men cut down the trees and sawed them into sixteen-foot lengths; some skidded the logs to the road that had been chopped through the forest; some loaded them on sleds; others drove the horses or oxen that hauled the sleds to the riverbank.

"In our camp," Pederson said, "there were three gangs of sawyers and as many skidders. So it was a constant race every day, each gang striving to outdo the others. It was a fine thing for the boss and also for the contractor. We were all onto the game. But we didn't care. Every gang strained itself to make the best showing.

". . . The teamsters and loaders had a hard life of it. It was seven miles from camp to the river landing and the schedule called for so many trips per day . . . They had to get up at 3 o'clock in the morning and often they didn't get in at night till 10, sometimes 11 o'clock. The trips had to be made, mishaps or no mishaps."

Pederson's schedule was a little shorter. As a sawyer, he could sleep until 4 A.M. and he was required to work merely from first light until it was too dark to see. For this, he got a bed of sorts, three hearty but monotonous meals a day, Sundays off, and something in the neighborhood of a dollar a day, less what he spent in the company store, or "wanigan," for tobacco and other necessities.

When he went home after that logging season was over, Pederson had a hundred dollars in cash, the hide of a bear he had shot and a bear cub he had captured. It was, he felt, recompense enough.

The era when men like him cut the primeval pine ended not long after the twentieth century began. It is a time that will never come again. Perhaps it's just as well. From Maine to Minnesota, enormous quantities of timber resources were wasted. Much of it was stolen from its legal owners, particularly the public. Dozens of now staid communities in Maine, New York, Pennsylvania, Michigan, Wisconsin and Minnesota were founded mainly to provide saloons, whorehouses and gambling halls to separate lumberjacks and sawmill workers from their earnings with maximum efficiency. And when the pines were gone—particularly in the three Lake States of Michigan, Minnesota and Wisconsin—vast regions were left a stump-filled wasteland.

But that is only one side of the story. The period when such men pitted muscles, axes and saws against a seemingly endless sea of green left memories of an epic period comparable only to the days of the old and equally wild West. The 400-year-old pines that fell before this hard-drinking army of men in mackinaws became raw material for housing half a continent at a time when America was young and full of beans, an era when it was rushing hell-bent across the treeless plains toward the Rockies and the Pacific.

Everything about this period was larger than ordinary life. The log jams in the rivers might stretch for twenty miles in the spring, when the big sticks floated to the mills—along with the bodies of a few men who had failed to balance themselves on the moving and treacherous river of pine. The forest fires were like nothing seen before or since. Lynchings, casual violence, death in icy rivers or from failure to dodge a widowmaker in the big woods—all these were part of the roaring period when most of the nation's white pine was cut.

The cutting made a few men rich. It turned tens of thousands of others into unwashed examples of Darwin's theory that only the fittest survive. They were a tough and agile breed, willing to work hard under miserable conditions, content with enough pay to finance a brief springtime fling.

There were exceptions, but in general the woods workers seemed to have a downright un-American disrespect for owning things. In a period when soaring ambition and a touch of greed were considered civic virtues, most lumberjacks said to hell with it. Pines were there to be cut, money to be spent, bottles to be emptied. When any of the three was gone, why worry? There would always be more over the next hill.

They knew their place, these men who called themselves shanty boys. When there were trees to be felled, that place was in the woods. When there were logs to be run, it was on the rushing river. And when there was action to be had, it was smack dab in the middle of it so there'd be something to brag about next winter on the deacon seat in the bunkhouse.

CHAPTER II

How It Began

BEFORE THE FORESTS of the three Lake States had felt an axe, the pattern for their destruction was established in the State of Maine and eastern Canada. A Maine lumberjack who passed out in a Bangor saloon and awakened in a nineteenth-century lumber camp in Michigan, Wisconsin or Minnesota would have felt right at home.

Still, America's first lumberjack boss was not a Yankee but a short-tempered Englishman. In 1607, Captain John Smith sent men of Virginia's Jamestown Colony to chop down trees to be sawed into boards to build houses. He ran into a predictable problem. The men started using language that, in the captain's opinion, endangered their immortal souls. So he decreed that each time a man used a naughty word, cold water would be poured down his sleeve.

Smith's forthright example in discouraging profanity was not followed by other logging bosses in the three centuries it took to convert the world's mightiest forests into boards and sawdust. Tackling giant pines was a task for the strong, so strong language seemed to help. So did sweat, long hours and the shimmering lure of a payday spree involving hard liquor and soft women.

Smith's crew hacked down enough trees to build fifty houses, but it's stretching a point to call these amateurs lumberjacks. Not until 1631, when the first sawmill in what became the United

States was erected on the Salmon Falls River in the future State of Maine, did felling trees become a specialized occupation.

That mill chewed through pine logs supplied by lumberjacks who challenged the nearby wilderness, standing on the eastern edge of an ocean of pine that seemed as limitless as the Atlantic at their backs. The pineries began in Maine and New Brunswick, stretching westward through Canada and upper New York to Michigan, Wisconsin and Minnesota before tapering off in Manitoba and Saskatchewan. There was enough prime lumber there to build the cities, villages and farms of two nations.

In 1631, no one knew what enormous resources lay to the west or, for that matter, cared. If there was one thing the new continent had in surplus it was trees. Only agents of the British king worried about how wastefully they were being used up.

Officers of the Royal Navy who looked at the forests saw not houses, not churches, not even taverns, but masts. No such trees as these had grown in Europe for a thousand years. To rule the waves, Britannia needed ships propelled by mighty sails. The admirals had been having trouble finding trees tall and straight enough to handle the billowing canvas. To a navy man, the new continent was a reservoir of tall masts which could help English seamen sail faster than Frenchmen or Spaniards.

A mainmast might weigh eighteen tons. The fact that New England pine was a fourth lighter than the Baltic fir formerly used was important. Besides, the trunks of two fir trees had to be spliced together to form a mainmast for a large ship, while a single white pine could do the job.

At first, there seemed to be no end to this naval resource. But that rude sawmill on the Salmon Falls River was only the first. Soon every New England community with a running stream wanted one. An unbeatable method of insuring neighborly cooperation to build a mill was worked out. A man ambitious to go into the sawing trade merely had to lay in a supply of strong drink. His friends gathered to put down his liquor and put up his mill, and soon his saws were beginning to chew up another part of the forest. There's a record of one such mill-raising in Connecticut in 1672. It cost the owner a bottle of brandy, two gallons of whiskey, three gallons of rum and a barrel of hard cider.

Nineteen years after those good neighbors recovered from their hangovers, the Royal Navy awoke to the likelihood that the colonists were going to waste all those lovely masts in the woods by making boards of them. The admirals spoke to the king. The king spoke to his ministers. The ministers issued rules. Any pine or oak that measured more than two feet at the butt and was within three miles of a stream belonged to the Crown. A settler or lumberjack who cut it could wind up in jail. If Captain Smith had been around when word of that order reached New England, he would have had to pour cold water down the sleeve of every male within reach.

To show he meant business, King William III sent men tramping through the woods marking trees with the sign of a broad arrow, which meant the pine or oak belonged to His Majesty, not some unwashed fellow with an axe. Timber stealing had not yet become the organized art it would attain in the Lake States two centuries hence. But the pioneers scorned the king's authority. If William III wanted a pine, let him grab an axe and chop one down. Otherwise, to hell with him and his broad arrow.

Each colony's surveyor general was charged with enforcing the law. Some tried. David Dunbar, for instance, let lumberjacks cut the king's pines and haul them or float them to the mill. Then he seized the boards made from the forbidden trees. So the colonists put on war paint and feathers and seized them right back, beating up the king's agents in the process. The New Hampshire surveyor general reported to London that the colonists there said they'd cut any tree they damned well pleased. Of seventy pines marked with the broad arrow near Exeter, he added, only one was still standing. The rest had been cut and hauled away.

Now and then, the king's men caught a logger red-handed. When he was brought to trial, one of two things happened. Either his friends smashed down the jailhouse door and turned him loose, or a jury of his neighbors declared he was not guilty.

The Pine Tree Riot took place in 1772 in Weare, New Hampshire, when a deputy sheriff tried to confiscate 270 of the king's logs, found in Clement's Mill Yard. Sheriff Benjamin Whiting and Deputy John Quigley arrested a timber cutter with the fine old Yankee name of Ebenezer Mudgett, ordering him to post bail. Instead, Mudgett and his friends grabbed the two lawmen, cut switches in the woods and whipped them out of town.

The matter of the Royal Navy's living masts caused no end of hard feelings on both sides, with the colonists losing some of their ancestral respect for the Crown and the British getting increasingly fed up with those scofflaws in the woods. Bostonians who dumped English tea got more attention from historians than the axemen who stole the king's pines. But around that portion of Massachusetts that would, in 1820, become the State of Maine, there was little doubt about why a revolution was necessary. In 1775, when news arrived that there had been skirmishes at Lexington and Concord, Colonel Samuel Thompson and his Maine men knew exactly what to do—they marched off and attacked King George III's mast agent, capturing several hundred felled trees and squared timbers. Even after the colonies became the United States, the loggers continued to set their own rules. They had little patience with distant authority, whether it was in London, Washington or a state capital.

After Maine became a state, no one was quite sure where the boundary line separating it from New Hampshire and Quebec should be drawn. While the politicians argued, tax collectors from all three jurisdictions tried to collect from timber owners and lumberjacks in an area that became part of New Hampshire's Coos County. So in 1832, the region seceded. The woods dwellers established the Republic of the United Inhabitants of Indian Stream Territory, elected Luther Parker president, adopted a constitution and issued currency. If an outside tax collector showed up, he was thrown in jail.

Neither Quebec nor New Hampshire acted with undue haste to restore sovereignty, but finally they made simultaneous plans for an invasion of the new republic. New Hampshire's militia arrived first. The soldiers threw Parker out of the presidency, released those imprisoned tax men and eliminated the republic. Still, it lasted three years, which wasn't bad for a nation with a population of a few hundred men and several women that defied the United States, Canada, Maine, Quebec, New Hampshire and anybody else who cared to join the argument. The Indian Stream Territory Republic helped persuade Washington and London that it was time to decide where the dividing line between Canada and New

England should be drawn. Daniel Webster and Lord Ashburton started discussing the matter.

Meanwhile, there was another flare-up in northeastern Maine. Loggers there complained that "Blue Nosers" from New Brunswick were cutting their logs. The Canadian lumbermen claimed the Yankees were also trespassing.

In the mutual stealing of timber that was going on, New Brunswick had a geographical advantage. The Aroostook River flows through Maine into that province, where it joins the St. John River. If a New Brunswick logger crossed the border and dumped a load of Maine pine into the Aroostook, then let nature take its course, the logs would wind up safely in Canada.

The War of 1812 had ended less than a quarter century before, and there was considerable sentiment in Maine for starting another with the British Empire. Rafts of logs floating down the Aroostook toward New Brunswick were seized and tied up. Blue Nosers sneaked through the underbrush and cut them loose again. Oxen belonging to rival outfits were shot. Stacks of wild hay, cut laboriously as feed, were set afire. Maine posses chased the invaders. There were battles with fists and axe handles along the Aroostook. The New Brunswick loggers were as rough a bunch as the Maine variety, the principal difference being that the Canadians were more apt to swear in French and wear red sashes.

Guns were considered a poor way to settle an argument when fists, feet and teeth were available, so fatalities were rare in the international skirmishing there in the woods. But combatants lost ears or came down with logger's smallpox, an ailment named for the characteristic print made by spiked boots on the skin of a fallen opponent's chest.

In 1839, pressure was brought to bear on Maine politicians and a dozen militia companies were sent north to reinforce the local combatants. The soldiers trudged two hundred miles through the snow, dragging a brass cannon, then threw up a couple of log blockhouses and settled down to fight the Aroostook War.

A problem quickly developed, however. The Maine men had walked as far as they cared to go, and the New Brunswick contingent saw little profit in attacking the forts. Action was confined to long-range sniping. But it began to be clear that there was a chance that a marksman would actually hit somebody, escalating the neighborhood dispute into an international crisis. So Webster and Ashburton began to negotiate more earnestly and in 1842 their treaty was signed, establishing the boundaries. The Aroostook continued to flow into Canada, the lumberjacks continued to fight in the saloons, but the militia marched home and the war was over.

Saloon fights were normal recreation in the woods towns of Maine, New Brunswick and points west. This became part of a pattern that was followed while the pines lasted, and it didn't matter whether the pines were in Maine or in Michigan, Minnesota or Wisconsin.

As the years went by, equipment for handling the cutting and transporting of trees improved. Crews became larger in number, better fed, better housed. But the basic techniques used were those developed in the State of Maine.

It was widely believed in the Lake States that the best lumberjacks came from there. A job applicant who could brag of experience along the Penobscot, the Kennebec or the Androscoggin was signed on at once. If his home address was Bangor, he might be made foreman—a Bangor Tiger was in a class by himself.

Bangor was the forerunner of a thousand settlements of various sizes that grew up to saw logs, supply lumber camps and separate the loggers from their pay. Unlike many of its counterparts, the city on the Penobscot did not depend entirely on logging and lumbering, however. It was also a shipbuilding center and a port for sailing ships that made their way from the ocean fifty miles away.

With two million acres of white pine and black spruce at Bangor's doorstep, its first sawmill began cutting logs before the Revolutionary War. When the United States first began to be settled, all but the biggest cities had enough trees handy to take care of their needs. But by the 1830s, many communities had outgrown the nearby wood supply and the pineries began to be exploited by specialists, such as the ones who converged on Bangor each spring with a winter's pay in their pockets and fire in their eyes.

Like the lumberjacks, operators of the establishments which grew up to relieve the woods workers of their earnings had to learn their trade. At first, it was the custom in the saloons to permit a man to help himself from an open barrel of rum, using a tin dipper hung from the side. The price was three cents per dipper-ful. For less than two bits, a 'jack could wash out the memory of fifteen-hour days in the winter woods. For a few cents more, he could wash out the memory of everything else, at least until morning.

There were two hotels in Bangor's early days where a man could sleep off his bender. If sleep was not what he had in mind, there were houses on Exchange Street with demure signs in front reading GENTLEMEN'S WASHING DONE. Now and then, a greenhorn actually knocked on the door with an armload of dirty shirts, causing no end of feminine hilarity.

Maine land originally sold at the rate of two acres for twenty-five cents, the price paid by a Pennsylvanian, William Bingham, who knew a bargain when he saw one. He bought two million acres of pines, a region vast enough so it took lumberjacks a century to harvest it. But by the 1830s, the cost of pinery land had soared to as high as ten dollars an acre and there were nearly as many real estate men in Bangor as saloonkeepers. One group of speculators took in $127,000 in a single day's sales, providing a washtub full of champagne to keep the bidding spirited.

Most of the Maine pinery wound up in a few hands, as was to happen with similar acreage in the Lake States. General Sam Veazie, for instance, acquired enough territory for a principality, along with sixty-two sawmills, the Penobscot Boom Company and his own town.

General Sam also had his own railroad eventually, but in the early days of lumbering the rivers supplied the only means of moving logs to the mills. This limited cutting to areas near enough to a stream so that oxen or horses could drag the logs to its banks on crude roads fashioned by men with axes and saws. The Merrimack, the Saco, the Piscataqua, the St. Croix as well as the Androscoggin and Penobscot were notable highways for this specialized form of commerce. But the longest of the New England logging rivers was the Connecticut, which crossed Vermont, New Hampshire and Massachusetts before reaching Connecticut and finally merging into Long Island Sound. The Connecticut had its dangerous stretches for the men who called themselves river pigs and drove logs to the mill. No less than twenty of them died at various times at a point called Fifteen Mile Falls, for instance.

There were other kinds of hazards in the towns that grew up along the Connecticut's banks. At Woodsville, New Hampshire, for example, there were enough saloons and whorehouses to accommodate even the spring rush of business. The lumberjacks who drove logs were the cream of a hardy crop and fully able to take care of themselves when sober. But not many stayed sober long in Woodsville. Some townsfolk were not above teaching them the hazards of drink by stealing their pay when they'd passed out.

A river driver, Ed Smith, demonstrated the potency of Woodsville alcohol by falling in love with a wax dummy in the show window of Sargent's Store. The manikin, dressed fetchingly in silk hose and corset, struck him as being exactly the girl he had in mind. He tried to give her a preliminary pat and was startled to find she was separated from him by plate glass.

"The hell you say," Ed muttered, backing up to get a good start, then jumping feet first through the window.

His friends found him lying morosely on a bed of jagged glass, still puzzled over the lady's lack of interest in romance but otherwise unhurt. The following year, Smith was killed by a log at Perry Falls. But his name went down in the oral history that was dispensed to newcomers in the logging camps.

So did the memory of Bert Ingersoll, who was swept over a dam in the Connecticut at Bellows Falls. With death clawing at him from below, he reached out and grabbed an iron peg set into the cement, pulling himself up to a log that formed part of the boom. He perched there, gazing thoughtfully down. Somebody yelled to ask what he was doing.

"I'm just looking at my fingerprints on that iron," Bert yelled back.

Bellows Falls was not far from North Walpole, best remembered in bunkhouse yarns as the headquarters of a professional woman known as Old Colorado. North Walpole was a lively village with eighteen saloons. When the spring drive on the Connecticut reached there, Old Colorado was waiting in her tent. But unlike most in her profession, she was willing to share her customers' hardships when business was slow. Each spring she headed upstream to First Falls and followed the log drive down. Old Colorado was no beauty, the river pigs said, but she knew how to get ahead of her competition.

Her rates varied between fifty cents and a dollar—that is, between half a day's pay and a full day's pay for a lumberjack. But she was willing to dicker, as demonstrated one morning when she encountered a logging crew. The drive had been going well, the men had been working hard, and the boss decided they deserved a treat.

"How much for the whole gang?" he asked Old Colorado.

"How many?"

"Forty."

"Eighteen bucks."

The deal was, you might say, consummated there in the woods. The wholesale rate figured out to forty-five cents each, a nickel rebate from Old Colorado's usual minimum.

New York State temporarily took the lead in lumbering in 1840, outdistancing Maine. Bangor was still the place men talked about when discussing logging, but by 1850 Glens Falls on the Hudson surpassed it. Maine lumberjacks were cutting more trees than ever, but the Adirondack region had more efficient methods of chewing up logs, having adopted the circular saw more readily than had the mills of Maine, some of which were still making do with the old-fashioned "muley" variety that moved up and down. The circular saw could create nearly as many boards in an hour as the muley could in a day. It cut a wide and wasteful kerf, the channel made in the wood with each passage of the saw. But the stock of trees was considered inexhaustible, so that was regarded as a minor drawback.

New Yorkers had heard of the roistering reputation of Maine lumberjacks, and attempts were made to change the pattern. The first temperance society in the nation was organized at Moreau, near Glens Falls. Forty-three loggers were persuaded to sign a pledge to drink only water, agreeing to a fine of twenty-five cents each time they downed something stronger. The society did not last long, however, and the woods workers of New York and Pennsylvania were not much different from those in New England, where it was said a lumberjack would eat a bale of hay if someone sprinkled it with whiskey.

Midway in the nineteenth century, more than six thousand sawmills were operating in New York State, many driven by steam instead of water power. By 1860, however, Pennsylvania had pulled into the lead in lumbering, with Williamsport on the Susquehanna the principal center. And beginning in 1835, with the opening of the Erie Canal, the eastern mills began to feel the first faint breeze of competition from Michigan, an indication of changes ahead.

Williamsport had thirty sawmills, but what impressed John E. Nelligan, a New Brunswick Irishman who worked there before heading for Wisconsin, was a new way of moving timber. A slide three miles long was built of logs. It descended gradually through a ravine to the river, with smaller slides feeding into it. When the weather turned cold, the slides were iced. Logs slipped merrily along them for a considerable distance by gravity, then were pulled the rest of the way by a rope attached to a team. The two horses, Nelligan reported, could drag as many as seventy-five logs at a time, thanks to the slippery slide.

Maine continued to live up to its reputation as the Pine Tree State, its production rising even though it never regained the lead in lumbering as the principal centers of that industry moved gradually westward. The co-operative sorting boom originated in Maine. A Maine blacksmith, Joe Peavey, improved the cantdog— also known as "the swinging bitch"—into a more useful tool. The peavey, a pole with an adjustable hook at one end, kept logs moving on the Lake States' rivers for several generations, carrying Joe's name with it.

The Maine influence was reflected in Lake States geography. There were at least three other Stillwaters and five other Bangors in the new lumber country. The St. Croix River, which forms part of the boundary between Maine and New Brunswick, is matched by a longer St. Croix that forms part of the boundary between Wisconsin and Minnesota.

Maine's white-pine period occurred mainly before the Civil War, but when those giants were gone there was still plenty of wood left to cut. The state remained a part of the world closely identified with lumbering even after the rise of the Lake States to leadership in that field. Maine's loggers were its most conspicuous residents. A few lived in fine mansions, drank imported wine and brought their horses and mistresses from distant places. Most lived in log hovels during the working season and were content with such amenities as raw whiskey and such temporary companions as Old Colorado.

Traditional logging methods were destined to last longer in Maine than anywhere else. What will presumably be America's last log drive took place on the Kennebec in 1976. A crew working for the Kennebec Log Driving Company spent the time from "ice-out to ice-in" superintending the waterborne delivery, ending 141 years of such activity by the company.

When that firm was organized in 1835, it had served sixty-three sawmills. By 1976, it served only the Scott Paper Company pulp mill. By then, the logs were mere four-footers, which early loggers would have considered unworthy of their skills. The legislature bowed to pressure from environmentalists, sportsmen and city folks and decreed that after 1976 it would no longer be legal to float logs to mills in the Pine Tree State.

Luckily for timid politicians, such distinguished earlier residents of Maine as Dirty Joe Bullie, Jigger Jones and Dick Sweat were no longer around to protest this end of a proud tradition. These men would either have ignored the law or taken after the legislators with a peavey.

Bullie, proud to be known as the dirtiest cook in the Maine woods, took direct action in a camp along the Kennebec one winter when he decided the rats were taking more than their proper share of the food. He balanced a board over an open molasses barrel and placed a chunk of salt pork on the end. When a rat went after the bait, it fell in the barrel.

Each morning, Dirty Joe fished out his night's catch before ladling out the molasses for the crew's pancakes. This went on for several days before Dick Sweat discovered why his breakfast had a new flavor. He finished his meal without comment—there was a rule against talking at the table. But after he and his friends had finished feeding, sopping up the last drop of molasses on their plates, he jumped onto the table and walked the length of it, kicking all the dishes to the floor. Joe got the point and found other methods to outwit the rats.

Jigger Jones was not at that camp. If he had been, it's unlikely he would have minded a few rodents in his molasses. Jigger didn't care what he ate, as long as there was plenty of it. Only once did he pass up his full quota of calories. He was working in a camp with a woman cook, which was bad enough. But her hair was worn long and had a tendency to fall out. Jigger startled his friends by refusing to eat her pie, pointing out that it needed a shave.

Like his predecessor, Captain John Smith, Jigger was a student of the Bible and frequently made reference to its characters in conversation, although not in a way that Smith would have approved. He favored such similes as "broad as Aaron's ass" and "as full of crabs as Job," along with a repertoire of profanity that could curl a beard at twenty feet. He was best known, however, for his habit of strolling around in subzero weather without shoes. A reliable witness, Stewart H. Holbrook, tells of seeing him in northern Maine on a day when the temperature was thirty-five below, walking through the snow with his feet as bare as a newborn babe's, although considerably bigger and dirtier.

Out in the woods, Jones might wear rubbers or rubber-bottomed footwear called shoepacks, but not socks. Socks, he said, were for funerals. When he died, his friends checked. Sure enough, he was wearing a pair for that solemn occasion.

CHAPTER III

Early Days in Michigan

BUREAUCRACY HAD NOT yet invented the environmental impact statement in 1815 when Edward Tiffin, surveyor general of the Northwest Territory, explored the area just west of Lake Erie, between the Maumee and Raisin rivers. He was assigned to determine whether 160-acre allotments in Michigan Territory might appeal to veterans of the War of 1812.

The impact that region's environment had on Tiffin was highly unfavorable. Michigan wasn't worth a damn, he told his superiors, unless you wanted to raise frogs or mosquitoes. Most of it was swamp, he added, and what dry land he'd seen wasn't fertile enough for crops.

While he was slogging around, Tiffin also noticed that Michigan had a lot of trees. He considered them a detriment. They kept the swamp from drying up. Before a farmer could raise wheat, he'd have to chop them down. No, Tiffin declared, Michigan Territory wasn't a likely place for a war veteran to locate, whether he wanted to homestead on the 160 acres of government land he was entitled to or preferred to sell it to someone else.

Tiffin's journey satisfied his bosses that Michigan was useless. Still, the territory was part of the United States and had to be governed. The man assigned to that thankless job was Lewis Cass. His reports to President James Madison implied rather strongly that Surveyor General Tiffin was full of undigested prunes.

Cass considered his territory—it included what would become Wisconsin as well as Michigan—a fascinating region, full of fine sites for new cities and likely places for farms. As a New Hampshire native, he also realized that Michigan's trees would become valuable as soon as a few New England lumberjacks showed up. It had the finest stand of tall white pine trees in the world, including the State of Maine.

Those pines were a long way from their markets. But lake ships could carry lumber east. Besides, the governor could foresee a time when demand for building supplies would skyrocket in Ohio and other nearby regions, giving Michigan lumber plenty of customers close to home.

Tiffin's report had discouraged settlement. Cass decided to counteract it by doing some exploration of his own. He took along nine officials and scientific experts, ten Indians to intercede with hostile tribes, and ten French-Canadian *voyageurs* to help the Indians paddle the expedition's three *bateaux*. The party left Grosse Pointe, Michigan, on May 24, 1820. Its goals: to visit the Indians, study the topography, select sites for forts and seek the source of the Mississippi River.

Left off the official list was an equally important reason for the trip—to counteract Tiffin's bad publicity. Cass understood public relations well enough to take along two men certain to spread the word of what was found. Henry R. Schoolcraft, a writer and geologist, was one. The other was James Duane Doty, the twenty-one-year-old secretary of the Michigan Territorial Legislature, who was assigned to keep a journal of the trip.

Doty later became the second governor of Wisconsin Territory. On the Cass expedition, he was nearly as optimistic about the region's future as he was about his own. Like the governor, he considered the forest an asset. He noted in his journal that there was a sawmill in the woods along Sheboygan Bay on the Michigan shore. Another backwoods crew was turning pines into boards at the rapids of the Black River, twelve miles before it joined the Mississippi. These were the only examples of lumbering the governor's party ran across. For hundreds of miles, the great forest was untouched by axe or saw.

Governor Cass understood that before his territory's timber could be harvested, the Indians had to be pushed out of the way.

A coalition of midwestern tribes had been whipped by Mad Anthony Wayne in northwestern Ohio in 1794, and the end of British support after the War of 1812 made it unlikely that the Indians could hold back the wave of white settlement much longer. But there were still forty thousand of the original settlers living northwest of the Ohio River, and their fighting men outnumbered the white militia by a considerable margin.

Cass participated in an 1817 treaty which opened up most of the remaining Indian lands in Ohio. Two years later, he met with Chippewa chiefs at Saginaw—then a collection of a few log cabins built by fur traders—and persuaded the Indians to cede six million acres of land on the Michigan peninsula. During his 1820 expedition, he met representatives from several tribes at Fort Dearborn on the future site of Chicago, obtaining title to additional Michigan land. Finally, in 1828, Cass got most of the remainder. During his years as governor, he made twenty-two treaties in all, acquiring for the United States roughly one fourth of all the land in five states that adjoined the Great Lakes.

Not all the Indians were moved west of the Mississippi, but they no longer represented a serious obstacle to settlers or lumbermen. Two other factors encouraged opening up the Michigan woods to loggers. Completion of the Erie Canal in 1825 made it possible to ship lumber by water from the Lake States to the East Coast markets. And an influx of New Brunswick loggers into the Maine woods drove down wages to the point where a lot of the natives were in the mood to migrate.

Some winters the pay in Maine lumber camps fell to as low as five dollars a month. In addition, a shanty boy got beans and a bed, along with enough lice and bedbugs to keep him from feeling lonely. But he had to buy his clothes and tobacco out of the five dollars, and by the end of the season he had hardly enough cash for a good drunk, let alone enough to patronize one of the young ladies who advertised that she took in lumberjacks' washing. Money meant little in camp, but it meant a great deal in town. If a Blue Noser was willing to work for a dollar and a quarter a week, a Maine man wasn't. It was a period when it was said that some camps had three crews—one going to Bangor, one coming from Bangor, and one working. A growing number of the discontented didn't stop long at Bangor, or even at the state border, but took a canalboat west toward a land worthy of a Maine man's skills.

In Michigan, the word was, pine floated like cork on the rivers, trees grew so thick a squirrel could travel five hundred miles without touching the ground and, best of all, the place wasn't civilized yet. Maine was getting too crowded. There were too many rules. The Prohibitionists were getting too thick. In Michigan there were plenty of jobs for a good hand. And at a living wage—twenty dollars a month, or even thirty dollars.

The Erie Canal towns had a reputation for being rough, but they weren't prepared for the invasion of transients from the Maine woods. Taverns were wrecked. Townies lost teeth. Barges were damaged. Dwellers near the Big Ditch remembered the shanty boys as a great nuisance, and so they were. But after they passed by, the logs they cut began floating eastward on barges in the form of boards and shingles, repaying the canalers manyfold for having to put up with the Maine men on their way to Michigan.

The average lumberjack in the nineteenth century was reasonably content with just enough money to buy liquor, tobacco, women and lesser necessities. But not all the Maine migrants felt that way. Some headed west to Michigan to get rich.

The going rate for government land there was a dollar and a quarter an acre, but plenty could be had for less. The 160-acre tracts given to veterans could often be picked up for eighty dollars or so. Properly chosen, an acre that cost fifty cents might yield hundreds of dollars' worth of timber, then be resold to a settler.

Charles Merrill of Maine was one of the advance guard of New Englanders, buying a large chunk of Michigan timberland in 1836. Other speculators followed, and soon the wilderness was acquiring a Yankee air. Augusta in Maine had a counterpart in Augusta, Michigan. As early as 1840, a New Englander reached the territory which would become Minnesota and founded Stillwater, named for the community on the Penobscot.

Daniel Wells, Jr., a tall Yankee from Waterville, Maine, who rationed his words as if they were jewels, started his land speculations around the twin settlements that became Milwaukee, but he was soon buying timberland in Michigan. One of his associates was Isaac Stephenson, who was born in New Brunswick but had

learned lumbering in Maine. Ike joined Wells in buying large holdings along the Escanaba, Ford and Sturgeon rivers for a dollar and a quarter an acre, starting his rise to the status of millionaire.

Dozens of other New Englanders headed west to get wealthy, and a surprising number managed to do so. Some wound up living in mansions, driving in fancy carriages, buying land and legislators, and otherwise enjoying their money. But most men who answered ads for lumber-camp workers in such papers as the Bangor *Whig & Courier* got little cash in the Lake States pineries. What they got was backbreaking work, primitive living conditions and, all too often, an early death and an unmarked grave—along with the chance to do the kind of job they wanted to do and lead the life they chose to live.

The saga of Michigan lumbering began around Saginaw, which was a backwoods fort and fur-trading station until the 1830s. One military report had suggested that Saginaw was suitable only for Indians, bullfrogs and muskrats. But after Harvey Williams, a skilled tinkerer with machinery, brought a marine steam engine to the Saginaw River, the community was on its way to becoming the temporary center of the nation's timber industry.

Williams' engine, used to power the first steam sawmill on the Saginaw, was nearly twenty years old when its owner brought it ashore from a Lake Huron schooner. It had been built for *Walk-in-the-Water,* the first steamboat to ply the Great Lakes. That ship sank off Buffalo during an 1821 storm, but the engine was salvaged and installed in another steamboat, the *Superior.* Williams bought the engine when the *Superior* was broken up. He adapted it to sawing machinery and started an industry that saw no less than 112 mills rise along the riverbanks between Saginaw and Bay City during the height of the boom, their saws converting pine trees into a billion board feet of lumber a year.

Thousands of square miles of forest were located along the Saginaw and its principal tributaries, the Titabawassee, Cass, Flint and Shiawassee rivers. Including brooklets that only an expert would consider suitable for driving logs, the Saginaw basin had 864 miles of streams capable of moving timber to the mills. Between the 1850s, when lumbering on a massive scale got underway there, and the 1880s, when the pine petered out, the Saginaw region was a principal source of supply for the settled East.

Some of the trees were so large that it took only four to provide enough boards to build a good-sized house, even though the cutting methods wasted a considerable percentage of each log.

Saginaw Bay offered a fine harbor on Michigan's Lake Huron shore. Much of the lumber sawed there and the logs that were to be processed at distant points were shipped to ports on Lake Erie and Lake Ontario or to communities served by the Erie Canal. Timber from the state's Lake Michigan coast supplied Chicago and other growing cities in the Midwest. In the vicinity of Escanaba, for example, such lumber kings as Stephenson, Wells, Jefferson Sinclair, and Nelson and Harrison Ludington added to their fortunes by hiring crews to slash through the woods and supply sawmills. The mills were built near Escanaba's harbor, which first flourished during the Civil War to ship iron ore needed for cannonballs.

As early as 1836, a land office at Ionia, Michigan, was opened to sell land around the Muskegon River in western Michigan. The following year, a sawmill was built at Muskegon, the forerunner of a community that became a rival of Saginaw as a lumber center. Muskegon's rivalry also extended to the question of whether it or Saginaw deserved the title of the most sinful center of lumberjack recreation.

One of the first New Englanders to arrive in Michigan predicted that "we'll never cut all this pine if we log it until hell freezes." Such misplaced lack of confidence was not characteristic. Still, next to the great woods, the brawniest lumberjack seemed small and insignificant. The double-bitted axe, crosscut saw and peavey that were his weapons seemed totally inadequate to the challenge of harvesting the nation's finest stand of pine.

Like a military campaign, the attack on the forest began with advance scouts being sent out to get the lay of the land. Few of these timber cruisers, or landlookers, had much book learning, but all were highly educated in matters pertaining to their special calling. Traveling alone or with a single assistant, they might disappear into the woods for months, living off the land. They must not only be able to estimate the board feet which could be obtained from a section; they had to study the terrain to determine whether there were streams suitable for driving logs, and take into consideration the obstacles, such as hills or swamps, that stood between the river and the timber. They had to be surveyors, able to locate a corner of a government section and step off the boundaries, two thousand paces to the mile.

Once a likely tract was found, the landlooker had to hurry to the nearest land office and enter the acreage for his backer. Sometimes another timber cruiser might have his eye on the same piece of property. Then it was a question of which man got to the office first. Even so, he might not be home free. Not all the land agents were honest. Desirable sections might be reserved for a speculator willing to cut the agent in on a share of the loot.

Among notable landlookers in Michigan's big woods was David Ward, who found a particularly promising stand of pine near the source of the Au Sable River in the mid-1850s. Another timber cruiser, Addison Brewer, had also spotted the same chunk of pinery. A race began to file for it first at the Ionia land office.

Ward walked eighty miles to the Tobacco River, paddled a canoe another eighty miles to Saginaw, rode by stagecoach to the nearest depot, caught a train for Detroit, picked up vouchers and cash from his employers, drove a rented horse and carriage for eighteen straight hours to Lansing, catching a stage there for Ionia. He barely won. A few hours after he'd filed his claim at the land office, Brewer's agent showed up to claim the same piece of property.

After a landlooker had done his job and the site of a lumber camp was determined, an advance party arrived in the woods in early fall to prepare for the winter's cutting. A log shanty, perhaps twenty-four by thirty-six feet, was built. The sides were three or four feet high, but the roof sloped up to a peak so a man could stand erect in the center of the hut. Another log building was put up to house the work animals. Sometimes the teamsters preferred to live with the oxen or horses because they had warmer quarters and clean straw.

The early bunkhouses would be considered nearly uninhabitable by modern standards. They were heated, after a fashion, by an open fire in the center of the single room, with a hole left in the roof for the smoke to escape. Cooking was done over this same fire. The men slept on the dirt floor, either curled up in a blanket or on beds made from hay or evergreen boughs. In some camps, a blanket big enough to cover a dozen sleeping men was provided so they could take advantage of their mutual body heat to keep warm. Often, the combination bunkhouse, cook shanty and dining hall had no windows. But no matter. Except on Sundays, the lumberjacks were never there when it was daylight.

The term *lumberjack* was seldom used before the 1870s. Until then, he was called a lumberman, woodsman, pinery boy or shanty boy. "I can smell a shanty boy a mile downwind," a Saginaw merchant once claimed.

This was a slight exaggeration, but it had some basis in fact. There were no facilities for taking a bath in the woods, and if the shanty boy bothered to wash his clothes—not all considered this advisable—it was in a futile effort to discourage vermin, not from any enthusiasm for cleanliness. Some of the men felt that bathing was unhealthy, a theory they shared with their Elizabethan ancestors.

In these early camps the food consisted mostly of dried beans, rice, salt meat, dried peas, prunes, molasses, brown sugar, tea, bread and, if the cook could manage it, pie. Fresh vegetables were sometimes raised in clearings and eaten in the fall until the supply ran out. Fresh venison was common and some camps assigned a man to do the hunting for the rest. Occasionally the larder was augmented when a camp ox broke a leg. The meat from what was called a "gore-stick steer" was so tough that only a shanty boy could chew it.

Supplies had to be hauled in from the nearest town, which might be several days' journey away. This was done before winter so the crew would not have to take time off from work once the season for cutting trees began. As a result, the food consisted mostly of staples that would keep indefinitely.

From necessity, the men who logged in the first half of the nineteenth century had to put up with food of a quality and variety that the generations of lumberjacks who followed them would have rebelled against. By the 1880s, the camps were larger and more comfortable and the menus were more diverse. Toward the end of the century, a few of the camps even had a privy, a luxury the early shanty boys considered quite unnecessary.

The Lake States' lumberjacks used techniques developed in

Maine, although there were gradual changes as the years went by. One notable improvement pioneered by Michigan crews was the practice of icing the logging road by sending a sprinkler along it at night. The sleds moved more easily, their runners sliding along in iced grooves in the roads. Loads could be increased accordingly. This method started early, but another change did not come until around 1880, when an improved crosscut saw became available, one that had alternate raker teeth to remove the sawdust. Before that, trees had been felled with axes.

The axemen took pride in being able to chop down a tall pine in a high wind, making it fall so accurately it hit a stake driven into the ground as a marker. The limbs were removed and the pine sawed into sixteen- or eighteen-foot lengths, with the crown and other branches left to rot or to burn in the next forest fire. An ox team dragged the logs over trails cut by swampers to the logging road that led to the river. The logs were dropped beside this crude highway, then piled on sleds for their journey to the bank of the stream that would carry them to the sawmill the following spring.

The workday was limited by the length of daylight, with most of the crew rising about 5 A.M. to hike to the scene of the day's cutting. The teamsters got up earlier to tend the livestock. The cook also started his chores early. Originally, one man handled the cooking. When the camps got larger, he acquired one or more assistants, known as cookees, who kept the fire going and handled other jobs no one else wanted.

It was also the cookee's assignment to roust everybody from bed. The teamsters were awakened quietly to avoid disturbing the ones who could sleep longer. But when it was time for the rest of the crew to get up, the cookee could make as much noise as necessary. His traditional shout of "daylight in the swamp!" was often augmented by blasts on a tin horn known as a "gaberel" or by beating on a triangular piece of iron, a "gut hammer."

The New Englanders in the midwestern camps had been joined from the start by Canadians and, in some areas, Indians. By mid-century, Irish began to arrive in considerable numbers, driven from their homeland by the potato famine, ready to take whatever work they could get. Freed slaves sometimes got jobs in the camps. Immigrants from a variety of countries showed up in the woods, with Germans particularly common in the 1850s and Scandinavians a few years later.

Camp bosses often assigned jobs according to a man's nationality. French-Canadians, it was believed, were too volatile to handle oxen or even horses, but were cocky daredevils well suited for river drives. Germans were considered too phlegmatic and cautious to ride logs, but they were steady and dependable. The Indians were best kept in a separate crew, it was felt. Otherwise the fights, which were a form of recreation in the woods, might get out of hand as old enmities surfaced.

Some of the Canadians who migrated to Michigan and its neighboring pineries did well. There was Robert Dollar, for example. He was an Ontario man who found work as a dollar-a-day shanty boy. Instead of investing his winter's wages in a springtime spree, he disgusted his companions by wasting it on real estate. He bought a few acres of pine lands at first, then more. He moved up the ranks to camp boss and his income increased accordingly. The time came when he owned mills as well as large amounts of timber, founded a community called Dollarville, and cut millions of board feet of pine on Michigan's Upper Peninsula. After leaving the Lake States for the West Coast, he got into shipping. The name of the Dollar Line became familiar around the world.

As the Michigan sawmills increased in number, disposing of the sawdust became a problem. It was used to cover mud roads, fill swamps, stuff mattresses. Along the Saginaw River banks, portions of the marshes were filled with forty feet of sawdust. A four-story hotel, the Bancroft House, was built on this shaky but appropriate foundation.

The Bancroft was the proud symbol of how rapidly Saginaw had risen in the world. It had a fancy cupola, cut-glass chandeliers, its own gas works. Every room had its own box stove, brass spittoon and red plush bellpull. The chef was imported from Paris.

When the hotel opened on September 7, 1859, every lumber baron in Michigan was there, with a single exception. Curt Emerson, who bragged that he hadn't been caught sober for thirty years, had been socially acceptable in Saginaw's early days. But now the town was getting some class and his old friends were a trifle ashamed of his uncouth ways. Besides, there was the prob-

lem of his mongrel, Caesar. The mutt and Emerson were insepa-
rable. One could not be invited to the Bancroft's opening bash
without the other. The rival lumber kings didn't like the dog and
they had reason. Whenever someone offended Curt—and he took
offense easily—he would yell for his pet and order: "Piss on him,
Caesar. Piss all over him." And Caesar would do his best to obey,
although his quarry usually fled first.

So Emerson was left off the guest list. He waited until the hour
set for the party, but no invitation came. He went to his office in
the sawmill and marched under the sign over the door that read
THE HALLS OF MONTEZUMA. He took a healthy jolt from the jug
he kept there. Then he headed for the grand new hotel.

The Parisian chef had done himself proud. The table groaned
with food. The champagne chilled in silver buckets. The ladies
were in their finest gowns. The men were shaved and barbered.
Some of them had even bathed.

Emerson stood in the doorway a moment, enjoying the sight of
such grandeur in a city that still had mud streets. Then, ignoring
his sixty years, he strode in, leaped nimbly onto the long head
table and kicked his way from one end to the other, cutting a
dozen guests with shards of flying glass.

That broke up the banquet. The next day, Curt paid two thousand dollars in damages and apologized to the injured. But he had
no apology for his dislike of the Bancroft House. It might be the
finest hotel in the big woods, but Caesar knew what he could do
to it.

CHAPTER IV

Wisconsin Logging Begins

COLONEL ZACHARY TAYLOR, who later won the presidency for the Whigs by defeating Michigan's Governor Cass, was in command of Fort Crawford in 1829 when he established what amounted to the first lumber camp in the territory that became Wisconsin. The outpost on the Mississippi at Prairie du Chien was in sad shape and Taylor was ordered to build a new one. He sent seventy men up the Chippewa River to cut trees, with Lieutenant John B. Gardenier and Lieutenant Levin Gale in charge.

One of the men, John H. Fonda, had a rudimentary knowledge of logging. The others were greenhorns in the woods. The expedition had numerous misadventures, including the only recorded instance of a democratic vote in the pineries on who would serve as entree at a cannibal feast.

The military lumberjacks worked all winter, producing enough square timber for two rafts. Fonda was put in charge of the larger one, Gardenier of the smaller. All the provisions were put aboard Fonda's raft, except for a barrel of whiskey. As they started drifting down the Chippewa toward the Mississippi, Gardenier's lads began dipping into the keg. By the time the two rafts became separated, they were in no shape to find the main party and its nonliquid provisions.

Fonda and another man chased Gardenier's raft in a canoe, but the canoe upset and by the time it had been righted and its occupants dried out the other crew was far downstream. Fonda finally found the raft two days later, hopelessly tangled in driftwood in a slough. The whiskey barrel was empty. Gardenier and his men had left on foot.

The lieutenant's party reached the Mississippi and built a flimsy raft of driftwood. It carried them to an island, where they went ashore to look for food. A windstorm came up, the raft floated away and they were marooned.

After nothing to eat for eleven days but acorns and roots, the group decided that one man must be sacrificed in the interests of a square meal. Balloting was held. Private Austin Young won the honor. Fonda, who is the authority for the story, failed to specify why Young was chosen, leaving posterity to speculate on whether he was the smallest and weakest, the least popular or, perhaps, the most robust and so most suitable to the central role at the feast.

At any rate, Young seems to have taken the result of the vote philosophically. He took a kettle to the river to fill with water while his buddies were casting lots to decide who would draw the duty of shooting him. As he was turning to take the kettle back to camp so preparation of the meal could begin, he saw Fonda's raft come floating to the rescue.

With the first logging expedition a partial failure, Colonel Taylor tried again. This venture was in charge of a young lieutenant, Jefferson Davis, but an experienced French voyageur went along to pilot the raft down the Chippewa and Mississippi to Prairie du Chien. The return trip went well until it neared the Chippewa's mouth. At that point the main channel veered to the right. On the left was a backwater called Beef Slough, later to become a favorite storage pond for lumbermen.

"To the right, hard," the Frenchman shouted as the raft neared the slough. But Davis thought he knew better.

"Here, you scoundrel," he yelled, "you are going to run this raft right to hell. Pull to the left where the main river is."

The voyageur shrugged. The oarsmen steered left. The raft wound up in a tangle of water-soaked driftwood. Davis led his men overland to Fort Crawford, living mostly on acorns, and tried to explain to Zach Taylor why he'd come back without the logs.

For this and other reasons, the colonel had little use for Davis, who had brought his body servant with him to the fort even though slavery was illegal in the territory. Taylor's family was with him, including his son Richard and two daughters. Zach noted that one of the girls, eighteen-year-old Sarah, was seeing a lot of Jeff Davis.

"I don't want to catch you two together again," he told her.

A dutiful daughter, Sarah was careful not to let the colonel catch them together. She soon left to visit an aunt in Kentucky. Davis resigned his commission and also departed. He'd been gone a half hour when Taylor learned the couple planned to meet. He ordered out his yawl, with nine soldiers to man the oars, and the future President of the United States went chasing down the Mississippi after the future President of the Confederacy. By the time he caught up to the couple in St. Louis, however, they were married. The Davises went to the lieutenant's Mississippi plantation, where Sarah died a year later.

Until the mid-1830s, development of Wisconsin's timber resources was delayed by the fact that, except around the forts at Prairie du Chien, Portage and Green Bay, the region was still controlled by Indian tribes. These original inhabitants had little use for lumber. They considered a sawmill an encroachment on their land, one that would encourage additional white settlers to come to the region.

For a time, the Indians managed to delay the inevitable. In 1819, for example, they chased away Colonel Daniel Shaw, a friend of Daniel Boone. Shaw arrived by birchbark canoe with plans to turn pine trees into boards, which could be sold for seventy dollars a thousand board feet at St. Louis. The colonel was a veteran of the War of 1812 and did not scare easily. But so many Winnebagoes showed up at the sawmill he built at the first falls of the Black River that he left. When he returned the following spring, the Indians had burned what he claimed was the first mill erected in western Wisconsin.

Three years later, a Kentuckian named Hardin Perkins put up a sawmill on the Red Cedar River, a tributary of the Chippewa. But a spring flood washed out the dam before he started work. When the Indians began threatening to burn him out, he abandoned the site.

Perkins' financial backers were Joseph Rolette and James Lockwood, who were getting rich in the fur trade at Prairie du Chien. They sent a crew to rebuild the dam. Chippewas chased them away. But Lockwood was a determined man. He met separately with chiefs of the Sioux and the Chippewa, both of whom claimed the region, and worked out a deal. In return for being allowed to cut trees and saw them into boards, he agreed to provide leaders of the two tribes with whiskey, blankets and beads each July. The federal government ratified the treaty. Lockwood led a mixed group of Menominees and French-Canadians to Wilson Creek, near its confluence with the Red Cedar, and built the first sawmill that ever operated in the pine-rich watershed of the Chippewa. The mill, located in what became Menomonie, Wisconsin, turned out a hundred thousand board feet of lumber its first year.

Menomonie later became the headquarters for Knapp, Stout & Company, one of the most successful of the Lake States' lumber operations. The firm could trace its beginnings to H. S. Allen, who built a mill there in 1839. He sold it two years later to a man named Green, who sold it to a fellow named Pearson, who built the first dam across the Red Cedar before selling out to David Black.

An Iowan, Captain William Wilson, explored the valley by canoe in 1846, liked what he saw and bought a half interest in Black's mill with the financial backing of John H. Knapp, forming a company called Knapp & Black. Black soon died. The name was changed to Knapp & Wilson.

By now the region was getting more civilized. In fact, it had already had its first murder. The victim was shot in the garret of his log house. The murderer was taken to Prairie du Chien for trial. Everyone was sure he did it, but there were no witnesses and he was acquitted.

In 1850, Captain Andrew Tainter bought a share of the company and the name was changed to Knapp, Tainter & Company. A new mill was built. More capital was needed. H. L. Stout supplied it and, at long last, the firm became Knapp, Stout & Company, the name under which it grew into what was claimed to be the largest enterprise of its kind in the world.

Its success came about despite an unconventional attitude toward strong drink. Neither Knapp nor Stout indulged and they refused to sell whiskey to their employees. Most mills made a good profit by ordering kegs of Goodhue's or some other brand and retailing the liquor to their men. But Knapp, Stout refused to go into the whiskey business and, as a result, Menomonie did not stand out as a particularly lively lumber town, although it was hardly the haven for teetotalers the owners had hoped it would be.

In one way or another, the thirsty managed to get their supplies. In fact, the first white to die in Menomonie, Mrs. Fanny Vale, was said to have succumbed to strong drink. Her husband, a local historian recorded, "dragged his helpmate down to his own level."

Mrs. Lorenzo Bullard, who had arrived on Knapp's keelboat some years before, went to visit the sick woman. She found the husband passed out near his wife's bed, but he aroused himself to inquire if she was dying. Mrs. Bullard nodded. Vale staggered up, opened his pocketknife and began to saw off a lock of his wife's hair, muttering: "It's all I ever 'spect to have of her now."

Mrs. Bullard was horrified. She persuaded Vale to put his knife away. That night, Mrs. Vale died. Told the news, the husband roused himself long enough to look down on the corpse and make a comment that the visitor remembered for years.

"Well," he said, "God thinks He done it, I suppose."

The body was laid out on a board resting on barrels which contained the winter's supply of pork and venison. Mrs. Vale had to be moved aside temporarily so her widower could get meat for his breakfast. The funeral was held that day. The remains were put in a rough box and carried by one-horse sleigh to the cemetery.

As long as the name of Menomonie has come up, it should be noted that the proper spelling of the name of the tribe for which it was named was uncertain. The uncertainty is still reflected in modern maps. The city which grew up around Knapp, Stout's five-hundred-acre establishment is spelled Menomonie. A river in Milwaukee County is spelled Menomonee. A river which forms part of the boundary between Wisconsin and Upper Michigan is spelled Menominee, as is the Michigan city on its banks.

It was on the Menominee River—the one in northeastern Wisconsin—where a Yankee fur trader, William Farnsworth, built that region's first sawmill in the winter of 1830–31, in partnership with a Detroiter, Charles R. Brush. The Indians in the neighborhood didn't want the mill. But they had decided that Farnsworth would do exactly as he chose, so there was no use to complain. Any man willing to blow himself up with a keg of gunpowder, the chiefs felt, must be dealt with very carefully.

Farnsworth won his reputation when he arrived with a stock of trade goods. He'd no sooner built his cabin when fifteen or twenty armed warriors arrived to tell him he had a choice—leave or be killed.

Farnsworth was a mixture of Scotch and Yankee and a stubborn man. He had defied the monopoly, John Jacob Astor's American Fur Company, in coming here. He was willing to defy the Menominee Nation as well. He grabbed hold of a keg of powder, set it in the middle of the cabin, lit a candle stump and placed the burning candle in a hole at the top of the barrel.

"You are braves," he said. "I am a brave of the white men. If my property and my life must be sacrificed, we shall all suffer the same fate. No truly brave man fears death."

Then he seated himself on the keg. The Indians showed no emotion. They sat or stood around the small room. No further word was said, as every eye watched the candle. Lower and lower moved the flame toward the powder. Finally, one Indian rose, ducked through the door and ran. Another followed. Gradually, the room emptied until only Farnsworth and one brave were left with the keg, the candle and their courage.

The flame was nearly touching the powder when the last Menominee rose with dignity and stalked out. Farnsworth extinguished the candle. As the white man who did not fear death, he became a legend there in the woods of northern Wisconsin. So when he decided to go into the lumber business, no one came around to protest that he was ruining the neighborhood.

Farther south and west, when lumbermen decided to exploit the Chippewa River country, the enmity between Sioux and Chippewa became a problem. Pressure was brought on Washington, which urged the two ancient enemies to make peace. A meeting was arranged in 1846 between the Sioux chiefs Wabasha, Red Wing and Big Thunder, and their Chippewa counterparts. The Sioux sent an escort of a hundred and fifty horsemen. They were joined at Chippewa Falls by an even larger contingent of Chippewa warriors.

The leading Chippewa approached the Sioux delegation with a large pipe made of red stone from Pipestone Mountain. In his other hand he had a hatchet. He hurled it with enough force to bury it partially in the earth. Then he lit the pipe, took a drag and handed it to a Sioux chief, who took a whiff and passed it on. When all the important men had shared the peace pipe, the speeches began. The Chippewa said they were anxious for peace. The Sioux said they were glad they could now hunt east of the Mississippi without fear. Finally, everybody repaired to the white settlement for an elaborate dinner.

When the conference was over, the whites assumed that the tribes were no longer enemies. The Chippewa weren't so sure, however, as was demonstrated a few years later when eight braves, assigned to escort ringleaders of a lynch mob to Prairie du Chien for trial, refused to get close to Sioux territory.

The lynching episode began in a saloon run by Tim Hurley, who had arrived along the Chippewa in 1848 with a Galena merchant who was looking for a site to build a sawmill. The merchant decided to go back home, but Hurley stayed to open the valley's first drinking place. It became headquarters for every gambler and tough in the region, including a Frenchman named Martial Caznobia.

In 1849, Caznobia and his friends celebrated the Fourth of July in their usual fashion. After the drinking went on for a time, they decided to visit a young Indian woman who lived nearby. They barged into the wickiup and, according to a primly worded account, "attempted to take liberties with the man's squaw." The Chippewa husband was home, however. He leaped to his wife's defense, plunging a knife into Caznobia up to its hilt.

That sobered the visitors considerably. They hauled the Frenchman back to the saloon, where they could watch him die without having to go thirsty. As it turned out, Martial's wound was not a fatal one. But his friends assumed that it was and, after a few more rounds, someone suggested: "Let's hang that damned Indian." A rope was borrowed. The crowd, led by Tim Inglar, went back to the Chippewa's hut, grabbed him, hauled him to a tree and strung him up.

If Inglar and his friends had been sober, they might have given a second thought to the wisdom of lynching an Indian in that neighborhood. There were more Chippewas than whites in the vicinity. The dead man's friends felt that hanging a man for protecting his wife from rape was unfair. Several hundred armed warriors threatened to burn Hurley's saloon and every other building in sight unless the murder was avenged.

The incident was so threatening that "King" Allen and his wife showed up to negotiate. An arrangement was worked out. Inglar and three other leaders of the mob gave themselves up after the Indians agreed that the four should be tried under white men's law. The prisoners were put aboard a boat and eight Chippewas went along to make sure they got to Prairie du Chien, the nearest location of a judge.

That meant going down the Mississippi. Its west bank was Sioux territory. The solemn peace treaty was only three years old, but the closer the Chippewas got to the river the less faith they had in the buried hatchet. Finally, they announced they would go no farther and would have to tomahawk the prisoners on the spot.

Inglar said he had a better suggestion. "The Sioux won't bother us, boys. Turn us loose and we'll give you our word we'll turn ourselves in."

Surprisingly, the Chippewas agreed. More surprisingly, Inglar and his three friends kept their promise. Leaving their guards, they paddled on down to Prairie du Chien and gave themselves up to the Crawford County sheriff. But when their case was called, no one showed up to accuse them. So they were turned loose.

Another lynching near Chippewa Falls was narrowly averted a few years later. She Sheep, an Indian, and a lumberjack named Frank Donaldson got into a drunken argument during a poker game. The Chippewa threatened to beat up the white, who pulled out his revolver and said he'd shoot him first. She Sheep stood erect. He pulled his shirt open, baring his chest.

"More big talk. You say shoot. So shoot."

Donaldson shot. She Sheep died. Donaldson was locked up in the root house of the H. S. Allen Company, the closest equivalent to a jail. Having learned civilized ways from their neighbors, the Indians decided to break in and lynch him. But Donaldson's lumberjack friends got there first. They smashed down the door and freed Donaldson. He left the country, surviving to be killed in the Civil War.

To survive in this tough new country, a man had to be able to take care of himself, whether he was dealing with nature or humans. As examples of the fortitude required, consider James Van

Slyke and Christopher Payne, who settled near Big Foot—now a southern Wisconsin resort town called Lake Geneva—in the 1830s. One was a farmer, the other a lumberman. Neither took a backward step when the going got difficult.

Mrs. Van Slyke could also meet her pioneer responsibilities, as she demonstrated one February day when her husband froze his toes while driving hogs from Squaw Prairie, Illinois, to Big Foot. He got the hogs penned, then hobbled into the house.

"My toes are gone," he said. "Cut 'em off."

She got out her scissors and performed the amputation. By spring, Van Slyke was well enough to break a hundred acres of prairie with his plow.

The lumberman who settled in the neighborhood was Payne. He had fought Indians in Pennsylvania before heading to Wisconsin to put up a sawmill. He couldn't read or write but he had a distinctive signature. He always made his X with a dot so it could be recognized.

Unknown to Payne, a party of surveyors had staked out the future site of Lake Geneva, marking the corners with their initials. The snow was so deep when Payne arrived that he failed to see the surveyors' signs. He cleared the underbrush and started a log cabin, then constructed a canoe out of a black walnut tree and, when the ice melted, floated down the Fox River to Illinois to get supplies.

When he got back, the surveyors were living in his cabin. He told them to get out. They grabbed their guns and chased him away. Payne walked back to his former home at Squaw Prairie on the Kishwaukee and rounded up seven friends to help him. By the time they returned to the sawmill site, the surveyors had also been reinforced. Both sides began shooting at long range. Several of Payne's friends were wounded. He helped get them back to Squaw Prairie, formed another small posse and headed back for Wisconsin.

By then, the surveyors had built two cabins across the river from Van Slyke's farm. Once again, the surveyors had more firepower. Back went Payne and his party to Squaw Prairie, but the lumberman was not giving in.

The third time he showed up, he had thirty men with him. They were armed with shotguns, rifles, pistols and Bowie knives. The Illinois army camped near the outlet and sent a messenger under a white flag to suggest a parley. The surveyors arrived, fully armed, to listen to Payne's proposition.

If both sides started shooting, he said, a lot of people could get killed. Instead, he offered to fight a duel with one of the surveyors. If he killed his opponent, they must give him back his claim. If he lost, they could bury him. Either way, the argument would be settled.

No one volunteered to take on Payne. The outnumbered surveyors made a counter offer. For two thousand dollars they would give up their claim to the site. That was a small fortune, but Payne agreed. He managed to make the payment, mostly in whiskey, blankets and other trade goods rather than cash. The Battle of Big Foot ended without further bloodshed and Payne built his sawmill.

Michigan Territory, which included what became Wisconsin in the days when Payne got into the lumber business, had plenty of laws on the books, including one that permitted public whipping and another providing that a convicted offender could be sold into slavery for up to three months. But in most of the region there was no one around to enforce the legalities. Frontier justice was whatever those in the neighborhood chose to make it, and often the party with the heaviest firepower called the tune.

When Michigan became a state in 1836, Wisconsin Territory was established. It included portions of what became Minnesota and Iowa. The original capital was at Belmont, a village in southwestern Wisconsin, the area where most of the territory's 11,683 residents lived. A few miles to the north was a region as large as France that contained one of the finest stands of timber in the world. But with so few sawmills to convert logs into boards, lumber had to be brought from a considerable distance. Wood to build the territorial capital, for instance, came from Chautauqua County, New York. The lumber was rafted down a tributary to the Allegheny River, down the Ohio to the Mississippi, then towed upstream to Prairie du Chien before being hauled by oxen to Belmont.

That same year, a Methodist missionary who had been transferred to Prairie du Chien decided that a log hut was not for him. He had his two-story house in Meadville, Pennsylvania, torn down and shipped by way of the Ohio and Mississippi to his new home, where the house was put back together again.

Belmont remained the capital only briefly. Thanks mostly to that former explorer turned politician and land speculator, James Duane Doty, it was moved to Four Lakes. Doty and his partner, Stevens T. Mason, Michigan's governor, had bought a large tract of land there for fifteen hundred dollars. By handing out deeds to corner lots to enough territorial legislators, Doty convinced them that Four Lakes would be a better place than Belmont for the capital. He renamed the place for former President Madison and prepared to cash in on the building boom.

Fourteen years earlier, when Doty wanted to build a house at Green Bay, he imported ten thousand board feet of lumber by schooner from Detroit. Unfortunately, the boards never arrived. The ship ran into a gale off Louse Island—later renamed Washington Island—and all his building material was thrown overboard to help the sailing vessel ride out the storm.

By 1837, when Doty and his fellow speculators founded Madison, it was finally possible to buy boards in Wisconsin. Daniel Whitney, a New Hampshire man, had started a sawmill on the Wisconsin River at Whitney's Rapids, about seventy miles above Portage. He had worked out an agreement with the Indians. They agreed not to burn down the place if he made annual payments of 50 pounds of powder, 50 pounds of tobacco, 100 pounds of shot, 200 flints, 100 pipes and 12 bushels of corn. This largesse was worth, in current prices, $67.50. Whitney charged $69 per thousand board feet for his lumber.

Doty knew that the new territorial capital would never be popular without a tavern. Luckily, a family named Peck had arrived to open one, and Madison's founder helped them expand. Doty considered the Pecks' original log hut inadequate, so he arranged for thirty-six workmen to make the ten-day trip from Milwaukee, ninety miles away, bringing four wagonloads of tools and provisions. Then Doty bought enough of Whitney's expensive lumber so the workmen could build a frame addition to the tavern. It was opened on July 4, 1837, with two hundred guests jamming the place to drink and dine.

Among the 1837 guests at Pecks' Tavern was an English geologist, George William Featherstonehaugh, who was gathering material for a book on the disadvantages of frontier life. Wisconsin, he informed his British readers, was a place "where man reverts without pain to his natural condition, which is little above the beast of the field." He admitted that the scenery was attractive, but he said it was spoiled by "drunken and brutal man."

The Englishman described a murder trial at Mineral Point. An "impudent and ill-looking fellow" named McComber had killed a man named Willard, shooting him in the back. Featherstonehaugh said the judge was "ill dressed, excessively dirty and unshaven," with his jaws tied up in an old silk handkerchief because he had the mumps. The second day's proceedings had to be postponed because the judge was too drunk to preside. The prosecuting attorney did not come up to British standards, either. His grammar was atrocious, Featherstonehaugh reported, and he was definitely from the lower classes.

McComber was found guilty. The judge ordered him to stay in the log jail until he'd paid a three-hundred-dollar fine. But the murderer broke out that night, the Englishman said, and no one took much interest in going after him.

Of the lawless men attracted to the Wisconsin frontier, the best known in this period was a gang called the Fearsome Finches. Old Man Finch and twelve sons had arrived from St. Joseph, Michigan, in 1836 and built a camp in a swamp near Lake Koshkonong. From that safe hideout they swooped down on farms to rustle horses and cattle, selling the animals in Chicago. According to legend, it was the Finches who first used the lasso in Wisconsin, demonstrating a talent for roping and riding later associated with outlaws farther west. For twenty years or more, backwoods mothers who wanted to quiet unruly children would tell them: "Hush. The Finches are riding by and they'll hear you."

When settlers caught two of the Finch brothers, they didn't waste time calling for the law. They shot them down. The surviving members of the family continued to rustle livestock and terrorize the countryside until the Civil War broke out, when they decided to fight Confederates.

A casual attitude toward civilized order was general not only in farming settlements but in the lumber camps of the period. The Reverend Cutting Marsh, a Congregational minister to the Indians, took an 1849 journey along the Wisconsin River, the first of the state's streams to be used extensively for getting logs to market, and was disappointed at the morality of the fifteen hundred or so men he found there in logging camps or working at the forty-seven sawmills he visited.

"Here and there was a live Christian," he said. "But it was painful to see how many had come into the new land as if to throw off Christ and the restraints of civilization."

The lumber barons might give lip service to the restraints of legality, but few paid much attention to rules against stealing timber. In 1849, the year after Wisconsin became a state, the register of the Green Bay land office estimated that fifteen million board feet of pine was cut in that region annually, every stick of it "plundered off the public lands."

Timber theft continued on a large scale for another generation, although sporadic attempts by government agents to enforce the law gradually made the practice less common. Eventually, most loggers had to buy the land or pay stumpage fees to its owners before converting the pine into boards and money.

Even in the relatively lawless 1840s, there was at least one company of the godly in the Wisconsin woods. In 1841 a band of Mormons traveled from their settlement at Nauvoo, Illinois, to the Black River pineries to cut lumber for a temple. They acquired a small sawmill and spent three years chopping down trees, sawing them into boards and rafting them to Nauvoo.

By the time the temple was completed in 1845, however, the Mormons' prophet, Joseph Smith, and his brother, Hyrum, had been lynched in Carthage, Illinois. After Brigham Young won leadership, trouble with the Gentiles continued. Finally, in 1847, the Mormons left their temple of Wisconsin pine and headed toward Utah.

Among those who arrived in the Wisconsin wilderness to cut trees in what he called "border times" was an Ohioan, Osborn Strahl. When he was an old man, he set down some reminiscences of what the region had been like before civil law was introduced:

"The Winnebago, the Menominee, the Chippewa and fierce, lawless whites often came in contact and made life hideous for any timid fellow. A lumberman had but primitive ways of prosecuting his business. He encountered many a difficulty, many a disappointment, many a hazard, many an escape for the dollars he sought. Aye, and there was many a doom, too. For the wild waters laugh at the puny strife of man."

In the 1840s, when Strahl arrived at the future site of Chippewa Falls, H. S. Allen was called "king of the Chippewa," owning not only the sawmill but the boom rights for what was to become the leading logging stream in Wisconsin. Few loggers could make a living above Allen's boom, a barrier of floating pine that trapped logs as they moved downstream so they could be sorted and credited to their proper owners, identified by markings stamped in the wood. Allen dictated the price paid for both logs and supplies—low for the former, high for the latter. Allen's house was the only private dwelling at the falls, aside from several shanties on the opposite side of the river and a boardinghouse near the mill.

"Every man employed was fed and some had a bunk to sleep in, but no bedding was furnished," Strahl recalled. "The [company] store, however, had blankets to sell as well as whiskey. Any good fellow could buy according to the amount of work he did. And especially did those who drank the most whiskey elicit the most admiration."

Strahl arrived in King Allen's domain in midwinter, when logging was in full blast. Whole trees were brought to the riverbank on a bobsled pulled by four oxen, driven by teamsters who rose at 4 A.M. to be ready for a day's work. The Ohioan noted that neither teamsters nor other lumberjacks got a cent of pay until the logs were sold in the spring—"and not always then." So he and several other free spirits decided to defy Allen's monopoly. They struck off on their own and established a camp upstream at Vermillion Falls, a rapids so dangerous it had never been run by raftsmen.

All winter the men chopped down tall pines, trimmed off the branches and snaked the logs to the riverbank. By spring, they had accumulated a small fortune in potential lumber. But when the ice melted and they saw how the swollen river plunged over the falls, even Strahl began to wonder if they could get their logs downstream—or, for that matter, live through the attempt.

"The perpendicular falls was at the foot of the rapids," he recalled. "A ledge extended straight across the river like a dam, ten or twelve feet high and obstructed by rocks on either side, save one place just wide enough for the raft. And one must make the right spot, for the force was terrific. Then, when one does shoot the rapids, one goes under furiously. But if one hangs on tight, one comes to the surface again."

The crew fashioned the huge logs into rafts, fastening them together with springy green timber to allow for twisting and bending. On a bright May morning, the first raft was launched a mile or so above the rapids. Strahl and the others climbed aboard to handle the heavy oars at each end of the raft, three men to an oar. A lumberjack named Norman began to sing a doleful song about the perils of a river pig's life. By the time he'd finished, the raftsmen could hear the roar of the falls ahead.

They rode on in silence. The current gradually picked up speed until they estimated they were traveling at twenty knots. At this point, Norman stepped between two logs and disappeared. The logs came together again. Strahl decided that was the end of Norman. But in a moment, the logs creaked apart. Norman's head reappeared. He was hauled back aboard, none the worse.

The first raft made it safely through the rapids and the falls. So did the second. But on the third try, Strahl said, "our raft was banged about amongst the rocks and crushed to pieces. We clung to a point of rock that stood a foot or two above the water. For half a day we waited there, feeling sure there was no help for us."

Then a Chippewa appeared in a bark canoe. Strahl shared the attitude of most frontier whites toward Indians—he didn't like them. But this was no time for animosity. He and the other half-drowned lumberjacks waved and yelled. The Indian headed their way.

"Dropping from rock to rock until our location was reached, and skipping across the mad waters from the eddy of one rock to another, with a dexterity only attainable by these savages that we assume to despise, he put us one at a time ashore . . . May the recollection of his favor ever soften the rancor of my thoughts toward him and his kindred."

The mutual distrust between Indians and whites did not always end so happily, particularly when rival crews were competing. Some years after Strahl's rescue by the daring Chippewa, Indian lumberjacks were working on one side of the Oconto River and a white crew on the other. When it came time to drive the logs, hard feelings that had been smoldering all winter broke out in numerous fights. The rival groups skirmished their way downstream until they got to Oconto Falls. Then the bosses of both crews decided too much time was being wasted in fighting. They worked out an agreement that each side would choose a representative to settle the dispute. The Indians put forward a strapping half-breed, John Galineau. The whites countered with an Irish brawler, Pat Golden.

Before the fight began, the cook of one faction ordered both sides to throw all carving knives into the river, insuring that the battle would be fair. A cook's word had weight—anyone offending him could go hungry. So the suggestion was followed. The men formed a ring, the opponents stepped forward and the fight was on.

It followed the usual rules. Fists and teeth were the primary weapons, but calked boots could be used if an opponent went down. Golden and Galineau whaled away, neither getting the upper hand for the first half hour. Then the Irishman took a mighty swing. It caught the half-breed on the side of the head, sending him staggering backward into a boiler filled with hot bean soup.

That ended the fight. The scalded Galineau admitted he'd had enough. The Indians went back to the woods, leaving the river to their rivals. That night's beans were served à la Galineau, giving them a special flavor.

In his account of early lumbering along the Chippewa, Strahl did not specify how many men were in his crew, but it's safe to assume the total was no more than a dozen. Such small-scale operations were typical of the period before the Civil War. What often happened was that two or three ambitious men—New Englanders, perhaps, who had headed west to make a fortune—got to talking at a saloon, rounded up a few men slightly more impoverished than themselves, and struck off into the pineries to cut timber. Some left descriptions of how it was.

John T. Kingston, for instance, who had explored the forests along Wisconsin's Lemonweir River as early as 1836, found himself in west-central Wisconsin in 1848, when the Treaty of Lake Poygan ended Indian claims to the region. Kingston and John Werner, Jr., a New Yorker, blazed trees on either side of the bank of the Yellow River, started to build a log cabin and laid claim to the site. Then they joined with a Vermonter, Thomas Weston, to form a lumber company. It was named after Weston. It's likely he supplied most of the capital.

The newly formed T. Weston and Company hired Uriah Hill and Usal V. Jeffreys to raft a small amount of lumber to the point where the Yellow joins the Wisconsin River, which in turn flows into the Mississippi. They were instructed to put up a shanty and fence in the adjoining land. Then Weston and Werner headed up the Yellow River to pick a site for a logging camp.

It was mid-November. The ground was covered with eight inches of snow. There were neither roads nor houses in the region, so their first task was to blaze a route for a tote road between the campsite and Point Bausse, the nearest landing on the Wisconsin where they could get supplies. At that outpost they bought three yoke of oxen, sleds and tools. They hired nine men, including three Canadians, an Irishman and Gilbert Adams from the State of Maine. It was agreed that the crewmen would be paid from eighteen to twenty dollars a month, depending on their jobs. A millwright and two other men were employed to put up a sawmill.

The lumberjacks left Point Bausse on December 22, 1848, to cut the road through to the Yellow River campsite, about twenty miles away. By now there was twenty inches of snow. Travel was slow. The party made four miles the first day. On the second, it ran into problems crossing marshes, with the ice frequently breaking under the oxen.

Once at the river, it took the men a week to build rude barns for the cattle and a shelter for themselves. The men's shanty, Kingston reported, "was built after the State of Maine plan, an open fireplace in the center with bunks and deacon seats on either side."

"Neighbors there were none," he went on. "Not even an Indian was seen at the camp until about the opening of spring, and not the mark of a white man was to be found on Yellow River."

The winter's routine followed the pattern established in Maine. By first light, the men were in the woods ready to work. At dark, they returned to the fetid bunkhouse, ate heartily and sat talking on the split-log benches called deacon seats until the 9 P.M. bedtime. On Sunday, with no place to go, the week's one day of leisure was passed in camp.

"Some had their old logging experiences to relate," Kingston recalled. "Others were fortunate in finding an old newspaper or perhaps a book, while others forgot the cares of life in a bunk."

Between November 5 and February 21, there was no sign of thawing in the shady spots. Then the snow began to melt a bit. Kingston set out with two others to get the oxen to Point Bausse before ice in the swamps became too weak to hold them. Weston and the others, except for Daniel Dugan, the cook, set off downriver to cut trees that leaned across the stream and formed potential hazards for the spring log drive. They traveled on the frozen river, hauling supplies on a hand sled. But after four days the ice began to melt and they took to the wooded banks, where progress was slower.

Kingston and his companions joined Weston's party at the proposed mill site. Most of the men were sent back upriver to get ready to drive logs. In crossing Cranberry Creek, they found the ice too weak to hold a man on foot. So each in turn lay down and rolled across the ice—"a manner of locomotion that might appear amusing," Kingston said, "but was more agreeable than to wade through the water at this time of year."

Dugan, the cook, was glad to see them, but he was in a sour mood. He'd been working hard, tapping trees in the hope of having a good supply of syrup for the work crew, but his work hadn't paid off. Kingston pointed out that he would have had more luck if he hadn't been trying to get maple sap out of a grove of yellow birch.

The winter's work had produced exactly 2,011 logs, scaling about 700,000 board feet. With Weston and three others going ahead to break log jams, and Kingston and two companions following to shove stranded logs back in the stream, the timber was floated to the site of the new mill, which began sawing the pines into boards that summer. Eventually, the lumber was sold at Galena, Illinois.

When Whitney opened the first sawmill on the Wisconsin and sold to such customers as Madison's first tavernkeeper, the price of lumber had been around seventy dollars per thousand board feet. Within a decade, so many sawmills had been built that the price dropped to less than eleven dollars, an indication of the rapid growth of the industry. Expansion of lumbering had brought an influx of men eager to get in on a good thing. By now, some settlements included wives and children. Schoolhouses appeared here and there. But most of those who headed for the pineries were young bachelors. The shortage of respectable women—or, for that matter, those who preferred cash to respect—remained a problem.

Some loggers solved it by taking Indian wives, generally making sure the marriages were not legal under white man's law to avoid future complications. An early history of the Chippewa River region notes with approval that after white women became less uncommon and the squaws were cast adrift, the loggers often provided for their half-breed children—and sometimes for the children's mothers as well.

"King" Allen permitted his Chippewa Falls mill to be used for dances, with Old Dan McCann playing his fiddle in the dining hall and every woman within miles invited. Even so, men always outnumbered the ladies by three to one. Those who couldn't find partners consoled themselves by getting drunk.

The guests at such affairs were a motley crew—New Englanders, Indians, French-Canadians, Irishmen, Germans and a contingent of Southerners who came armed with revolvers and Bowie knives. As the evening wore on, there were always several fights going on outside the hall, along with what one historian described as "haphazard shooting."

A man who came armed was careful not to hit a woman, however. Such a mistake could get him lynched. There in the pineries, it was understood, women were too scarce to waste.

CHAPTER V

Wisconsin Loses the Twin Cities

IF IT HAD NOT been for Caleb Cushing and his dreams of a Minnesota lumber empire, Minneapolis and St. Paul would be in Wisconsin.

Thanks in considerable part to its growing logging activity, Wisconsin Territory's population had increased rapidly in the 1840s. When Wisconsin entered the Union as the thirtieth state in 1848, the St. Croix River was established as part of its boundary with Minnesota Territory. Cushing and several influential New England friends were directly responsible for drawing the line there instead of a considerable distance to the west, as had been planned.

Cushing was an influential politician from Newburyport, Massachusetts, best known for having negotiated the first trade treaty between China and the United States. He arrived on the St. Croix in 1846 to try to increase his fortune.

Nine years earlier, the St. Croix Falls Lumber Company had built a dam, sawmill, stores, shops and shanties for workers. But by the time the New Englander got there, the project had gone broke. The owners were ready to sell.

Cushing was interested. But first he climbed into a canoe and paddled up the river to take a look at the pineries. He was impressed. He saw enough trees to supply the mill for generations. And he was aware that the St. Croix flowed into the Mississippi, offering cheap and ready access to such downstream markets as St. Louis.

Cushing joined two wealthy Boston friends in a grandiose scheme to develop the timber, waterpower and mineral resources of the region. They bought out the bankrupt St. Croix Falls company and prepared to establish a timber monopoly.

With Wisconsin approaching statehood, Cushing decided it would be easier to control the St. Croix Valley under the easygoing administration of a territorial government than to be subject to the whims of state legislators in Madison. So he and his rich friends headed for Washington to buttonhole congressmen.

Wisconsin had already lost Chicago and adjacent territory to Illinois, and the Upper Peninsula to Michigan, so there was precedent for stealing another chunk of its territory. The original plan was for Wisconsin's northwestern boundary to be along the Rum River, a considerable distance west. The New Englanders persuaded their friends in the Capitol to draw the line instead along the St. Croix.

Cushing was less successful at getting himself named governor of Minnesota Territory when it was organized in 1849, perhaps because he had to quit politicking and march south as colonel of the First Massachusetts when war broke out with Mexico over the annexation of Texas. When he got back to the St. Croix, he not only found that another man had been chosen governor but his lumber empire had been taken over by the resident manager, William S. Hungerford. It took Cushing and his friends from 1849 to 1853 to win a court battle and be declared the rightful owners. By then, their dream of monopolizing development of the region had evaporated. Cushing's company continued to be a factor along the St. Croix for years, but the former congressman's principal monument is the location of the Wisconsin-Minnesota boundary line.

The St. Croix begins at an inland lake twenty-two miles south of Lake Superior, twisting south and west until it reaches the Mississippi about twenty miles southwest of the present outskirts of the Twin Cities. The region was opened up to settlement in 1837, when a treaty was signed with the Indians. One of the first whites to head for the newly exploitable region was young Franklin Steele. He headed a party that paddled a canoe and poled a scow up the river as far as the falls of the St. Croix. It was there that they decided to establish the river's first sawmill. Steele went to St. Louis for financial backing, returning the following spring aboard a steamboat which carried thirty-six workmen, supplies and members of the newly formed St. Croix Falls Lumbering Company. Another company soon built a sawmill on the Minnesota side of the river at a community called Marine—its manager, a Vermonter named Orange Walker, had formerly lived in Marine, Illinois. Within twelve years, there were also mills at Arcola and Stillwater on the Minnesota side, and at Osceola as well as St. Croix Falls on the river's east bank.

Plenty of hardwoods grew near the sawmills, but the lumbermen had no use for such trees just yet. The white pine was located mostly above the falls of the St. Croix, along the main river and around such tributaries as the Snake, Kettle and Namekagon. As early as 1849, over thirty-seven thousand logs were floated down the river, representing something like eighteen million board feet. The St. Croix mills could handle no more than two thirds of this pine harvest. The rest had to be stored or sent downriver to the Mississippi.

The logs belonged to a number of different outfits, each of which stamped its identifying mark on its timber. During the drive the logs became mixed. They had to be sorted to determine the owner and destination. The various logging companies hired a scaler who measured each log and kept track of its ownership, maintaining books which were balanced at the end of the season. It was a cumbersome method. Martin Mower and another Maine man, John McKusick, who had founded Stillwater, Minnesota, and named it after his hometown, knew a better one. They decided to establish a boom company similar to those they recalled from Down East.

Minnesota Territory and the state of Wisconsin issued their first boom charters in 1851 to the St. Croix Boom Company, giving it authority to construct a movable barrier of huge logs chained together across the river six miles below Taylors Falls, Minnesota, and Osceola, Wisconsin. The company was permitted to charge forty cents per thousand board feet for the logs it collected, sorted and distributed to owners, plus an extra dime for logs delivered between the foot of the boom and McKusick's growing community of Stillwater. The charters specified that the company must not block the river's navigation—a provision that any lumberman or logger knew would be impossible to obey during the busy season, when thousands of logs would be massed behind the boom.

By the summer of 1851, residents of what was still largely a wilderness congregated at the newly constructed boom, busying themselves buying and selling logs, contracting to cut more, sorting and scaling the pine that had floated down the St. Croix from lumber camps to the north. Rafts were formed and sent downstream.

A visitor who stopped at a friend's home to find him was regarded as out of touch with what was going on: "Is Henry home? Hell, no. He's down at the boom like everybody else."

Makeshift saloons and gambling halls grew up near the boom site to cash in on the sudden prosperity. Several enterprising whores made the difficult trip north and were kept remarkably busy. There were the usual frontier brags about how the St. Croix folks had shown how to bring order out of the chaos that had been traditional when rival loggers all tried to get their winter's crop to the market at once.

The boom company soon ran into trouble, however. It couldn't keep its pledge not to interfere with navigation. When the steamboat *Asia* arrived with supplies for Taylors Falls in the late spring of 1853, the river was so jammed with logs above the boom that there was no way it could proceed. To avoid legal trouble, the company paid to transfer the goods to mackinaw boats and hauled them to their destination. This set an expensive precedent for other shipping that was stopped by the boom.

An even more serious problem for the company was the decision of many sawmill owners to build at Stillwater twenty-one miles south, instead of in the upper valley. Shortly before the boom was built, there had been only a single small mill at Stillwater. By 1854, the saws at that community and others downriver were producing more than two thirds of the lumber sawed in the valley. The Stillwater lumbermen complained about having to pay to have their supplies of logs rafted from the boom.

As so often happened, it was a Maine man who decided to do something about it. Isaac Staples, who had worked on a log boom at Old Town, Maine, formed the Stillwater Boom Company in 1854, getting a charter to build a boom five miles above his mill. Within a year, he and his eastern partners acquired ownership of much of the stock of the St. Croix Boom Company and in 1856 formed a new outfit, the St. Croix Boom Corporation, which built the Stillwater boom, tearing down the upriver barrier after a few years. The result was that Stillwater became the principal lumber center along the St. Croix.

The Stillwater boom, which antedated its principal rivals in Wisconsin and Michigan by a decade, handled more than thirteen billion board feet of logs during the next fifty years. The St. Croix Valley did not produce as much timber as the Chippewa in Wisconsin or the Saginaw in Michigan. But the boom at Stillwater outlived the Beef Slough boom on the Chippewa and the Titabawassee boom in Michigan.

Eastern capital and Maine lumbermen were particularly influential in Stillwater's growth. By 1855, when the community's population had risen to 1,200—an increase of 1,131 persons in six years—the Down East accent was common on its streets. Most of its six sawmills were owned and operated by Maine natives. A leading figure was Staples, who had interested the Hersey family of Maine lumbermen in investing in Minnesota. The Hersey, Staples & Company mill burned slabs and sawdust to make steam to power its saws. Its gang saw could make twenty cuts at once, an improvement on the circular type still generally used in the Lake States at that period. The company later branched out into logging, manufacturing, distribution, retailing, banking and transportation, growing into one of the largest business enterprises in the region.

Finding it sometimes easier to exchange lumber for grain instead of cash, Hersey, Staples also got into the flour-milling business, along with such Minnesota competitors as John S. Pillsbury. A New Hampshire man, Pillsbury started his Minnesota career by opening a hardware store for lumbermen, branched out into investments in pinery lands and finally, in 1872, joined a nephew, C. A. Pillsbury, in making flour.

Even before Minnesota entered the Union in 1858, it was a favorite destination for European immigrants looking for a toehold in a new land. The Scandinavian influx mostly came later. The early migration, as in neighboring Wisconsin, was mainly from the German states. This was encouraged by political troubles at home and by such publications as the *Emigrant Journal,* published in German and English by Ignatius Donnelly. As founder of Nininger, Minnesota, which he hoped to make into a metropolis, he shipped thousands of copies of his publication abroad to encourage Germans to move there. Donnelly's dreams never came true. The bottom fell out of the real estate market in 1857 and Nininger became a forgotten portion of what is now South St. Paul. Germans who had hoped to find prosperity there wound up swinging axes in the big woods instead.

One of Nininger's neighboring communities fared better. It was originally called Pig's Eye, in honor of a one-eyed saloonkeeper. By the time it had grown into a village of five hundred residents, it was decided the designation was undignified. So in one of the most thoroughgoing name changes on record, Pig's Eye became St. Paul.

Germans who gravitated to the pineries were mostly young bachelors. But now and then one showed up with a woman in tow, as happened in 1851 when a party of German lumberjacks passed through Eau Claire on their way to camp. John—his last name is no longer remembered—had a young woman, Louisa Ehrmann, with him. He said they were married, but this was apparently a gallant exaggeration. He was persuaded that a lumber camp was no place for Louisa and left her behind as housekeeper for James Reed and Simon Randall, partners in a local sawmill.

When John returned the next spring, Randall told him he wanted to marry the girl and was willing to pay the lumberjack two hundred dollars for her. That was more than he'd earned in a winter's labor. The deal was struck. Randall and Louisa were married. Their son Allen became the first white child born in Eau Claire. As for John, all he got was a two-hundred-dollar note, and he never cashed it. His friends kidded him about selling his "wife," and finally, in a temper, he threw Randall's IOU in the fire.

The last Indian claims to eastern Minnesota were given up by treaty in 1851, but trouble between lumberjacks and the original settlers continued on both sides of the St. Croix. As an example, two men who set out from Stillwater to pick a site for a lumber camp were ambushed by a pair of Indians. The braves shot them, cut the bodies into small pieces and tossed the remains in a lake.

The lumberjacks' friends organized search parties, with as many as three hundred men tramping through the woods on both sides of the St. Croix. But the disappearance remained a mystery until a band of Chippewa encamped near Chetek heard a rumor that troops were on the way. The rumor was false, but a chief who believed it sent a messenger to James Bracklin, superintendent of logging for Knapp, Stout. Bracklin was in charge of a lumber camp at Louseburg, an appropriately named community in Wisconsin's Barron County. Samuel B. Barker, a big man with a reputation as a good fellow to have along in a fight, agreed to accompany him to Chetek for a powwow.

After the preliminaries were over, the chief asked if the two missing men had been found. Bracklin had no knowledge of what had happened to them, but he didn't let on.

"Oh, yes. They were killed by Indians."

The chief smoked his pipe for a while, considering the matter. Then he said, "That is true."

He went on to assure Barker and Bracklin that his tribal band had nothing to do with the murders, but he knew what had happened. One lumberjack had been carrying fifteen hundred dollars, the chief said. He gave the white men the names of the braves who had done the shooting.

Barker and Bracklin went back to Louseburg. Not long afterward, one of the murderers showed up there with a large party of his friends.

"They were feeling good and had plenty to eat and were gambling," Bracklin recalled. "One game was to lay a blanket on the ground and the leader had two moccasins and a bullet and he moved them around over the blanket. And then betting would commence as to where the bullet had been left, under which moccasin. These Indians bet anything, from their moccasins to their souls."

Bracklin and Barker waited for a chance to get the killer alone and grab him. In a temporary lull in the gambling, the Indian went with several friends to Barker's trading post, but he stayed just outside the door. Bracklin took down a fiddle and began to play. To hear better, the Indian moved inside.

Barker pounced on him. Dropping the violin, Bracklin rushed over to help. Surprised by the suddenness of the attack, the other Indians fled. Bracklin slammed the door and locked it. But it was quickly knocked off its hinges and the Chippewas rushed back in to rescue their companion. A tug of war began, the two whites clinging grimly to their prisoner and his friends trying to haul him outside.

"He was dragged back and forth in that store from one end to the other a great many times," Bracklin said. "He was so bruised up that he was practically useless. He could not help himself or he would have got away."

The room was so small the Indians were unable to take advantage of their numbers. Finally, they went outside, leaving the prisoner, and sent a messenger to ask for help from another band of Chippewas encamped at the forks of the Yellow River. Among the reinforcements was an old man named Krokodokwa, who parleyed with the two whites. When he heard the captive was wanted for murder, he agreed to take a note to Henry Sawyer at Chetek.

Krokodokwa was chased by some of the prisoner's friends—the whites could hear sporadic shooting for the next half hour. But he got away and delivered the message. Sawyer rounded up all the lumberjacks he could find and headed to the rescue. They had only one gun, so they arrived armed with axes and peaveys.

The whites were still outnumbered ten to one. They crowded into the trading post, now and then ducking when someone shot at the log walls. After dark, a young Indian asked to palaver with the prisoner and was allowed inside. The only light was from flickering candles made from deer fat.

The murderer and the youth talked in low voices for half an hour before the latter left. Then the prisoner went to the wall. With his face at a crack between two logs, he began singing his death song. About 9 P.M. a shot rang out. Bracklin realized that the visitor had smuggled in a weapon and there was confusion in the cabin, with men dropping to the floor to make smaller targets. But the gun did not sound again and Barker finally walked over with a candle to investigate. He found that their prisoner had blown a hole in his belly with an ancient two-barreled pistol.

"He was a good Indian," Bracklin said, in telling the story. "That is, he was dead."

A seventeen-man army contingent arrived the next day, after the funeral. The whites had buried the prisoner, watched by a delegation of Indians. Bracklin explained to the onlookers that the dead man had killed a lumberjack and cut up his body.

"Yes," one of the Chippewas said. "And he cut off his ears, too."

Despite what happened to the Stillwater lumberjacks, travel in the Minnesota woods was generally safe enough for a man who knew how to deal with a wilderness. Landlookers disappeared into the forest for weeks at a time, searching out places where pines were thick and the lay of the land made logging easy. Most traveled on foot. A few used dog teams. They lived off the land, eating what they could shoot or catch.

Among notable Minnesota landlookers was Daniel Stanchfield, who explored the Rum River region in 1847 for Cushing and returned with word that "seventy mills in seventy years can't cut all that pine out there." Another was Lyman W. Ayer, son of New Englanders who had come to Minnesota as missionaries to the Indians. Ayer never wore white men's shoes until he enlisted in the Civil War Army. Besides being a timber cruiser, he carried dispatches from Fort Snelling, Minnesota, to Winnipeg, a considerable hike. He hunted buffalo, taught school, traded for furs. He never used liquor, tobacco or profanity, which made him stand out in the neighborhood. He was still cruising the woods when he was in his seventies, striding beneath the tall pines with his white beard flowing out behind him.

The discovery of gold in California nearly depopulated some frontier towns in the Midwest as Forty-Niners headed west to dig for their fortunes. The excitement got Minnesotans to wondering if there might be metallic riches closer to home. Midwestern Indian tribes had used native copper for hundreds of years before the first whites showed up. There were tales of braves who had found silver deposits in the region. A number of gold rushes occurred in what came to be known as Minnesota's Arrowhead country, with hopeful prospectors pouring into the region. The boom collapsed as quickly as it was born, although some years later there was a temporarily prosperous gold mine near Rainy Lake, close to the Canadian border.

Most prospectors for precious metals went away disappointed. Some came to realize that in the Arrowhead country the wealth was colored green, not gold or silver. They stayed to cut the pine and to start a flourishing lumber industry in the region. The first sawmill in that area began cuttings logs at Oneota in 1855. But it was not until well after the Civil War that logging was conducted on a large scale in the Arrowhead country. In the early days, it was considered too remote to compete with forests handier to the markets.

Until around 1850, eastern lumber—some from as far away as New England—was sold along the Mississippi, with Chicago acting as a transshipment point. Then the supply from the St. Croix, the Wisconsin, Chippewa and lesser rivers became more than adequate to meet the demand from St. Louis and smaller river ports. The lumber was bought by settlers who were pushing west into Iowa, Missouri, Kansas and more remote points.

After the Civil War began what one authority called a "forty-year frenzy in the pine woods." But the period just prior to that conflict saw lumbering change in the Lake States from a local and small-scale industry into a well-organized method of giving fortunes to the few and hard work under primitive conditions to the many. Michigan lumbering was flourishing. Minnesota was getting into the competition. Wisconsin was gearing up to supply enough boards to settle half a continent as covered wagons headed west into the Great Plains.

There were six principal logging rivers in Wisconsin. Besides the St. Croix, which it shared with Minnesota, there were the Chippewa, the Wisconsin, the Black, Wolf and Red Cedar. Another principal lumber center was what was known as the Green Bay and Lake Shore district. This included production along the Menominee River, which divides Wisconsin from the Upper Peninsula of Michigan. Together with the Wolf River sawmills, this area looked to Chicago and the East for its markets, shipping boards and sometimes logs by way of Lake Michigan.

The Wolf River district made lumber towns of Fond du Lac and Oshkosh and contributed to the bustle at the port of Sheboygan, where schooners were loaded with lumber for Milwaukee, Chicago and ports to the east.

Oshkosh grew up around a dozen sawmills that were built to handle the flood of logs coming down the Wolf from the north. By the late 1850s it was calling itself "The Sawdust City." As the principal center of the region's lumber trade, it used its ready supply of cheap pine to lead the nation in the manufacture of wooden matches and became a major manufacturing location for producing wagons, carriages, doors and other products whose chief raw material floated down the Wolf each spring.

Across the state, La Crosse became the Black River district's chief lumber town. Located at the point where the Black and La Crosse rivers meet the Mississippi, it had early ambitions to outdistance St. Louis as the Mississippi Valley's principal market for pine. On the eve of the Civil War, La Crosse had two banks, six carriage and wagon factories, a sash and blinds factory and more than a dozen sawmills. At a time when hogs still ran at large on its mud streets, it had an opera house and eight newspapers, three of them dailies.

Chippewa Falls and Eau Claire were the principal lumber centers along the Chippewa River. They were located some distance from its junction with the Mississippi. Along the Wisconsin, an early center was Big Bull Falls, where George Steele filed his claim in 1839. Within eight years, the settlement had 350 residents and had changed its name to Wausau.

In Michigan, exploitation of the lumber resources of the Upper Peninsula lagged behind, but by the 1850s there were a few scattered lumber camps and sawmills operating there. Captain John G. Parker built a mill in 1852 on the Ontonagon River, for example. He was soon joined by others, including Allen Gardner, remembered more for his ability to win logging camp brawls with his fists than as a lumber baron.

Most of the boards produced by the Upper Peninsula mills were used in the vicinity. Not until pine became scarce in the lower peninsula did the northern region begin to compete for distant markets.

As for Minnesota, its logging industry was growing rapidly in the 1850s despite a scarcity of locally grown crops to feed horses, oxen and men. There was, as yet, a lack of farmers. But the lumberjacks shot deer and moose to supplement their larders and fanned out along the rivers.

In the winter of 1852–53 there were twenty-two logging crews on the Rum River, each averaging better than a million board feet for the season. Two years later, eighty-two crews were cutting timber along the St. Croix and its tributaries. Other lumberjacks were working along the Minnesota River and the upper reaches of the Mississippi.

The activity was brisk enough to impress eastern observers, especially those who hoped to cash in on investments in the region. But not everybody was optimistic about the territory's future. Horace Greeley, an editor with an opinion about nearly everything, remarked that Minnesota was still an importing region. And what it was importing just then, he added, was "bread, whiskey and loafers in great abundance."

Luckily, the men who were chopping down trees from dawn to dark were too busy to read Greeley's New York *Tribune*.

CHAPTER VI

Stealing the Public's Timber

THE OUTBREAK of the Civil War in 1861 disrupted the marketing pattern for lumber in the Mississippi Valley. But wartime prosperity more than made up for the loss of former markets in the Confederacy. An expanding railroad network provided a more versatile method of distributing boards from the Lake States sawmills.

In the war's early months, when marching south to put down the rebellion seemed like a lighthearted adventure, lumberjacks and mill workers joined volunteer regiments, causing shortages of workers in the woods. Canadians drifted south to fill the gap. A few women played a role, mostly as cooks or clerical workers but in a few instances as landlookers. As the war wore on, enthusiasm for enlisting waned with each new casualty list, and lumber camps became reasonably secure hideouts for deserters and men who were dodging the draft.

Lumber workers who joined the Army were used to a rugged life and usually made good soldiers, although there was little call for their specialized skills. An exception to this came during an 1864 expedition by a Union force on the Red River in Louisiana. Knowledge of how to persuade a stream to float logs made a hero of a Wisconsin lumberman.

Joseph E. Bailey, who was from Kilbourn City (now Wisconsin Dells), had learned logging skills along the Wisconsin River. On the 1864 expedition, he was a lieutenant colonel in the forces commanded by one of the Union's political generals, N. P. "Nothing Positive" Banks. Along with a fleet of transports and gunboats commanded by Commodore David Dixon Porter, General Banks and his men moved up the Red River in the hope of capturing Shreveport. When the fleet got to Springfield Landing, however, it found the stream blocked by a scuttled steamer. Meanwhile, Banks's ten thousand troops were being routed by the Confederates. The soldiers rallied under the guns of Porter's ships. The commodore and the general agreed to retreat back down the river to Alexandria before they got in any more trouble.

A little above that community, Porter discovered that the river level had fallen so far that there was no longer water enough to float his ships over the shallows. There seemed to be no choice but to abandon the fleet and slink back to New Orleans on foot, the ultimate disgrace for a sailor.

Bailey came forward with a plan. Up north, he said, when a river didn't have water enough to float a winter's log crop, the boys had some tricks to make it behave. If he could have the use of some of the army's former lumberjacks, he'd build a dam and get the fleet out of its trap.

Porter wasn't much impressed. But he was desperate enough to be willing to try anything, saying: "If he can dam better than I can, he must be a good hand at it. I've been damning all night."

Banks was also skeptical, but he told Bailey to go ahead and see what he could do. The colonel could have twelve days. After that, the army was leaving and the ships must be abandoned. The general added another proviso: Bailey could use whatever equipment was available, but he must not spend a dime of government money.

The colonel picked a crew of three thousand men. A contingent of freed slaves was included, along with lumberjacks from two Wisconsin regiments and one from Maine. Porter's sailors lined the rails to make witty remarks while the axemen went to work.

They began by anchoring two 170-foot coal barges in the river, leaving a 66-foot gap between them. They lengthened the sides of the barges, filled them with rocks and let them sink to the bottom to form part of the dam. Meanwhile, trees were being chopped down. Horses dragged them to the river and they were floated between the sunken barges and the banks, with the treetops pointing upstream. The butts of the trees were fastened together with cross timbers. Stones were poured on top of the trees.

The water was beginning to rise by now. Porter began to feel faint stirrings of hope that Bailey knew what he was about. The pinery boys and the blacks worked around the clock, torches lighting the river at night. They added brush, small stones and earth to the dam. Then wing dams were built upstream to force the river into a narrower channel.

When the water had been raised by seven feet behind the dam, Bailey asked the commodore to get ready. Dixon indicated he was not only ready but eager. An opening was made in the log and dirt barrier. Several vessels sailed through before another part of the dam collapsed. The lumberjacks went back to work, rebuilt the barrier and raised the river level again. This time, when an opening was made, the remaining ships moved through like pine logs in the spring drive, getting safely past the shallows to deeper water.

Bailey admitted to Banks that the operation had cost the taxpayers fifty axes, which had been lost in the river, but no one was disposed to complain. The thirty-five ships saved were valued at two million dollars. President Lincoln made Bailey a brevet brigadier general.

Lincoln's assassination on the heels of the northern victory changed the President from a controversial politician to a heroic martyr. In the booming sawmill town of La Crosse, the saloon sentiment turned ugly.

"Let's hang Brick Pomeroy," someone suggested.

All of a sudden, that seemed like an excellent idea. Mark Pomeroy was the editor of the La Crosse *Democrat,* a supporter of the Copperhead wing of the party. During the 1864 campaign between Lincoln and General George McClellan, he had written that "it would be well were some bold hand with a dagger to pierce Lincoln's heart for the public good." In view of what had happened in the Ford Theater, that now sounded like treason.

A mob formed to call on Pomeroy, wreck his paper and string him up. Luckily for the editor, the line of march led past a brewery. Thought of the lynching had made throats dry. Pomeroy could wait while they stopped for a quick one. One drink led to another. By the time Lincoln's admirers finally left the brewery, hanging Pomeroy seemed like too much trouble. Brick did not wait until his critics sobered up, however. He took the next train for New York.

Lincoln's death proved a major political asset for his party, with Republicans triumphantly taking over on the strength of the Union victory and their leader's martyrdom. Feelings against Democrats sometimes ran high, even if the member of the opposition party had fought for the North. William Pope discovered this when he returned to his old job at the Peshtigo Harbor sawmill after his military service. It became known to the owners that he was the only man there who admitted he voted Democratic. They issued an ultimatum: Change your politics or be fired.

"I fought against slavery for four years," Pope told his boss, "and I don't plan to become a slave to such tyranny now."

The speech gained him respect around the lumberyard—and a chance to start hunting for another job.

The lumber barons took a keen interest in political matters, particularly those involving state and local elections. A workman who couldn't be counted on to vote right was not welcome. The nation was entering into one of the most corrupt periods of its history, with many legislators for sale to the highest bidder. The logging interests had no intention of letting rivals outbribe them.

Local elections were particularly important because of their effect on the tax rate on timberland. The companies had a built-in voting bloc in the lumberjacks, who were often transients with little interest in local affairs. They could be coerced or persuaded by their bosses to vote right. Reinforcements were also easy to recruit in the saloons, where idlers were delighted to trade a vote for a drink. If all else failed, ballot boxes could be stuffed.

The stuffing was not one-sided, however. Local residents often had an equally strong interest in the election, which would determine whether they could finance improvements by raising taxes on land owned by lumbermen and other outsiders. There were strong-arm tactics and other illegalities practiced by both sides.

As one lumberman put it, when he was an old man and could speak freely, the transfer of timberlands from public to private ownership in Minnesota, Wisconsin and Michigan constituted "one of the greatest periods of graft and exploitation" in the nation's history, with the railroads and lumber companies dividing the profits.

The Homestead Act of 1862 provided that a settler could obtain a quarter section of land if he built a house with at least two windows and lived there for five years. Lumber companies paid their men to stake out such claims in prime pine country and construct some sort of shack, with the understanding that after the claim was approved the acreage and its trees belonged to the sponsor.

Many federal land agents shared in the graft and went along with schemes to cheat the government. But now and then an honest agent showed up, causing problems. If he couldn't be bought or chased off, other methods were tried.

An honest agent proved an annoyance one year in Ashland, Wisconsin. Lumber companies wanted to cut several million board feet of pine on a nearby Indian reservation, but the agent wouldn't agree to approve the deal even after he was offered a share of the profits. Threats were tried. The agent stood fast. Finally, at considerable expense, the lumbermen imported a young woman from Chicago who managed to catch the land agent's eye. They were in bed in her hotel room when the door was kicked in. A large man with a gun in each hand demanded:

"What the hell you doing with my wife? Get out of town before I kill you!"

Snatching up his clothes, the agent ran. He caught the next train. John Nelligan, the lumber camp boss who told the story, said the gunman took his fee and headed west where, according to rumor, he wound up a millionaire. The land agent was never seen in Ashland again.

Most companies considered it poor business to cheat the landlookers who worked for them, but others took advantage of them. After a man had spent weeks in the woods, he would return with information about a likely tract of pine, suggesting that the land be acquired and he be given a quarter interest for his trouble. If a lumberman was unscrupulous, he would turn him down. Then, before the landlooker had a chance to interest anyone else in the opportunity, the company would file a claim for the property at the land office.

To keep land prices low, lumber company owners would often get together before an auction to divide up the acreage, each agreeing not to bid on the portion allotted to the others. This was illegal, of course. But as long as no one but the public or some distant land speculator was hurt, it was socially acceptable in the vicinity.

There was some criticism of an Oshkosh millionaire for his dealings with a small competitor from Oconto, Wisconsin, however. In 1875, the North Western Road offered several thousand acres of good pine land between the Wolf and Oconto rivers for sale to the highest bidder. The Oshkosh lumberman told his rival it was foolish to drive up the price by bidding against each other.

"I'll do the bidding for both of us. After the sale, I'll sell you the part you want at what I've paid for it. That way, we'll both save money."

The Oconto man was agreeable to cheating the railroad, and when the auction was held the fellow from Oshkosh got the entire tract for a dollar or so an acre. When his competitor showed up to claim his share, the millionaire was cordial. He offered him a cigar. He bought him a drink. But he said he'd changed his mind. He was sorry, but he was going to keep the whole thing.

Land grants for railroads and canals eventually totaled one tenth of the entire area of Wisconsin. Michigan and Minnesota followed a similar pattern. Other public land was sold at low prices for schools and to support land-grant colleges. Veterans of several wars were given bonuses in script which represented acreage in the Lake States, with most of the former soldiers and sailors selling their acquisition rights at low prices to speculators. Homesteaders could get 160-acre parcels free if they made certain improvements—or pretended to make them. As a result of all this cheap land floating around, much of the three states was owned for a time by Easterners, including some who were well known. Daniel Webster, the New Hampshire senator, for instance, along with Wade Hampton of South Carolina and the Biddles of Philadelphia. Charles Augustus Murray, an Englishman, owned 20,000 acres, hanging onto a portion of this impressive Wisconsin estate he'd never seen until 1879.

The Minnesota Legislature at one point called on Congress to preserve public lands for bona fide settlers, but no one in Washington paid much attention. Absentee ownership discouraged settlement by farmers and made life more complicated for loggers.

But in most cases, the latter simply cut the trees without worrying unduly about who owned them.

Speculators who'd bought land early resented latecomers to the high-stakes game. The lumbermen considered it proper for Knapp, Stout & Company to monopolize the pine on the Red Cedar River by buying up 135,000 acres near its mill at Menomonie, or for Isaac Stephenson and his associates to acquire 138,000 acres in Upper Michigan and northern Wisconsin. The logs such outfits cut would be sawed in nearby mills, giving work to residents. But when New York, New England or Pennsylvania capitalists bought up good pine land and held it in the hope of a rise in price, that was sorely resented. If a local lumberman could get away with stealing such absentees' timber, so much the better.

By the mid-1860s, most of the best timberland in Michigan's lower peninsula had been sold. That brought a rush of Michigan speculators to Minnesota and Wisconsin. A group that included a Detroit millionaire, Francis Palms, and William A. Rust of Saginaw acquired 309,000 acres in Wisconsin's pineries, causing considerable hard feeling over such "foreign" encroachment on the part of Wisconsin lumbermen, who had too little capital just then to compete.

Even more aggravating to local interests was the acquisition of 600,000 acres in northern Wisconsin by Ezra Cornell and two of his fellow New Yorkers, Henry W. Sage and John McGraw. Sage and McGraw were already lumber kings in Michigan, owning two of the largest sawmills in Bay City, which they had helped found. Cornell bought nearly half a million acres along the Chippewa and its tributaries. McGraw and Sage picked up another 100,000 acres, giving the three something approaching a monopoly of timber resources in what had become the richest lode of white pine in the world now that trees were getting less plentiful in the Saginaw watershed.

Cornell was an Ithaca contractor who invested in Western Union Telegraph Company stock when that company was organized. The investment made him a millionaire. He decided to give his hometown a college which would teach farmers how to operate more scientifically. After Cornell University was chartered, its founder began to acquire land-grant scrip which could be exchanged for acreage in the Lake States, pledging to use the anticipated profits to increase the school's endowment fund, less 7 per cent he would retain for his trouble.

There was plenty of such scrip around. Over the protests of most congressmen from Michigan, Wisconsin and Minnesota, Congress had passed the Agricultural College Act, giving 30,000 acres of federal land to the states for each representative or senator they had in Washington. In New York's case, that amounted to 989,920 acres. Scrip representing rights to more than 900,000 acres was obtained by Cornell on behalf of his college. He used it mostly to buy land in Wisconsin and Minnesota.

By 1867, Cornell was the largest private owner of pine land in the nation, aside from one or two railroads. He sold his investment gradually over a lengthy period, holding most of the land until prices rose with a growing scarcity of prime timber. In all, he grossed nearly $6,800,000, making a net profit for Cornell University of about $5 million. By contrast, the state of Wisconsin sold its 240,000-acre allotment for a mere $300,000.

Thanks to a stubborn willingness to hang onto the land until the price went up, Cornell benefited his university and fulfilled the goal of the 1862 legislation. He was a rare exception. Most states, like Wisconsin, unloaded their allotments as fast as they could find buyers, selling the land for as little as forty-two cents an acre. As a historian has noted, disposal of the agricultural college scrip was marked by "neglect, carelessness, incapacity and something closely akin to corruption."

Minnesota, Wisconsin and Michigan each had a million acres of federal land earmarked for sale under this huge dispersal plan. By 1868, all of it had been bought. The clamor for Michigan pinery holdings was so great that Congress amiably added another 400,000 acres to the allotment in that state.

The absentee ownership created by much of the land-grant sale encouraged a continuation of the tradition of timber stealing, which went back to the region's early days.

The original settlers in the north woods felt that trees were a public resource, like air and water, free for the taking. This attitude gradually changed as it was demonstrated that pines could be bought and sold, but the feeling persisted that stealing timber was not as sinful as stealing other things—whiskey, for instance. If you stole a man's last bottle, he might perish from thirst. If you stole his pine trees he could always walk a little farther into the woods and find more.

Some timber thieves became folk heroes of a sort. For example, a French-Canadian named LeCoq, who operated around the Cass River region in Michigan, was notorious for the brazen way he went about his work. But even LeCoq could make a mistake. One spring, he and a confederate rounded up logs that someone else had cut and fashioned them into two rafts. The rafts were floated down to Saginaw, arriving there after dark. The wind was blowing hard and LeCoq persuaded his partner that it would be better to wait until morning to get the stolen lumber to the mill.

The two shared a room in a nearby boardinghouse. LeCoq waited until his friend started snoring, then crept out of bed, dressed, tiptoed down the hall and went outside. He untied one raft and poled it to the mill, where he collected the money. Then he sneaked back into bed without disturbing his partner. The next morning, LeCoq pretended to be surprised that only one raft was left.

"Tough luck, eh? Your raft got loose and drifted away."

The friend ran over to take a closer look.

"Oh, no," he told LeCoq. "Here's my mark. This is my raft, tied up safe and sound. You're the one who's out of luck."

And so LeCoq's reputation grew along the Cass and the Saginaw. There were plenty of timber thieves. But who else had ever stolen a raft from himself?

The small-time specialists in making off with somebody else's pine had little to lose and took their logs or finished lumber wherever they could. The logging companies had to be more careful, having assets which could be attached in a lawsuit. A favorite practice was to buy a forty, the smallest unit sold by the state or federal government, then tell the camp foreman: "Log around that forty." If it came to an argument someday, the lumberman could swear he'd meant that his crew should cut trees only on the land he owned. But the foreman understood that he was expected to misunderstand his instructions, taking them to mean he should log the forty acres to the west, the east, the south and the north of the original forty.

Absentee owners were considered fair game, but the favorite victim of timber trespass was the public. Washington was a long way off. The state capitals were not much interested in how the pinery boys behaved as long as they voted right.

Now and then, legislators made a gesture. In Wisconsin, for instance, the first law forbidding timber trespass was enacted in 1849, the year after the state was admitted to the Union. The measure's effectiveness is indicated by the fact that another such law was passed in 1855 and still others in 1860, 1864, 1865, 1876, 1885, 1891, 1893 and 1901. The enforcement of such wistful attempts to stop thievery improved somewhat as the nineteenth century waned. But the problem of how to keep people from stealing pines was not really solved until there were no more pines worth stealing.

The federal government was nearly as impotent. Even when it seized stolen lumber, no one in the vicinity would bid on it without the consent of the man who'd stolen it. If it sent out agents who were willing to try to enforce the law, they were jeered at, circumvented, threatened and made to feel like outcasts. At least one was shot to death—a deputy land agent who was killed near Dubuque in 1854 while trying to take possession of stolen logs that had been floated down the Mississippi from Wisconsin.

An agent in western Michigan tried to arrest some timber thieves but local law-enforcement officials refused to back him up. He finally had to call in the Navy. A ship happened to be in port nearby and the bluejackets shouldered rifles and marched to his support.

At one point, sixteen sawmills on Wisconsin's Black River were cutting nothing but stolen government pine, using two hundred million board feet of it a year. Of half a billion board feet shipped from eastern Wisconsin and northern Michigan between 1844 and 1854, it was estimated, 90 per cent was stolen. Tens of millions of dollars' worth of pine was taken from government-owned land in the three states between 1856 and 1877, but Washington collected exactly $154,373.74.

Things changed a bit when Carl Schurz was made Secretary of the Interior in 1877. A German immigrant who had settled in Wisconsin and helped gain the support of his compatriots for the Republican Party, Schurz took his job of protecting the nation's forest resources seriously. He announced a crusade against timber thieves. Before the year was out, his men had arrested twenty-five of them in Minnesota and Wisconsin. But as soon as the heat was off, thievery resumed. During the next two years, federal agents estimated, fourteen million board feet of logs was stolen and only two million recovered. Often the lumber had changed hands so many times when the agents caught up with it that they didn't know whom to indict. Sometimes, after a tract of public land was logged it was set afire, destroying evidence of the illegal cutting.

One reason why Washington disposed of its wilderness lands so rapidly in the nineteenth century was that authorities kept warning that the property was losing its value because so many of the trees were disappearing. The full might of the United States could not stop such massive pilferage. Numerous spokesmen admitted this, among them a land agent who said that when he tried to stop the thefts he was considered "an Ishmael, with my hand against every man and every man against me." According to one reliable estimate, there wasn't a forty-acre tract of government land in the three Lake States that hadn't lost at least a few pines to illegal cutting.

It was not true, however, that the rule was "anything goes." Public opinion held that it was all right for local folks to steal trees, but not strangers. When a group of Minnesota trespassers begun cutting pines on state-owned land near La Crosse, Wisconsin, for example, the sheriff organized a posse and chased them back across the Mississippi, declaring: "Such foreigners are not welcome in my district."

Washington periodically took note of how much of its timber was being lost and authorized land agents to seize logs that had been cut illegally, a method that had already been tried in colonial days by the king's agents. But the federal rules were more lenient than the Crown's had been. If a government agent seized logs a company's men had cut on federal land, all the lumberman had to do was buy the land at the going price, usually $1.25 an acre.

That gave a logger an interesting option. If he wanted to cut pine on a thousand acres of public land, he had the choice of paying $1,250 for the acreage or taking a chance on cutting the trees without owning them, knowing that in the unlikely possibility that he got caught it would still cost him $1,250.

"No one will buy, of course, so long as he can steal with impunity," the Green Bay register noted in a letter to the general land office.

Even when a timber thief was brought to trial, he could usually escape penalty if he had stolen the trees from the public or an absentee owner. Local prosecutors and judges knew they would be voted out of office if they took action against companies that controlled so many votes in the neighborhood. Frontier juries were seldom willing to convict unless the offense had been committed against an owner whose local connections were good.

Only those speculators who were able to hire honest agents to guard their acreage from illegal cutting were likely to profit from their investment. There were more losers than winners, but some people did quite well. Abner Coburn, a millionaire lumberman from Maine, for instance, sold acreage in the Eau Claire River Valley for $600,000 that had cost him $30,000. Cyrus Woodman, who arrived in Wisconsin early to manage fifty thousand acres owned by Bostonians, soon persuaded his employers to sell out to him at a low figure. Over the years, he added another fifty thousand acres and managed to fight off such hazards as high tax assessments and encroachments by timber thieves. He wound up a rich man.

Unless he was on the scene to protest, pull strings, buy votes and otherwise participate in frontier democracy, an owner of timberland was often at the mercy of residents of the region. Absentee owners wound up footing most of the bills for courthouses, roads, schools and bridges, as well as paying subsidies out of local tax money for railroads. Local voters, especially those with no land to be taxed, found it profitable to organize a new township or a new county, elect themselves or their friends to office, then hand out construction contracts, making sure that most of the taxes were paid by absentees.

In northern Chippewa County, Wisconsin, for example, land was assessed at 100 per cent of value, but in the southern half it was assessed at 33 per cent. The northern half was mostly absentee owned. The southern half was occupied mostly by homesteaders and their friends.

County and local governments in the pinery regions were often corrupt and poorly managed. In Clark County, Wisconsin, for instance, three treasurers in a row defaulted, producing a $50,000 loss for the sparsely settled region. In other counties, railroad subsidies were handed out so lavishly that the public debt mounted alarmingly. But as long as absentee landowners had to pay most of the bills, no one in the vicinity got too disturbed by such things.

At a time when the Wisconsin county of Ashland had a permanent population of three hundred, a referendum was held on whether to issue $200,000 worth of county bonds to be exchanged for stock in a proposed railroad. Ezra Cornell owned much of the land that would be taxed to pay for this generosity. He and his agents, along with other absentee owners, fought vigorously against the proposal. For a time, it looked as if they would be able to persuade or hire a majority of the voters. But at the last minute, seventy Irishmen were brought in from Chicago to cast ballots and the subsidy carried.

When graft and poor business practices started affecting the resident lumber companies, of course, that was another matter. The local lumbermen usually could make sure their interests didn't suffer. Sometimes they had to take strong measures. In 1859, for instance, when Knapp, Stout decided it couldn't run Polk County, Wisconsin, it was instrumental in having it divided in two, hoping the smaller pieces would prove more manageable.

In another northern Wisconsin county, Barron, a $50,000 courthouse was authorized at a time when the total public resources amounted to $2,000. Lincoln County paid a member of its board of supervisors $4,000 for a poor farm, then discovered it had only one pauper within its borders. Buffalo County paid $5,000 for its poor farm and, with no demand for its facilities, soon sold it for $700.

A large tract of land belonging to a distant owner might be attached first to one school district, then another, until everybody in the vicinity had a fine new building. The cost of other civic improvements was mostly paid by New Englanders, New Yorkers and other absentees. Land taxes had to be paid at the county seat, either in person or through an agent. Unless the distant owner kept close check on when taxes were due on each of his properties, he might find that he'd lost his title.

The resident lumbermen understood how to take advantage of the prevailing dislike of absentee owners, adding some tricks of their own. In 1869, for example, the government decided to hold a public sale of 247,680 acres in the Chippewa pinery which had been kept off the market until then in case it was needed to encourage a railroad to send its rails into a new patch of wilderness. This was choice property. So many rich lumbermen showed up in Eau Claire that both of that community's taverns were quickly filled and several millionaires had to rent beds in private homes.

The early bidding was brisk. Some of the land went for as high as $6 an acre. Then cooler heads arranged a meeting of the lumber barons and that ended competitive bidding. Knapp, Stout got 14,000 acres at $1.25 an acre, the minimum Washington would accept. Thorp, Chapman & Company got a similar amount on the same terms. William A. Rust, who was already well on his way to a fortune on the Saginaw, was allotted 13,000 acres. Philetus Sawyer, Oshkosh's entry in the competition, was content with 5,600 acres. Lesser lumbermen got smaller amounts. When the sale was over, there was great satisfaction in the knowledge that the cozy arrangement had cheated the government out of close to a million dollars.

Pinery owners bought up weekly newspapers to control public opinion. Once the land was stripped of its trees, they refused to pay taxes, letting the cutover acreage go to the local or county governments. Many of the owners delayed payment of taxes for years even on land that was still valuable, knowing that the hard-pressed local governments would have to issue tax certificates against such delinquent acreage. Then those certificates could be bought for as little as ten cents on the dollar and used to pay the tax bill. There was widespread speculation in such tax certificates and much dickering back and forth between large landowners and politicians.

Because taxes were often high on valuable timberland, the companies found it profitable to log them as rapidly as possible, almost regardless of the market for lumber. This provided one more impetus for wasteful cutting.

It has been estimated that close to 90 per cent of the "homesteaders" in the pinery region were actually front men for the lumber barons, hired to file a claim for 160 acres which could be turned over to their employers. A special agent of the U.S. land office, sent to Duluth to look into such shenanigans, found that of fifty-six Minnesota homesteads he examined, only one had a habitable dwelling. About half showed no faint sign of human life. The remainder, he told Washington, had "log pens from one to four feet in height, without any semblance of door, window, floor or roof." He summoned the fifty-five men who had filed false homestead claims, but none showed up. Anyway, the agent said, it was unlikely that a local jury would have upheld the law. It was as hard to convict such men of fraud, he added, "as it is in Utah to get evidence of bigamy."

Lumber companies employed gangs of men to go into the woods and stake out claims. Some were Great Lakes sailors, who could make a hundred dollars by spending a day or two as make-believe homesteaders. Under the law, they could pre-empt a claim for thirty-three months without paying for the land. By the end of that time, of course, the trees would have disappeared and the government could have its property back.

To qualify for a homestead, a settler had to be an adult. Some of those willing to earn some easy money by bilking Uncle Sam were lads still in their teens, but the lumberman knew a way around that. He'd mark "21" on the floor of his office with chalk and tell the boy to stand on that spot.

"Son, can you swear to me that you're over twenty-one?"

"Sure can," the lad would say, grinning.

"Okay. Now you remember you told me you were over twenty-one if the subject ever comes up."

A homesteader, regardless of age, was supposed to build a house on his 160 acres. Often the speculator would supply one in the form of a large packing case with a couple of holes cut in the side for windows. An empty whiskey bottle might be fastened in one of the holes so the owner, if he was unlucky enough to be challenged, could swear he had glass in his window.

It was specified that the dwelling must be at least fourteen by sixteen. Dragging a packing case that large into the woods was a lot of trouble, so sometimes the buildings erected to fulfill the legal requirements were considerably smaller. Still, the owner could say his house was fourteen by sixteen, as long as no one got stuffy and asked whether he meant feet or inches.

One commissioner of the General Land Office regarded the matter with weary cynicism. "The vast machinery of the land department," said William Sparks in 1885, "appears to have been devoted to . . . conveying the title to public lands upon fraudulent entries under strained constructions of imperfect land laws and upon illegal claims under public and private grants."

Because the lumber companies controlled such a high percentage of the human musclepower available in the vicinity, they could often intimidate the opposition at public land auctions. An outside bidder who tried to compete with a timber king's representative might find himself surrounded by a group of tough lumberjacks. They seldom had much difficulty in persuading him to withdraw his bid.

Sometimes a lumber baron would bid generously for a tract of public land he wanted, agreeing to pay $15 or even $20 an acre. A few days later, when the auction was over and the other bidders had left, he would withdraw his offer. That meant the tract would be sold by the government for what it could get. Then the high bidder's agent could work out a deal with his friends in office to get the land for the $1.25 minimum.

When a bidding pool had been formed to buy auctioned land cheaply, those in the ring sometimes would later hold an auction among themselves to distribute the acreage. One such sale held in Madison caused a scandal when word leaked out that a pinery tract which had brought $3 an acre to the state was soon sold for as much as $50 an acre by members of the pool. The state land commissioners canceled the deal, bringing down on their heads the nearly unanimous criticism of weekly newspapers in the logging counties, most of which were owned or controlled by the lumber interests. The commissioners held fast, but the Wisconsin Supreme Court was persuaded to rule that the state agency could not withdraw from the market any land that had once been offered for sale.

Pinery politics were summed up by a Wisconsin candidate for Congress, seeking to represent one of the principal strongholds of the lumbermen. Somebody asked him how he expected to get enough votes to get elected.

"God damn it," he explained, "money counts in Chippewa County."

It counted in local town halls, county courthouses and the state legislatures, too. In the post-Civil War period, the favorite methods of making money in Minnesota, Wisconsin and Michigan were railway promotion, land speculation and lumbering. As all three depended to a considerable degree on being treated favorably at the public trough, a number of lawmakers felt they ought to get their share of the spoils. Buying friends in the capitals of the Lake States was easy enough.

Of the three states, Horace Greeley claimed, Wisconsin was the worst. After visiting Madison on an 1869 speaking tour, the Manhattan editor said he had never seen "such a pack of drunken rogues and ruffians" as the legislators there. Coming from a New Yorker acquainted with such experts in corruption as those in Albany, that was considered quite an accolade. But there were critics in Minneapolis and Lansing who claimed Greeley had slandered local roguery by putting Madison in first place.

CHAPTER VII

Rivers of Pine

THE CLIMAX OF a winter spent in the woods was the spring log drive. Everybody looked forward to it. The owners, because it meant their logs could be converted into cash. The lumberjacks, because it meant their tree chopping was over, payday approached and it was time for a spree. The respectable townspeople anticipated hearing the distant grumble of the mass of waterborne logs, a noise that was a symbol of prosperity, progress, and a break in the monotony. Those townies who were not notably respectable eagerly waited for the spring breakup for reasons of their own.

But the ones who looked forward to the log drive the most were the river pigs, as the men were called who escorted the lumberjacks' pinery harvest to the sawmills. Working conditions were often miserable on the drive. Food was plentiful but had to be snatched on the run. Duckings in icy water were common. Death under the logs was a single misstep away. Still, what did such things matter? The pay was good, the drive went toward the saloon lights instead of away from them, and, best of all, a river pig was a man who could demand respect. He was rough. He was tough. He was rugged. And when he made his brag, people listened.

Before a drive began, an advance crew was sent downstream to clear out brush or fallen trees along the banks and, if possible, move rocks likely to cause a log jam. Wing dams might be built to channel the current. Barriers to seal off backwater sloughs where logs could be caught and immobilized might be built. If the stream was small—some of those used by the loggers were hardly more than brooks—dams would long since have been constructed to catch the runoff when the snow melted, making sure enough water would be available to keep the logs from getting stranded. In many cases, a series of dams was built, each impounding in its turn the water released by the dam farther upstream.

Such impressive feats of engineering were performed under the direction of bosses who might not know how to read or write but had been educated in the skills needed to cope with the problems of moving logs. The techniques had been handed down from one generation of woods workers to the next, with a succession of minor improvements made by anonymous lumberjacks seeking better ways to get the job done. The men who got ahead in this competitive game were those who watched how a respected veteran tackled the challenge of getting the pine to the mill before low water, then figured out a way to go him one better.

During the log drive, the men were divided into three crews. There was the driving crew, which might be spread out over as much as ten miles of river. Its job was to keep the logs moving and to try to steer them out of shoals and backwaters. There was the jam crew, which stayed close to the head of the drive. Its duty was to keep the leading logs from piling up and, if a jam did develop, to break it. Finally, the sacking crew followed along behind, slogging through swamps and sloughs hunting for logs and shoving them back into the main part of the stream. The rear crew demanded the least skill, its chief attribute being a willingness to stay wet and to lift and shove logs when the boss gave the word.

In command of the crews was the boss driver, also known as the head push. He had to know how to keep logs from jamming and what to do about untangling them. He also had to command the respect of as unruly a group as could be found anywhere. There were boss drivers who could command without having to whip anybody into line with their fists, but this was unusual.

Sam Hunter, the head push on drives around Grand Rapids, Minnesota, was more typical. As soon as a new man signed on, Sam would throw him in the river. When the fellow surfaced amid the floating ice, Hunter would yell: "Now get busy and you'll warm up."

There were those who came ashore ready to beat the boss over the head with a peavey. Then Sam would have to throw them in again. Eventually, they got the message and either quit or started working hard enough to keep from freezing in their soggy clothes.

The lore of the woods held that a man from the State of Maine was the king of the choppers and sawyers, but the premier river pigs were considered to be either French-Canadians or Indians. The job demanded a devil-may-care attitude and the surefootedness of a squirrel. The most skillful men were picked for the jam crew. They took pride in the honor and the danger that went with it. They were not modest about their talents.

"Hell's fire, boys," a whitewater man would say, bellying up to the bar, "I can ride anything that floats. Throw a bar of yellow soap in the river and I'll ride the bubbles to shore."

A jam pike—a five-foot hardwood stick with a steel point—was used to help balance while riding a log or skipping from one to the other. But the river pig's most useful tool was the peavey. Its pointed end could be used to prod a log, and its adjustable hook provided leverage for rolling a heavy length of pine to one side. A man who lost a peavey had the three dollars' cost deducted from his pay. If a river pig fell into the churning sea of logs, the shout went up:

"Never mind him. Save the peavey!"

Drownings were common enough to be taken as a matter of course. For example, in one nine-day period on the Chippewa during the 1871 drive, ten men died. The Chippewa Falls *Democrat* recorded this statistic as a matter of mild interest, much as traffic accidents were reported a century later.

One notable hazard was "getting sluiced." When it was time to send a batch of logs through a dam, the gates were opened and the logs went churning and tumbling down the sluiceway. If a river pig was careless enough to go with them, he was likely to wind up in a shallow grave on the riverbank, his boots hung on a tree limb as his only monument.

If a crew member survived a ride through the sluice, his name might go down in the oral history that formed a staple of the conversations in lumber camps and saloons. John Powers, an Irishman from Canada, became temporarily famous after an incident at a dam in Lake Nocquebay in Wisconsin in the early 1880s.

Powers was working next to the sluice, keeping logs from jamming. He was smoking a short clay pipe when his foot slipped. He disappeared under the water and the logs, which stretched back for half a mile or more behind the dam.

Luckily, the man working on top of the dam saw John go down the sluice. Moving fast, he dropped the gates that closed the sluiceway. At the foot of the dam, the water level fell abruptly. To the amused astonishment of his friends, Powers was revealed standing on the bottom, the pipe still clamped in his teeth, none the worse for the experience.

Breaking a log jam was a particularly hazardous phase of the river pig's duties, as an Indian working at Sturgeon Falls on the Menominee River along the Michigan-Wisconsin border discovered. The Indian had started his day's drinking early and was in no shape to handle his job, but he was trying. The logs had piled up. The head push was yelling orders on how to break the jam before it got worse. The Indian ran out on the logs just as the jam gave way unexpectedly. He was swept over the dam in a churning chaos of foaming water, chunks of ice and tons of pine logs.

His companions hardly bothered to look for him, certain he was dead. But somehow he survived, although his clothes were ripped from him as he went tumbling down the river with the pine. A considerable distance downstream, he was thrown ashore. He hobbled back to where the other men were working. When he arrived, those who were there claimed, the Indian was as sober as a Methodist preacher.

On a drive, the company provided a floating cook shanty known as a wanigan, where the cook turned out four large meals a day. Often crew members had to eat while sitting on a log in the cold woods, but if the wanigan was close enough they would try to reach it and get the food while it was hot. The usual method of travel was to ride a log—a river pig shared with the cowboy a dislike of walking. A riverman named Bell, participating on a drive on the Fence River, was a mile from the cook shanty when lunchtime came, so he jumped on a log to ride to the end of the log jam where the wanigan was tied up. On the way, the log hit a rock. Bell was thrown off and carried under the jam to his death.

The Fence River is a tributary of the Michigamme, which flows through Upper Michigan to the Menominee. Another drowning there involved an Iron Mountain man whose body was later found at Golden Rapids. For some reason, it was decided not to bury him on the spot but to send the body to Witbeck, Michigan.

The corpse was loaded aboard a supply wagon pulled by four mules. Six river pigs who had run picks into their feet or had sprained their ankles also climbed into the wagon. The load was completed by adding three hundred pounds of dynamite, needed elsewhere. It was a fifteen-mile trip, the tote road was rough and the night was stormy. When the mixed cargo finally reached Witbeck, the teamster headed straight for the saloon.

"That was the worst God-damned load I ever hauled," he told the barkeep. "A dead man. Six cripples. Six boxes of dynamite. And I could have lit my pipe with the lightning."

Another Michigan log drive ran into an unexpected hazard when a train wending its way from Channing to Ontonagon was wrecked on the Nett River bridge shortly before the river crew arrived. They investigated this interesting accident and discovered a miracle—a boxcar full of whiskey had jumped the track and lay on its side.

There were thirty or forty men in the vicinity, all thirsty. Still, they couldn't drink up all of this unexpected gift at once. While they could still walk, they hauled away the surplus and hid the bottles in the woods.

The railroad rounded up several section foremen at Green Bay and sped them north to take charge of the whiskey. But most of them turned out to be as ready for an open-air party as the river pigs. It took the crew a full week to finish the cargo, with help from their newly acquired railroad buddies. Then the log drive resumed and the trainmen hauled the empty cases away.

Generally, men who worked on the floating logs were too busy to get in trouble until the drive was over. But there were exceptions. There was a time, for instance, when a crew was sent to Port Sanilac, Michigan, to salvage logs that had floated ashore from a raft that had broken loose from a tugboat in a storm. There was no particular hurry and the men rented rooms in the hotel to rest up for the chore of wading around looking for the scattered pine. The next morning they ordered a hearty breakfast in the hotel dining room. The waitress came in with a heavily loaded tray, nervous over the prospect of serving so many rough-looking characters. She tripped, fell, and the tray went sprawling.

"Jesus H. Christ," Wes Kenney yelled. "You ought to look where you're walking."

The waitress burst into tears. Another river pig, George Betz, leaped to his feet.

"You can't use such language to a respectable woman, you son of a bitch! I'm going to lick you."

When an argument began in a dining room or even a bar, it was proper etiquette to postpone the fight long enough to go outside where nothing but heads would be broken. But Betz was hungry and in a hurry. He knocked Kenney down there in the dining room. When Wes got up, he knocked him down again. After the fight, everybody finished breakfast and headed for the job, including the loser. But Kenney brooded about the insult. Getting licked in an alley was one thing. Being humiliated before the waitress and the hotel guests was quite another. So, a night or two later, when Betz was in a saloon, Kenney stuck a revolver against his back and killed him. He spent the next eighteen years in the state prison.

Gunplay was rare among lumberjacks, including those who put down their axes in the spring and turned into river pigs. Fists, feet, knees, elbows and teeth were the usual weapons. Shooting a man was considered unsporting by Kenney's friends. What he should have done, they agreed, was wait for his chance to knock Betz down, then jump on his chest with calked boots.

These boots were worn mostly in the spring log drives, although at any season they were a useful weapon in a saloon brawl. The sharpened spikes on soles and heels were designed to dig into the bark of a slippery log. Used on an opponent's back, chest or face, they could take the fight out of him in a hurry.

During the winter, most lumberjacks wore rubber overshoes and clothes of woolen flannel, often including a red shirt. But on the river drives, they preferred overalls, which dried faster, cutting them off just above the boot tops with an axe to create the desired "stagged" effect. After a day spent wading in ice water, the men's feet often were swollen and sore but they had a remedy for this occupational hazard. The wanigan kept a keg of pure white lead on hand. This was smeared thickly on the foot and a cotton sock pulled over it, then a woolen sock put on over the cotton one. The cotton sock was left on until the foot healed.

As the logs headed toward the mills, they could be heard a mile or more away. In the forgotten little lumber towns, the signal brought men, women and especially children running to the river-banks to watch the excitement. By the time the spectators arrived, the first logs would be rushing by on the current. Soon this advance guard was replaced by the main army of sixteen-foot lengths of pine, some of the logs four or five feet across.

"You scarcely could see the water between them," an early settler recalled. "The river became a mass of sluggish bodies, rolling this way and that, grumbling all day and all night. No door could shut out that noise."

But sometimes the sound of the moving river of pine suddenly stopped. If that happened late at night, children would wake from heavy sleep to sit up and listen to the unexpected silence. Then they would leap up, dress and head for the river because they knew what had happened. There was a log jam. That meant excitement, danger, the possibility of witnessing heroism, accident, even death.

For the logs' owners, a major jam could mean financial disaster. The drive depended on high water, which wouldn't last forever. Getting a good price for the pines sometimes depended on delivering them to the mill quickly before the market was glutted. The men shared the anxiety because, if the company couldn't cash in on the winter's work, they might not get paid. The drive boss was under the gun. Everyone knew that log jams happened. But a head push who got the reputation for letting them happen too often might be back in the ranks the next season.

Every locality where log drives took place had a record jam it boasted about when strangers were around. Over the years, the size of such backups tended to grow as the evening got older. Still, some jams were worth bragging about, such as the one on the St. Croix River in 1886, a mile or so above St. Croix Falls, Wisconsin. What was known as the jam at Angle Rock backed up an estimated 150 million board feet of pine in a spectacular tangle that stretched for miles. The logs filled the river from bank to bank. A man could walk from Wisconsin to Minnesota across the watery boundary line without getting his feet wet. It took two hundred good men, working night and day for more than six weeks, to break that jam, with the help of a hundred horses, two donkey engines and two steamboats. Residents of Minneapolis and St. Paul spent much of their spare time that June and July standing on the banks of the St. Croix, watching the struggle.

A jam in the Mississippi near Brainerd in north central Minnesota proved impossible for the men to break without dynamite. There wasn't enough on hand, so the foreman sent downriver for more. While the river pigs were waiting, they whiled away the time in such Front Street saloons as the Last Turn, the Number One and the Dolly Varden Club. Otto Olsen made so much money playing mustang and chuck-a-luck that he announced he was quitting the river for good. He and another riverman, Abba Hall, entered a roller-skating contest and won first prize by covering one hundred miles in seven and a half hours. To celebrate, they checked into the Headquarters House, Brainerd's best hotel, which bragged that it contained over six hundred joints of stovepipe.

As soon as Olsen got to bed, he was awakened by a loud voice in the hall. He leaped up, ready to take action. The noisy one turned out to be a preacher who was striding up and down, rehearsing his sermon. Throwing a preacher out of a second-story window would not have been considered polite, so Otto said to hell with civilian life. He reported back to the head push, arriving in time to help pack the dynamite around the logs that were causing the jam.

"Greenhorns ashore!" the boss yelled. Everyone scrambled for safety. The dynamite blasted pines into splinters and Olsen rode down the river on the sea of moving logs.

The Angle Rock jam was spoken of with respect even outside the St. Croix district, but it was no worse than the one near Chippewa Falls in 1869 when logs extended for fifteen miles up the Chippewa River and were piled in tiers that reached thirty feet above the water. In 1876, there was a jam an eighth of a mile wide, three miles long and thirty-feet high on the Red Cedar above Menomonie. The Jump River loggers could get into the conversation by bringing up a thirteen-mile jam that clogged that stream in 1879.

Each jam was a crisis for the men charged with getting the crop of pine to the lumber towns downstream. Oxen as well as horses were often used to break loose the logs near shore, but toward midstream the work had to be done by men wielding pikes and peaveys. It was dangerous work. A jam could give way of its own accord. The huge sticks were often piled higher than a man's head, waiting to crush the fellow who dared dislodge them.

Such a mankiller jam developed one spring below Lower Clam Lake Dam on the West Fork of the Chippewa. A huge pine stump washed through the sluice gate, then got hung up, forcing the logs to pile up behind it. Charley Ouillette was the boss. He sent upriver for his two best whitewater men—Joe Dumel and Joe Cascanette. By the time they arrived, the riverbed in front of the jam was nearly dry. Back of the obstruction, the river was piling up a great head of water. Riding in the widening lake behind the dam were thousands of logs.

"I tell you what we do," Ouillette said. "We build a causeway of logs out to the jam. Then we knock out the key log and run like hell."

The escape route was pushed and prodded into place. Then the boss motioned to Dumel. He took his axe and was about to start out when Cascanette grabbed him.

"You're crazy," he told the boss. "Once she goes, nobody can get back."

Dumel took a second look and agreed with his friend. Ouillette started jumping up and down, waving his arms, calling them every name he could think of. Finally, he shook his fist at the sullen clouds overhead and offered to fight whatever god or devil was responsible for his troubles, man to man. The two Joes listened impassively. When Ouillette finally calmed down, he began suggesting ways to break the jam and get back alive. Somebody could go down in the dry riverbed in front of the jam and chop away the pine stump that was holding up the mass of logs. The two Joes shook their heads. Well, then, he could lower a man from the top logs in the jam by a rope and have him do some chopping. Dumel took a pinch of snuff and made no comment.

"I want a volunteer," the head push said. No one answered. "All right, God damn it, I'll appoint one. Cascanette, you get out there."

"I wish to see the padre before I die," Big Joe told him.

"You know we got no preacher here, you dumb Canuck."

"Then I don't go. Touch it off with dynamite."

Ouillette had known all along that dynamite was his final recourse, but he'd hoped to avoid it. Blowing up logs was not only dangerous, it was wasteful. Still, if Dumel and Cascanette wouldn't go out there, none of the lesser men would do it. So dynamite it was.

The charge was set. There was a mighty blast, with splinters flying. The avalanche of white pine began to move with a roar, huge logs bouncing like jackstraws as the jam broke. It was plain that if a human had been out there on the river when the jam gave way, he would have died.

Ouillette could see this as well as the others, but he merely shrugged and walked off without admitting to Dumel and Cascanette that he had given them orders that would have killed them. The fact that he didn't fire them on the spot because they'd disobeyed was considered apology enough.

According to experts in such matters, the notion that a single "king log" held back a jam was generally a myth. Usually, there were a number of key logs, each of which had to be moved before the jumble could be unsnarled. But sometimes, after much painstaking effort around the edges, a single log remained to be cut away. An Oshkosh newspaperman described such an incident.

The river pig chosen for the dangerous assignment was twenty years old. He stripped down to his long underwear—never mind the women spectators on the bank. A heavy rope was looped under his arms. Half a dozen men kept hold of the end, ready to pull, as he walked out on the jam, picking his footing like a cat. He got to the log that was holding back those tons of floating wood and started chopping it in half. On the bank, no one spoke. No sound was heard except that of the axe as it bit into the pine. The notch deepened fast. It was halfway through the log when a cracking noise was heard. The axeman paused, ready to jump, but the log held. He raised his axe high and brought it down once more.

"There was a crash like thunder and down came the wall, to all appearances on the axeman," the reporter wrote. "Like many others, I rushed to help the poor fellow. But to my great joy I saw him safe on the bank, certainly badly bruised and bleeding from sundry wounds, but safe."

Such episodes did not always turn out so happily. But death was not permitted to slow the drive. Mourning for a friend or hunting for his battered body could wait. The logs had to be moved. Pine was king. The logs came first.

In return for the long hours, hazards and hardships of the log drives, the men were paid from two dollars to five dollars a day, plus board. That was considered good money, and it was all profit. What little sleeping was done was usually a matter of curling up on the ground, which was free. If dining facilities were lacking, the food was plentiful. For instance, a crew of forty men, superintending the journey of a batch of logs from Grand Rapids, Minnesota, to Minneapolis, consumed an average of a hundred pounds of flour a day, along with numerous other eatables, during the forty days it required to make the 320-mile trip.

Until railroads penetrated the pineries, sawmills in the river towns operated only from the time the logs arrived in the spring until the supply gave out. That meant that some lumberjacks turned into sawmill workers when they were through in the woods, spending the summers in town, sometimes supporting legal wives and families. Others did a little farming in the warm months, before it was time to head back for the woods.

Still others, broke after their spring spree, got jobs as raftsmen, riding cribs of rough lumber turned out by sawmills, floating down the Mississippi or its tributaries to places where the boards could be sold.

On such lesser rivers as the Chippewa, about half a dozen cribs —each sixteen feet long and from twelve to sixteen feet wide— were fastened together to form what was called a string. When the Mississippi was reached, several of these strings were hooked together to form a raft worthy of that river. Some Mississippi rafts covered three acres.

The rafts were guided by oversized oars, each sixteen feet long, attached at the front and rear of the lumber. If there were rapids or falls to go over, the oarsmen had to be skilled, surefooted and willing to risk drowning. A considerable number of the rafts were knocked apart on rocks or other obstructions, so that losses were common. Everything considered, nearly half of the cost of converting a north woods pine into boards to build a house on the treeless prairie represented money spent on transportation, even though the rivers provided free motive power. An estimated 10 per cent of the logs and lumber were lost in the rivers.

Like most techniques used in the early days in the Lake States' pineries, methods of rafting lumber on the Mississippi and its tributaries were imported from New England and Canada. In 1842, Charles Dickens noted huge rafts fitted with little houses that were floating down the St. Lawrence. But the method went back considerably earlier than that. During the forty or so years when rafting was the chief method of moving boards to market in Minnesota, Wisconsin and, to a lesser extent, in Michigan, the techniques changed hardly at all from those used in Maine a century earlier.

The upper reaches of the Wisconsin River were particularly challenging to lumber raftsmen. Rafts designed for that gauntlet of rapids, falls and dams were fastened together with particular care. Even so, the accident rate was so high that the remains of rafts were strewn on the banks of the lower Wisconsin for years after rafting on that river ceased.

A raft pilot might earn as much as a thousand dollars a season, but without his expert knowledge the system would have broken down. He had to understand how to deal not only with natural hazards but with the challenge of going over man-made dams. The dams were provided with slides about fifty feet wide, but taking a raft down the steep incline required not only skill and daring but a bit of luck.

If the water's flow was too slight, a raft could get stuck part way down on the slide. If the flow was heavy—as it usually was in the rafting season—the pilot's slightest miscalculation could smash up the raft. Anywhere from two to eight men were riding it. If the raft broke up, they were in immediate and sometimes mortal danger.

Watching rafts go down the slides was a fine spectator sport. Sometimes the feat was accomplished easily, which spoiled the show, but there was always the possibility of disaster. Michael Cassidy, a Wisconsin River raft pilot, described in 1865 a fairly typical ride down a slide by one of his fellow pilots, Jack Hawn:

"The moment the bow entered the slide it was literally jerked down and disappeared beneath the wild waters. His men were lifted off their feet, thrown back upon the raft. Hawn for a moment was overboard, but was caught and pulled aboard. All came out right, the men thoroughly soaked, yet saved the raft."

The oars were swung up out of the water and made fast with rope halters as a raft nosed between the rude wooden piers that guided it into the slide. Then the men threw themselves flat and grabbed a rope, the "sucker line," strung down the center of the raft. If all went well and the raft didn't break up on the way down, it plunged underwater at the bottom of the slide, so the men had to hang on until it shook itself free and surfaced.

Between dams, there were rapids. Each little settlement on the upper Wisconsin had its own choice for the title of most dangerous rapids. Wausau bragged about its Big Bull Falls. Mosinee claimed Little Bull Falls was worse. Around Stevens Point it was said that Conant's Rapids could wreck a raft with the best of them. And at the community that became Wisconsin Rapids, the mile-long stretch of white water called Grand Rapids was a source of local pride. A raft traveled through this rough water in eight minutes, but it seemed longer to those aboard.

Big Bull Falls featured an added attraction known as Lumberyard Rock, an outcropping that earned its name by smashing up rafts. But Mosinee's entry in the competition for most hazardous passage probably deserves the title. Little Bull Falls consisted of a sixteen-foot ledge over which the Wisconsin plunged, then a narrow gorge a quarter mile long. Above the gorge was a huge rock, partly above water. Below the gorge was a submerged rock, which sent the current swirling in unpredictable patterns. And beyond that rock was what was called a bottomless eddy, a maelstrom that could keep its grip on a massive timber for several days or rip apart a crib of lumber.

Only the most experienced river pilots dared run a raft through Little Bull. The others deferred to such local specialists as William Cuer, a "standing pilot," who did nothing except guide rafts through that stretch of the river. Cuer's fee was one dollar per trip. When he finished taking a raft through, he'd jump on his horse and ride back to pilot another. On a good day, Cuer could make as much as thirty dollars.

That was a lot of money in the 1860s. Now and then, someone

tried to cut in on Cuer's business. A young Polish immigrant, for instance, after standing with other spectators on the bridge in Mosinee to watch the excitement of running Little Bull, decided he'd become a standing pilot there. He talked someone into letting him try. He and the raft survived, but after that one ride the Pole left town, not even waiting to eat breakfast.

The Dells, at what was then called Kilbourn City, have become a major tourist attraction in modern times. In rafting days, Wisconsin Dells was a hazard, all right, but not in a class with some of those farther upstream. A dam that was built there in 1859 to provide power for mills was another matter. Numerous rafts were smashed and several lives lost. Finally, a posse of angry raftsmen descended on the dam and started to tear it down. The owners worked out a compromise, improving the slide and lowering the dam until it was no longer a major barrier to rafting.

In the lower Wisconsin, a wide and peaceful stream, rafting was easy enough. An inexperienced pilot could wind up in a slough instead of the main channel, but that was not the river's fault. Once the Mississippi was reached, the raft was enlarged, shanties resembling pig sties were built as sleeping quarters, and facilities were provided for the cook. The raft cook was hired more for his muscles than his skills with a skillet. He was expected to be able to lick any of the twenty-five or thirty men aboard. According to one raft pilot, Walter L. Blair, this was a good thing, considering the kind of grub the cooks turned out. Among those he remembered from his river days were Steubenville Slim, Slufoot Murphey, Double-Headed Bob and Hayden the Brute. None of them, he indicated, could cook worth a damn.

Still, the lazy journey down the Mississippi to St. Louis or some other port, such as Mark Twain's hometown of Hannibal, was usually pleasant enough. There was the chance to stop at the river towns and a few shots of Forty-Rod. In the early days, when the current did the work instead of a steamer pushing a covey of rafts, there was little to worry about except running onto an island or sandbar.

The most famous Mississippi raftsman in the mid-nineteenth century was Stephen B. Hanks, a Kentuckian whose cousin, Abraham Lincoln, also made a name for himself. Hanks started work in the St. Croix Valley in 1841 as a lumberjack. Three years later, he took his first raft to St. Louis, floating down the river from Stillwater, Minnesota, a 700-mile trip that had never been attempted before by a lumber raft. Later on, he switched to steamboat piloting.

When rafting was new on the Mississippi, numerous tales made the rounds about the hazards of that mighty river. Henry Merrell, a Utica (New York) native who moved to Wisconsin, had heard the stories, but he decided to take several lumber rafts from Portage, Wisconsin, to St. Louis in 1839. He and his crew built a shanty to sleep in and brought along a dugout canoe. When they sighted a town, someone would jump in the canoe and paddle ahead, seeing the sights and passing the time of day until the raft caught up, then getting back aboard.

When they left the Wisconsin for the Mississippi, Merrell and his men fastened the small rafts together to form a bigger one and continued on their way. At some river towns, passengers would come aboard to travel a few miles with them. Among them was an old fellow from Ohio, dressed in a hunting shirt and worn trousers, carrying a flintlock rifle. A Texan also joined the travelers, bearing a lighter and more modern gun. He began bragging about his prowess. The Ohioan finally accepted the Texan's challenge to shoot at a mark, the loser to buy drinks all around at the next port. Merrell fastened a board to one end of the raft and added a paper circle about the size of a silver dollar. The Ohioan fired and missed. The Texan fired and came a little closer. Then Merrell borrowed the flintlock, rested it over one knee and, as he put it, "drove the nail." The Texan left the raft at Fort Madison, Iowa, neglecting to say anything about buying the drinks.

"The old man thought that was mean," Merrell recalled, "but he could not get over his delight at my beating him."

Merrell's crew consisted mostly of French-Canadians, some of whom had done some rafting in Canada. At Dubuque, several Frenchmen came aboard with a warning that unless a pilot was hired the raft would never get past some fearsome rapids downstream. But Merrell had questioned several steamboat men about the river and been assured there was no danger, so he ignored the warning. He waited until the raft was nearly through the rapids before he spoke up.

"Boys, these are the great rapids you've been so much afraid of."

There was a great shout and much laughter. It was agreed that, to men used to rafting on the treacherous Wisconsin, the Mississippi's rapids provided "the best running we had on the river."

When conditions were favorable, a raft could go from Wausau to St. Louis in three or four weeks. But during a dry spell, the journey might take considerably longer. In 1840, when rafting on the Wisconsin was in its infancy, a man named Barnes left Point Bausse with a load of lumber for the Mississippi. He made his way over the upstream hazards and through the Dells at Kilbourn City by June 1. But by then the water level had fallen. Waiting for a rain, Barnes whiled away the time by planting several rows of potatoes at what was known as Dells Eddy. The low water continued for much of the summer. In late August, Barnes and his crew had progressed no farther than Sauk Prairie. They were out of food. So they tied up their raft, hiked back to the Dells, harvested the potatoes and returned to take the lumber the rest of the way to St. Louis, reaching there in October.

Particularly on the Wisconsin River, rafting was a hazardous way to make a living. In 1873, a fairly typical year, forty men were drowned at Clint's Dam at Grand Rapids (now Wisconsin Rapids). Another forty raftsmen died at Big Bull Falls (Wausau) the year before. Lesser accidents were routine, often from getting a leg or arm crushed between rafts or by being caught by a snubbing rope. Records indicate that most raftsmen were satisfied with a single trip on the Wisconsin River, either shifting to a quieter stream or getting into another line of work. As a result, there were periodic shortages of labor and the Wisconsin raftsmen were supplemented by young men from Illinois who came north in the spring to try their hand at rafting. Most soon returned home. The resemblance of their migratory habits to those of a fish called the sucker gave the strangers a commonly used nickname.

Old hands who stayed on season after season as raftsmen were generally lumberjacks who spent their winters cutting trees. Many had a regular routine: Work hard all winter, collect the season's pay, have a spree until the money ran out, hire on as a member of a rafting crew, collect the wages, spend them in St. Louis saloons and bawdy houses, walk back home and prepare to repeat the process. As one raft pilot noted, pointing out the obvious, most of the crewmen "celebrated their release with drinking and fighting."

A fight could break out over almost anything, including enmities brought over from Europe. For instance, John Nelligan tells of an incident in a saloon at a place called Metropolitan, where a river driving crew of seventy-five men crowded into the establishment, which was run by Mike Horigan. By nightfall, "everyone was pleasantly drunk" and a French-Canadian cook named Joseph Gousaw was playing his fiddle between belts of whiskey. Then an immigrant from Ulster, William Knox, yelled out:

"Let's hear 'The Protestant Boys,' Joe."

John and James Enright swore that no such Orangeman's song would be played. To make sure, they knocked down the men closest to them at the bar, a hint to everyone that it was time for the music to stop and the fighting to begin.

"A good many of those present, including the poor fiddler, didn't know what it was all about," Nelligan said. "But that didn't prevent them all from participating in a good fight. In a short time, the place looked like a cross between a hospital and a morgue."

The Enrights got their way. "The Protestant Boys" was not played. Those who could still talk the next morning agreed it had been a fine party.

Such milder sports as birling never replaced the barroom brawl in popularity. Still, contests to see who could stay on a floating log longest were another method of deciding which man could back up his brag. If a saloonkeeper could be induced to donate a jug as the winner's prize, birling could draw a considerable crowd on the theory that the victor would divide up the spoils with his friends.

Birling contests have persisted into a time when they are chiefly a diversion for summer tourists. The rules are simple. A suitable log is placed in the water and two contestants climb onto it. Each tries to keep his balance while rotating the log in a way that will throw the other fellow into the river. At first, birling was confined to competitions in lumber camps or, more typically, outside a waterfront saloon. But toward the end of the white pine era, local champions were brought together in regional contests.

Around the turn of the century, such a match was held in

Ashland, Wisconsin. By a process of elimination, Tom Oliver and Jim Stewart became the finalists. Oliver was the champion of Michigan, Stewart the top birler of Wisconsin. Along the crowd's edges, considerable betting went on, the Wisconsinites backing Stewart, the Michigan contingent betting on Oliver. The Minnesotans, whose champion had been eliminated earlier, placed their bets without any distracting considerations of sentiment.

The contest began at noon. It was soon clear the men were evenly matched. Stewart was bigger and stronger. Oliver was more agile. By 7 P.M., when it got too dark to see the log, neither man had been able to make the other fall off. An intermission was declared, with everyone repairing to the bar.

The next day, Oliver and Stewart climbed back onto the log at 10 A.M. and the match resumed. It kept going until 4:30 P.M., except for an hour off for lunch. At that point, the Michigan champion collapsed and fell off the log into the water. Stewart collected the one-hundred-dollar prize and a gold medal attesting that he was the champion birler of the Lake States. A year or two later, a Minnesota challenger, Bill Delyea, beat him.

Competition among workmen was encouraged—demanded, in fact. In the woods, each crew was urged to try to beat the others. On the rivers, raftsmen or those in charge of a log drive were persuaded they must try to outdo everyone else. The pinery boys understood that such contests mostly benefited the owners, getting more work done in a shorter period of time. But trying to beat another good man at chopping down a tree, riding a log or getting the product to market was part of the game and appealed to their competitive instincts.

There was also competition among lumber companies, particularly in the early days before combinations of loggers and lumbermen were formed to bring order out of an often chaotic system. The competitiveness of rival lumber barons was reflected in skirmishes fought with fists between crews working for opposing interests. A more serious reflection of the bitter rivalry was what is known in the history of the Chippewa Valley as the Beef Slough War.

The war was named for a swampy backwater of the river that formed a natural haven for storing logs. The opponents included some very large guns in the lumber business. The home team was composed of those who wanted to saw the pine logs that floated down the river at their mills in Eau Claire, Chippewa Falls and nearby communities. Their opponents were mainly lumbermen who wanted to do the sawing in mills along the Mississippi.

The local contingent included such big lumbermen as Daniel Shaw of Eau Claire and the Knapp, Stout interests of Menomonie. The downriver men were headed by Frederick Weyerhaeuser, already well on his way to becoming a lumber emperor, not a mere king or baron. Associated with him were W. H. Laird and other important lumbermen from Winona, Minnesota, and several allies from another center of the industry, Clinton, Iowa.

The home team won the first skirmish, acquiring control of the land around the slough to keep it from being used as a storage pond for logs which could be made into rafts and floated down to the Mississippi. In 1867, the local interests formed the Beef Slough Manufacturing, Booming, Log Driving and Transportation Company. It had backing from a Detroit lumberman, Francis Palms, who had substantial holdings on the Jump River and was interested in stepping up the competition between the Chippewa River mills and those on the Mississippi.

The battleground then shifted to the state capital, with each side buying up as many legislators as it could afford. The out-of-staters had a built-in disadvantage here and might have been prevented indefinitely from using Beef Slough if the Wisconsin contingent had maintained a united front. Instead, the lumbermen in Eau Claire and Chippewa Falls began feuding over a proposal to build a dam on the river and some of the Chippewa Falls group went over to the enemy. When the dust cleared, the Mississippi interests held the state franchise for the Beef Slough Company. It erected facilities to shunt logs into the backwater, sorting them there before sending them on to a rafting works at Alma, a Mississippi River community six miles below the Chippewa's mouth.

The Eau Claire lumbermen struck back. They erected booms upstream and stopped all logs that floated down the Chippewa, including those belonging to their Mississippi rivals. It was then that talking and lobbying stopped and the war began.

The Mississippi interests recruited a hundred of the toughest lumberjacks in the region. They were armed with pike poles, peaveys and a sprinkling of revolvers and marched up the riverbanks to cut the Eau Claire booms. Before the home forces could gather, something like twelve million pine logs were released to float down to the Mississippi.

No one got shot trying to defend the Eau Claire booms, but there were some broken heads. Word spread that the finest fight in years was in the offing. From miles around, lumberjacks came pouring out of the woods to get in on it. The county sheriff had no trouble forming a posse of two hundred men. They arrived too late to save the logs, but in plenty of time for a battle. To nearly everyone's disappointment, however, the Beef Slough contingent was ordered to retreat.

The organized part of the war was over. But for weeks, there were battles on the streets of Eau Claire and neighboring towns between representatives of the rival factions as well as between lumberjacks who had come to town to get in on the fight and weren't going back to the woods without knocking somebody down. Most of the fights were between hired hands, but a few bosses got mixed up in the trouble. T. B. Wilson, for instance, was thrown into the river even though he was resident manager for Knapp, Stout Lumber Company and a very important man. The Mississippi interests claimed he had cut ropes holding a portion of the Beef Slough's boom. The brawling continued until the battlers' credit ran out at the saloons and they had to go back to work.

The war was finally won by the Mississippi interests, but by that time they'd spent so much money buying legislators and hiring gangs to fight their battles that the Beef Slough Company was nearly bankrupt. Weyerhaeuser and his friends had plenty of cash left, however. They formed the Mississippi River Logging Company, capitalized it at $1 million and bought out the previous owners of the Beef Slough Manufacturing, Booming, Log Driving and Transportation Company.

Within ten years, the conglomerate headed by Weyerhaeuser had absorbed or bought out the Chippewa River lumbermen, giving the Mississippi River Logging Company command of virtually all logging and lumbering in the valley and its tributaries, with one notable exception. Knapp, Stout and Company held out. For years, it remained a major rival of the Weyerhaeuser interests.

CHAPTER VIII

No More Shanty Boys

THE ERA WHEN a rough-hewn army chopped and sawed its way through the Lake States' primeval inheritance of white pine can be divided into the period of the shanty boy and the time of the lumberjack. While the terms often are used interchangeably, lumberjack was not a word that was much in favor until about 1870.

About the time that the logging railroads began to change life in the big woods, shanty boy became something of a misnomer. The crews' quarters never became luxurious, but the days when the oxen lived better in camp than the men gradually ended.

The shanty boy generally slept on a dirt floor. The lumberjack had a bunk—either a muzzle-loader or a breech-loader, depending on whether he crawled in from the end or from the side. In the early camps, an open fire in the center of the log hovel provided a place to cook and took a little of the chill from the air. By the final quarter of the nineteenth century, this source of heat had been replaced by a box stove in a container of sand. There was also a cookstove, usually in a separate room, for preparing the meals.

The lumberjacks' bunkhouses had windows. Some even had skylights which could be opened when the air got so foul from drying socks that even a woods worker noticed it. The camps by then had grown larger, with crews of eighty men or more not uncommon. The facilities usually included an office, presided over by a clerk, as well as stables, a granary, sheds to store hay, a blacksmith shop, a carpenter's shack for the saw filer and "wood butcher," a root cellar to store fresh vegetables. Kerosene lamps made it possible to read or play cards before the 9 P.M. bedtime.

The food had improved by the time the shanty boy metamorphosed into the lumberjack. A typical breakfast included flapjacks, pork hash, beans with molasses and fried cakes. Coffee was gradually replacing strong tea in favor. Tea was a Maine drink. Coffee was demanded by the Scandinavians, and their companions were gradually converted. The noon meal, delivered to the men where they worked, was also a hearty one. When the moon came out and it was time to quit chopping, the cook and his cookees were ready with pork, salt beef, more beans cooked in a hole in the ground, potatoes, bread, pudding, cookies the size of pizzas, doughnuts, molasses cake and such treats as larrigan or shoepac pie, made with liberal amounts of brown sugar and somewhat resembling butterscotch.

Some logging companies had farms where they not only raised hay for camp animals but vegetables for the men. Another reason for the improved diet was that the three states were filling up with farmers, including some who settled near camp tote roads or railroads and were eager to sell supplies to loggers. Such things as potatoes and beef no longer had to be hauled impossible distances.

The camp wanigan, once merely a locked box containing a supply of snuff and chewing tobacco for the men to buy, expanded with the times. It became a comparatively well-stocked store, often occupying part of the clerk's quarters, and sold most of the things a man was likely to need, generally with the exception of whiskey. Liquor was discouraged in most camps by then, but friends of the cook could get a glow from lemon extract, which was 44 proof.

By the 1870s, camp dining rooms were provided with long tables, some of them covered with oilcloth. A flunkey known as the bullcook—often an old 'jack who could no longer keep up with the others in the woods—supplied wood for the stoves, hauled water, swept the floor, filled the lamps, and even, now and then, washed the single roller towel that was the camp's chief gesture toward cleanliness.

Some things hadn't changed, of course—the cookee's cry of "Daylight in the swamp!" or the nature of the job. The work continued to be hard and long, although equipment was gradually improved. Beginning in the 1870s in the Lake States, trees were sawed down instead of chopped down. Until then, a crosscut saw was impractical for such work because the sawdust kept clogging it. But the Disston Company turned out a model with the teeth arranged to provide alternate cutters and rakers, the latter clearing out the sawdust. That made it possible to cut the tree closer to the ground, eliminating a small portion of the waste. The ideal two-man crew consisted of a right-hander and a left-hander. Axes continued to be used to lop off branches and to cut a preliminary wedge in the tree to direct its fall.

It was during this period of change that oxen began to give way to horses for skidding logs and pulling sleds. The horses were not as strong but they were faster and more nimble. The use of iced ruts in the logging roads made it possible for a team to pull an amazingly large load. Old-timers grumbled about the downgrading of the oxen. An ox cost less to feed than a horse. Besides, when he was too old for anything else, he could be butchered and eaten, although that was not necessarily an advantage to those who tried to chew the beef. Oxen could live on a diet of marsh hay and rutabagas. Horses required timothy and oats.

Over the years, so much hay was hauled to camps on the tote roads that when the trees were gone and farmers moved in they found fields of timothy and clover spreading from the seed dropped there by the camp suppliers.

Among the aspects of camp life that did not improve was the necessity to put up with lice, known as "traveling dandruff." The common superstition among lumberjacks that it was unhealthy to take a bath before spring may have had some bearing on the problem. Some 'jacks regularly boiled their clothes on Sundays, but others contended that it didn't pay to change your underwear.

"Them bugs like to be clean," an old-timer explained to a greenhorn. "If you get dirty enough, some of 'em will leave. Ask any old lumberjack if that hain't right."

Burly Dick Phelan's camp in the Michigan pinery was notorious for its bugs, but it had plenty of competitors. Men in such camps spent their leisure time picking lice and bedbugs off each other, and sometimes nearly burned down the bunkhouse by using a firebrand to singe the pests in their bunks.

A variety of other methods were used to discourage the graybacks. It was believed that fresh balsam boughs in a bunk drove some of them away. Lumberjacks shredded chewing tobacco and mixed it with their blankets on the theory that the smell offended the resident vermin. Some preferred using snoose or "Scandihoovian dynamite"—damp snuff used for chewing. The rumor was that one pinch of snoose had floored heavyweight champion John L. Sullivan, but it failed to bother the lice. Another favorite way to deal with the problem was for the victim to turn his long underwear inside out just before going to bed. By the time the bugs had made their way back inside the longies, the host would be asleep.

Such human ingenuity may have mitigated the problem, but it never solved it. At least as late as World War I—when soldiers in the European trenches had similar difficulties with what they preferred to call cooties—the louse was as much a part of logging-camp life as the baked bean. Not until spring came and the lumberjack could soak in a tub in town without endangering his health did the scratching stop.

Contests were sometimes held in the bunkhouse, a crab louse matched against a body louse in a battle to the death while bets were made. There was never any difficulty in finding plenty of worthy contestants for this north woods sporting event.

Eldon Marple, who worked in northwestern Wisconsin lumber camps as a lad, recalled a remark made by Robert L. McCormick, manager of a Hayward lumber company, while he was watching one of his camps burn in a forest fire:

"Well, we got all the men and horses out. Only two million lives lost."

By the final quarter of the last century, the camps were no longer totally isolated from the outside world. Peddlers sometimes showed up to sell clothing or watches—a gold pocket watch was considered almost a necessity because it was easy to pawn when the need arose. Preachers followed sinners to the pinery, mincing no words about the need for repentance.

"You are giants of the woods picking diamonds from the snow," one migratory minister declared. "And in the spring you will give those diamonds to the saloonkeepers and whorehouses in Chippewa Falls."

A priest named Goldsmith visited camps in the Chippewa River region, accompanied by several nuns. They not only offered religious consolation but sought donations. A hospital in Chippewa Falls was built with the money kicked in by pinery workers.

Standard, Peerless, Climax and Spearhead tobacco sold for half a dollar a pound. Pipe smoking or the use of snuff and chewing tobacco was almost universal. Cigarettes, however, were considered a sign of citified ways. Most camp bosses would fire a man caught smoking a "pimp stick."

With the arrival of railroads, it became less difficult to get to town. Some 'jacks managed to escape camp life after work was finished on Saturday and stagger back in time for Monday breakfast. But most Sundays were still spent in the bunkhouse, hemmed in by the snowy woods and the subzero cold of a northern winter. The favorite recreation, judging from accounts by those who were there, was lying. But nonverbal sports were also known, including a variation of drop-the-handkerchief known as hotass. Whoever was "it" knelt with his face in a hat or a sack. Someone would give him a mighty swat. If he guessed who it was, the swatter had to take his place.

The men were proud of their skills, which were often considerable, and held contests to settle arguments about who was the best man. Bets were made—seldom in cash, which was scarce, but in tobacco, which could be bought on credit at the wanigan. Bucksaw contests were held to see who could cut a log fastest. Contests matched muscular men in lifting a log, a barrel or even the front end of a horse. Axe-throwing competitions were common, with the men lining up thirty steps from the butt end of a large log and aiming axes at a mark.

Wrestling matches and fistfights were held for sport as well as in anger. The battle continued until one man was down and asked for mercy. Then the victor was pulled off.

There were times when the fights got more serious. Louie Blanchard, who logged the north fork of the Flambeau River in 1885, told of an international incident involving a German sawyer and a Frenchman called Frosty. To keep the crosscut from sticking in the pitch from the pines, the men carried pint bottles of kerosene in their back pockets. But such bottles tended to get broken and there was a chronic shortage of them.

Frosty had one. The German didn't. When he finished work,

the Frenchman stashed the pint of kerosene in his bunk. It disappeared. Frosty accused the German of stealing it.

"You're a liar," the other man replied.

"I'll fix you," Frosty said, heading for the pile of double-bitted axes in a corner of the bunkhouse. "I'll chop your head off."

But the German moved faster. He grabbed an axe, sharp enough to shave with, and started chasing Frosty around and around the camp, swinging the weapon around his head. No one dared interfere until the camp scaler emerged from his office, tripped the pursuer with a piece of wood, jumped on him, wrestled the axe away and told him to collect his pay and get out.

"That's about as close to having a funeral without really having one as I ever saw in my logging days," Blanchard observed.

There was an established pecking order in a lumber camp. The job with the lowest wage and least prestige was that of "road monkey," or "chickadee." He was assigned to shovel horse manure out of the iced ruts on the logging road. He ranked even lower than the bullcook or the cookee and was usually either a boy just getting started or a man too old to do anything else.

The practice of creating iced ruts started in Michigan and moved west, reaching Minnesota last. During the night, a sled hauled a large wooden barrel of water slowly down the road, with twin streams of water directed into the ruts. The next morning, sleds containing ten thousand board feet and more of logs could be hauled along the two tracks of ice toward the riverbank.

In laying out such a road, hills were avoided as much as possible. Each downward slope was a danger spot for the horses and the man who perched high on the load of logs to drive them. Hay was scattered on the ice to slow the descent, but it was not unusual for a sled to get out of control, piling into the horses and sometimes sending the load tumbling down on top of them. The teamster had to be ready to jump. If he miscalculated, he would wind up crippled or dead.

A good teamster might be paid as much as forty dollars a month, a wage equaled only by the tophand who directed loading the logs on the sleds. The skidder, who snaked the logs to the road to be picked up by the sled, got about a dollar a day. The chain tender, who branded each log by hitting it with a sledgehammer bearing the company's mark, could do as well. Down the scale a considerable way was the swamper. He cleared roads, cut under-brush and did other minor chopping jobs.

The bull of the woods was the camp foreman, who not only directed the work and settled arguments but often kept order by the force of his personality, backed by a heavy fist and the power to hire and fire for any cause or none. His authority was close to absolute. Toward the end of the white pine era, a more demo-cratic arrangement was worked out in some camps with a commit-tee of workers meting out punishment to anyone who broke the rules, fining the culprit a specified amount of tobacco for minor offenses and beating him up for more serious ones.

The camp boss could fire a man for disobeying an order, dam-aging property, disorderly or riotous conduct and, at least in theory, for getting drunk or bringing liquor to camp. These offenses were considered breach of contract. A man fired before the end of the season automatically lost one fifth of the pay that was due him. His credit at the company store was cut off. A strike was defined as riotous or disorderly conduct, grounds for immedi-ate dismissal. In at least one case, recorded by the Bureau of Labor and Industrial Statistics, a Norwegian was docked 20 per cent of the pay due him because he was killed in the woods and so failed to fulfill the contract to work until spring.

The camp boss was long on muscle and on the techniques for dealing with trees, but often uneducated in other respects. Some could neither read nor write, which caused occasional compli-cations. There was the time, for instance, when a foreman needed a new grindstone and sent his order to Chippewa Falls by a lad who worked in the camp. The foreman drew a sketch of a grind-stone on a piece of paper and told the boy to hand it to the mer-chant. The boss hit new heights of profanity when the messenger brought back a round of cheddar. When he'd cooled off, however, he admitted it was his own fault. He'd forgotten to draw a small circle in the center of the large circle, indicating the hole in the middle that would make the picture look like a grindstone instead of a cheese.

Jack Nelson, who bossed camps along the Namekagon River, was once asked by a brash sixteen-year-old camp clerk, George Jenson, why he'd never learned to read.

"When I can pay a damn young fool like you to do it for me, why should I bother?" he growled.

Women temperance workers occasionally showed up in the lumber camps and some of the lumberjacks gallantly signed the pledge, staying on the wagon until the next time someone sneaked in a bottle. It was said, apparently with considerable truth, that a respectable woman had nothing to fear around the woods workers, although the foreman was uneasy until feminine visitors had left.

One winter, two young women from a charitable organization in Houghton, Michigan, arrived at a camp on the Upper Peninsula to seek donations. The foreman gave them his office as sleeping quarters, moving his blankets to the bunkhouse. He stoked up the stove and even, in a grand gesture of hospitality, provided a clean towel. The visitors were still sleeping soundly when the men sat down to breakfast. The cook took advantage of his status as the only man allowed to talk during meals and started making insinuating remarks about women who would walk so boldly into a lumber camp, implying that they had something besides donations in mind. Nobody else said a word until the eating ended. Then one man stood up with a suggestion:

"Let's lynch the son of a bitch."

The crew bore down on the cook. He grabbed a cleaver, then changed his mind and decided to run instead of fight. Luckily, he was fast on his feet and got away in the woods. A new cook was appointed while the old one made his chilly way through miles of snow to the nearest town. The women collected contributions and went on their way without ever knowing they'd been insulted.

Some camps had a woman or a married couple to do the cooking. Toward the end of the era, there were even camps where children were allowed. Mrs. Victor Curran, who was Margaret Andreae when she was an eight-year-old living in a logging camp near the now-vanished community of Shanagolden, Wisconsin, wrote down her recollections many years later.

Her parents did the cooking for seventy lumberjacks, aided by a cookee and a bullcook. There were two bunks in the corner of the cookhouse, with Margaret assigned the top one. She was required to stay there and read a book during mealtimes, following strict orders not to talk with the men.

The bunkhouse was off limits to the little girl. But once her father, George A. Andreae, took her there when the men were gone. She remembered it as a large room with wooden bunks, straw mattresses and the persistent odor of chewing tobacco.

Christmas Eve came. Margaret hung her stocking on a two-by-four that supported her bed. In the morning it was filled with homemade taffy, popcorn balls and that traditional holiday treat, the only orange she was likely to see all year. Her big present was a copy of Owen Wister's *The Virginian*. She and her father read it together, crying over the chapter where Shorty had to sell his pony.

It was a lonely life for the little girl, but she kept her eyes open. She noticed that the supply sled had brought a hundred bars of a yellow laundry soap called Santa Claus. She had heard that if you sent enough labels from this soap to the company it would send you a prize.

Like everything else in camp, the soap wrappers belonged to the company. If Margaret wanted them, her father told her, she'd have to see Emil Terpe, the camp boss. That was asking a lot. As far as she knew then, Terpe was the most powerful man in the world. Still, she wanted the prize so she walked to his cabin, knocked timidly on the door and inquired if she could please have those soap wrappers.

"Of course, little girl," Terpe said. Then he pointed to a small black box, topped by a tin horn. "Would you like to hear this?"

She nodded. The boss put a black cylinder in place, turned a handle, set down the needle, started the cylinder turning. A voice spoke: "This is the Edison Record Company." And then music began to play. More than half a century later, Margaret Curran could still recall her delight.

The makers of Santa Claus soap came through. In return for the hundred labels, they sent her cheaply bound copies of *Black Beauty, Grimm's Fairy Tales* and *Alice in Wonderland*. Lying in the top bunk, with thousands of snowy Christmas trees outside the window, she was content until spring.

Christmas was one of the few holidays that changed the winter routine. No work was done that day. The cook baked pumpkin pies. If he chose, a lumberjack could have an entire pie to himself. There might be fiddle playing, clog dancing, card playing, or a friendly competition to see who could spin the most unlikely yarn.

Sometimes there was square dancing, with the ladies identified by a grain sack tied around their waists. These temporary representatives of femininity smelled of snoose or cut plug. Trodding on a partner's toe might result in a broken jaw.

Homesickness was a less desirable attribute of December Twenty-fifth. Men with wives and children missed them more that day. A lumberjack far from home remembered pleasanter holidays. One veteran of the Minnesota woods recalled in his old age a Christmas he spent near Bemidji when he was seventeen and newly arrived from his native Norway. On Christmas Eve he ducked out of the fetid cabin he shared with the others and walked far enough into the forest to be sure he was unobserved. Then he began to sob like a child and call for his mother.

The logging camps became a little less lonely with the arrival of the railroads. Some of the intercity railways, encouraged by liberal land grants, began to penetrate the Michigan, Wisconsin and Minnesota pineries as early as 1860, when the North Western reached Green Bay. It extended its line to Menominee, at the southern edge of Michigan's Upper Peninsula, eleven years later. With the arrival of rail facilities, sawmills in the backwoods could compete with those along the Mississippi.

Equally important to the pinery owners were the narrow-gauge logging railroads which snaked into the forests and hauled logs to a central point to be sawed into boards or transferred to the major railroads. For the first time, it became practical to cut pine the year round. Spring log drives continued, but the companies were no longer entirely dependent on them. Pines located too far from a suitable stream to be worth chopping down before could now be cut.

According to one authority, the region's first logging railroad was laid near Red Keg (later Averill), Michigan, in the early 1870s. By the end of that decade, lumber companies had fashioned makeshift roadbeds in the woods of all three Lake States and a new kind of logging had arrived.

There were other changes in the techniques of dealing with logs. In some sawmills, the circular saw—it had come into general use in the 1850s—was replaced by the band saw. That device was a continuous strip of metal about fifty feet long with teeth on one side, operating like a continuous pulley belt. It had been invented in England in 1808, but it took another seventy years to become popular in the Lake States. Its big advantage was that it wasted less wood. The circular saw converted half an inch of each cut into sawdust. The band saw cut a kerf as thin as a knife blade.

Sawmill operators also learned to keep the pond where logs were stored free of ice all winter by piping steam from the mill boiler into the water. Michigan lumbermen pioneered in the use of the "bull chain," which kept logs moving in a disciplined line from the "hot ponds" to the saws, with each log fastened to heavy hooks on the endless chain.

Some lumber camps experimented with a device called, logically enough, "big wheels." Created by a backwoods inventor, it consisted of a set of wheels ten feet or so in diameter, the axles far enough above ground to clear stumps. It made it possible to haul logs even in warm weather.

A more astonishing machine to come upon unexpectedly in the woods was the steam hauler, invented by A. O. Lombard, a Maine man. It was a caterpillar tractor with skids in front, powered by a steam engine and weighing as much as sixty thousand pounds. It could haul three double sleds at a time over an iced road.

The early version of the "Lombard" was steered by a horse, but later a human pilot was used. He sat on a light sled ahead of the crawling monster, so close to the smokestack that he had to keep beating out embers in his clothes, steering the machine with a massive iron wheel that twisted the runners. The steam hauler was considered hell on a downgrade. If it ran away, all the pilot could do was steer for his life, knowing he'd be crushed if he jumped.

The Lombards were the most dramatic sight in the woods— behemoths belching smoke, fire and steam, dragging trains of sleds piled high with pine that might stretch for five hundred feet. But they were expensive to buy, dangerous to drive, difficult to keep running. The steam hauler never became a major factor in the white pine era. But what a sight it was to see!

By making year-round logging possible and opening up new territories, the railroads hastened the day when the vast acreage of white pine would be gone. Locomotives, belching sparks from fat smokestacks, became a new hazard in the woods, starting fires that devastated large regions. Within a few years of the arrival of the first railways, the predictions that doomsayers had been making no longer sounded ridiculous to lumbermen. As early as 1867, a Wisconsin committee, headed by a farsighted fellow named Increase Lapham, warned that wasteful cutting methods were ruining a natural resource that could never be replaced. The report was filed away and forgotten. But by the 1880s, even the most optimistic experts said the white pine would be gone within thirty years, and pessimists said it would be gone in as few as seven.

In public, most lumber barons scoffed at such forebodings. In private, some took steps—not to start replacing the forests they had ruined but by investing in virgin pine lands in the South and the Pacific Northwest.

An indication of the impending shortage of white pine, as well as a reflection of the greater freedom of operation brought by the railroads, was the fact that toward the end of the century some companies began to cut hardwoods, formerly scorned. Such logs did not float well in the rivers, but that no longer mattered if a railroad was handy.

To the average lumberjack, none of this mattered very much just yet. He was a member of a strange breed of American, an untypical sort whose acquisitive instinct was dormant. If he was the instrument that wasted much of the pinery, he was often equally wasteful in his personal life. Trees were made to be cut, and if they ran short, what the hell? There would always be more just over the next hill.

CHAPTER IX

Forest Fires and Other Hazards

IF A LUMBERJACK had to get sick, it was generally agreed, the best thing to have was the ague. Not that the fever and other miseries that accompanied malaria were pleasant. But the treatment had its advantages. Farm families in the Lake States used quinine, but woods dwellers had their own medicine. The accepted remedy was to slice up roots of the blue flag, dug from a swamp, and add liberal quantities of Forty Rod whiskey. After letting the mixture stand for a while, it was administered to the patient three times a day until he felt better or the whiskey ran out.

When Dr. F. G. Johnson went directly from medical school to Lake Nebagamon, a lumber town in northern Wisconsin, in 1895, he found malaria common in lumber camps. A few years later he also had to deal with a typhoid epidemic. Johnson had been taught that the way to combat this mankiller was a combination of intestinal antiseptics, a liquid diet and cold baths. His lumberjack patients didn't object to the diet or the antiseptics, but there was considerable resistance to the baths. Some years later, medical opinion decided the treatment was worthless. By then, the woods workers who'd contracted typhoid were no longer interested, some of them because they'd recovered.

Smallpox was also a recurring problem in the big woods. When an outbreak was discovered in camp, the boss isolated the victim in a pesthouse built on the premises and issued a strict order against mingling with the rest of the crew or visiting other camps. But lumberjacks were a gregarious lot and the order was often disobeyed. The result could be a full-scale epidemic, affecting an entire region.

That was what happened one year to the Musser-Sauntry Lumber Company, which had six hundred men in several camps near Hawthorne, Wisconsin. Instead of isolating the ill men in individual camps, the company built a central pesthouse in the village, hiring Dr. Johnson to take care of them. The doctor brought his wife along. They checked into the Hawthorne hotel. But drunks were so numerous and so noisy there that they moved out again after an hour and found a cottage to rent.

The Hawthorne pesthouse became something of a civic asset. Lumberjacks used the excuse of visiting a sick friend to come to the village. Patients on the road to recovery were ready to do their recuperating at a bar. Business boomed. A contingent of gamblers arrived to set up shop. Saloons were full. Madams were turning away customers. All in all, the smallpox epidemic livened things up considerably. It wasn't considered a bad thing to have around, except perhaps by those who died.

By the 1880s, lumber companies were encouraging their workers to be vaccinated. Some even hired a physician to visit the camps with his needle. In 1886, for example, Dr. B. J. Merrill went to thirty camps around Stillwater, Minnesota, vaccinating any man who'd hold still long enough. Particularly among some immigrant groups, there was deep suspicion of vaccination, but Merrill found such opposition had lessened that year. The men remembered one of the worst epidemics in the north woods, which had killed several hundred lumberjacks in Minnesota camps in the winter of 1882–83. That outbreak was blamed on a cook who became ill at a stopping place on a tote road that led to Trout Lake. Some of his blankets wound up at a camp on Caldwell Brook. From there, the infection spread to the entire logging region that centered on Grand Rapids, Minnesota. After the epidemic finally ended, state health officials burned every building where ill men had been housed.

Most camp bosses took quick action when a man was suspected of having smallpox, trying to stop the disease from spreading to others, which would cut down on the work force. A foreman named Lindsay was running a camp near Oscoda, Michigan, at the mouth of the AuSable River, when Charlie Goule told him he was feeling poorly. Lindsay decided Charlie must have the pox. He locked him inside a ten-by-ten tarpaper shanty, a few feet from the logging railroad's tracks.

Charlie Beever, a sympathetic railway brakeman, decided to slip Goule a pint of medicinal whiskey. He fastened the bottle to a long pole and, as the locomotive inched by, held it up to the shanty's window. Goule was not too sick to reach out and grab it.

Whiskey was easy to come by for trainmen. Lumberjacks riding back to camp often left bottles behind in the train or hid them in the woods so they wouldn't get fired for breaking the rule against having liquor. So Beever made a regular habit of supplying the patient on each day's trip. Before long, there was a second head in the window. He recognized another lumberjack, Huey Buchanan.

"Huey's got it, too," Goule yelled, grabbing the bottle.

As the days wore on, the trainmen spotted increasing numbers of patients in the pesthouse. A pint was no longer sufficient. In view of the soaring number of smallpox victims, the train crew kept increasing the allotment. Finally, they were attaching four quarts to the pole each time they passed the shack. At that point, Bill Hardy, superintendent of the AuSable and Northwestern Railway, ordered a halt.

"Lindsay's raising hell," he told Beever. "He says his chore boy picked up two bushels of bottles and three gallon jugs. He says the whole bunch is fighting drunk. And he says he thinks none of them ever had the smallpox in the first place."

A north woods physician had to handle everything from obstetrics in an Indian village to injuries from a saloon brawl, taking the unexpected in stride. Dr. Thomas Torpy, who worked out of such tough lumber towns as Minocqua, Wisconsin, was ready for anything that came along.

In those days, Minocqua's main street was lined with saloons. One night, the discussion at one of these bars turned to the prowess of Jack Bolger's pit bulldog. The animal had whipped every other dog in town, its owner claimed, and had even made a wolf turn tail and run.

"Bet you five bucks I can whip him," a lumberjack yelled.

"You're on," Bolger said, and went home to get his dog.

To make things fair, it was agreed that the lumberjack could not use a club and had to get down to the dog's level on all fours. He was game. He started growling at the dog, ready to slug the beast when it made its rush. But the animal moved too fast.

When Doc Torpy got to the saloon, the lumberjack's face had been ripped from jaw to cheekbone. The physician sewed up the wound without anesthetic. The 'jack never winced.

"Come back and see me in a week or two," Torpy said, and left to patch up survivors of a brawl down the street.

It was several months before the man who'd lost to the bulldog returned to Minocqua. He didn't stop at the doctor's office but Torpy met him on the street. The man was wearing a full beard.

"Who took your stitches out for you?" Torpy asked.

"Stitches?" The lumberjack looked puzzled. Then a light dawned. "Oh. So that's why I haven't been able to shave."

Another tale Torpy liked to tell had to do with a winter night when he got a call from a saloon and found a lumberjack lying there, more dead than alive. He'd been caught under the wheels of a logging train when he tried to jump off to head for the bar. The only other physician in the vicinity was Dr. A. B. Rosenberry. Torpy sent a messenger to get him. Rosenberry brought along his young nephew, Marvin.

Some years later, Marvin Rosenberry became the chief justice of the Wisconsin Supreme Court. That night he was pressed into service as the anesthetist. Two sawhorses and some planks were the operating table. A bed sheet was ripped up for bandages. A blacksmith's light was hung overhead. Torpy decided if he used ether, the sputtering kerosene lamp would blow the place up. He handed young Marvin a bottle of chloroform and told him to do his best.

The two doctors amputated one leg and patched up the patient's other injuries. After they were through, they filled empty whiskey bottles with hot water and tucked them under the blankets. Then everybody went away, leaving the injured man to recover if he could. Torpy rose at dawn and woke up the saloonkeeper, who grumbled about the hour.

"Hell's bells, Doc, what's the hurry? All we're going to find over there is a stiff."

But the lumberjack was not only alive, he was feeling much better. Within a few days, he'd carved a set of crutches for himself and hobbled off into the woods toward his camp. Torpy met him several months later. By then, he'd fashioned a wooden leg and bragged that he could still do a good day's work with a peavey.

Incidents like that gave Doc Torpy a lot of respect for his lumberjack patients. He continued to practice medicine when he was past eighty. By then, the north woods was getting a new crop— summer residents from the city. The salty old man considered them a pretty poor lot, as he made plain one day when a wealthy woman living in a fancy summer cottage scolded him for making a house call without wearing a jacket or necktie. She was sitting up in bed, wearing a silken negligee, looking bored. Torpy made his examination, then stepped back to give her his diagnosis.

"There's absolutely nothing the matter with you, you lazy old bitch," he said, and stalked out of the house.

Logging companies of the late nineteenth century usually paid for the initial treatment if a man was injured on the job. If he needed further care, that was his problem. The men were encouraged to take out accident insurance. But many of the insurance companies that sought their business went bankrupt and failed to pay off.

A better system was the practice of buying hospital tickets. For a modest fee, usually around five dollars a year, a man got a card which entitled him to treatment at the issuing hospital, providing he could get there. Some agents who visited the camps to sell such tickets pocketed the money, but in general the method worked out pretty well.

Among the hospitals for lumberjacks was one established by Dr. John M. Dodd in 1895 in an abandoned bawdy house in Ashland, Wisconsin, then known as "The Garland City of the Inland Sea." Ten thousand loggers were working in the vicinity and Ashland's ninety saloons stayed open twenty-four hours a day. Its bordellos also prospered, but a large one at 610 Ellis Avenue had been abandoned after the owner's wife, Sadie Mahoney, was shot and killed there by Jack Linsey five years before the doctor bought the place.

There was a doubledeck porch around the front, wainscoting on the walls, a ballroom, numerous small bedrooms for patients, even a large bathroom on the second floor with a tub big enough for two. The doctor not only converted the place into a hospital but lived there with his wife and children for ten years, treating such cases as that of a lumberjack who was hauled across the ice from one of the Apostle Islands by dogsled after having his bowel perforated when he was hit by a log. The injured man survived, as did a patient from a sawmill who was hit in the chest by a slender, twelve-foot stick that passed through his body, front to back, protruding four feet behind his shoulder blades. Fellow workmen sawed off the end and whittled it down so it could be pulled out. Bits of bark and clothing were imbedded in the man's chest cavity. But Ellis patched him up and he went back to work.

It was good business for a lumber company to get an injured man back on the job as soon as possible, so some hired physicians to treat their employees. Dr. P. P. Stewart, for example, worked out an agreement with a Weyerhaeuser logging operation in which he would be paid one hundred fifty dollars for the season to deal with minor injuries. For major ones, it was specified, he could charge the company his regular fee.

It was a busy year. Stewart worked hard dealing with broken legs, fractured skulls, smashed chests. The accidents in the various camps kept him jumping, but he comforted himself with the thought of all those fees for major injuries he was piling up. It turned out, however, that the company considered every case he had treated as not only minor but routine. All he got was his one hundred fifty dollars.

Physicians were scarce in the north country and lumberjacks relied mostly on their own resources. Broken legs or arms were often set, after a fashion, by a friend who was handy. Nostrums were purchased from Indians. Spring tonics were made from goldenrod, sassafras, ground hemlock or black cherry. Such ingredients were boiled down and stored in a jug until spring, when the owner took a swig each morning and night. Every man swore by his own recipe. If someone suggested that a tonic was worthless, the 'jack had a ready answer:

"I'm still here, ain't I?"

It was hard to argue with that. If a man could survive the life in the woods, he must be doing something right.

The dangers of disease, accident and saloon brawls were not the only ones that cut short life expectancy for the weak, the unwary and the unlucky. Flame was another accepted hazard. The lumberjacks' own carelessness was often responsible for the forest fires that were common whenever the woods were dry.

One such fire in the fall of 1871, which claimed more lives than any other in American history, devastated large sections of northeastern Wisconsin and a portion of Upper Michigan. It wiped out the thriving lumber town of Peshtigo, Wisconsin, and several smaller communities. It killed perhaps twelve hundred people, five times as many as the Chicago fire that occurred the same day.

Like many similar disasters, the Peshtigo fire was an example of what happens when men ignore what Increase Lapham called the doctrine of usufruct. That is a legal term, having to do with the obligation to use another's property without injuring or destroying it. In his 1867 report to the legislature, Lapham deplored the waste of pine trees taking place, declaring that "man has too long forgotten that the earth was given him for usufruct alone—not for consumption, still less for profligate waste."

Usufruct was a word that was not familiar to either lumberjack or lumber baron. The concept was not one they found useful. They considered "cut and get out" a better motto. Never mind that the process resulted in a wasteland of stumps and slashings—great heaps of tangled branches left behind when the logs were hauled away.

The Peshtigo fire was actually two or three nearly simultaneous conflagrations on both sides of an arm of Lake Michigan called Green Bay. It had a number of causes—an unusually dry summer, a shift in the wind, the lack of any organized method of fighting such catastrophes before they got out of hand. But the primary cause was, as usual, human carelessness.

It was the custom for settlers in the Lake States to set what they called "pasture-maker" fires, burning off the stumps and debris left behind by loggers. Some of these fires got out of hand that fall. The railroads constituted another danger. They made no effort to keep locomotives from spewing sparks in forested country, and fires were frequently burning along the rights of way. Hunters sometimes failed to douse a campfire. And the slashings left by loggers created huge piles of kindling, ready for the burning.

Every late summer and early fall, before the snows came, there was heavy smoke in the air in the pinery region that stretched across three states. Nobody paid much attention to such fires, as a rule. In 1871, because the smoke was worse than usual and conditions were abnormally dry, there were some forebodings. Around some of the small communities, men with shovels dug trenches or set backfires to keep the danger in the woods, where it belonged. But in general, life went on much as usual.

The day before the night when every building but one in Peshtigo was destroyed, workers from Peshtigo Harbor and lumberjacks from the surrounding camps arrived in the village for their customary weekend spree. Peshtigo's fourteen saloons were crowded. The bawdy houses at the edge of town did a brisk trade.

A railroad line connected the community with the harbor settlement, seven miles away. The Peshtigo Company, which provided work for most residents of the two communities, had cut close to 5.7 million board feet of lumber in its sawmill that summer. It was nearly time for the sixty logging camps in the vicinity to start felling pines to be floated down the Peshtigo River to the holding pond above a dam at the center of the village. The North Western Railroad was pushing its right-of-way northward from Green Bay, so railway crews augmented the usual Saturday night crowd at the bars.

There is no way of knowing how many fewer persons would have died the night of Sunday, October 8, if everyone had been cold sober. When a wall of flame came roaring down on the lumber town, some lumberjacks and their drinking buddies were sleeping off the weekend drunk. A considerable number of others were in no shape to make the life-or-death decision on where to run. Most who survived took refuge in the river. A man who lingered long on the way was apt to wind up dead.

The fire struck about 9 P.M. By then, according to one eyewitness, many of both "the virtuous and the vicious were seeking the God-given boon of sleep." Father Peter Pernin reported that earlier in the day he'd been annoyed by drunks outside a saloon near his church. Their condition, he wrote, was "plainly revealed by the manner in which they quarreled, wrestled, rolled on the ground, filling the air the while with wild shouts and horrid blasphemies." It was, in other words, a normal Sunday in a lumberjack town.

When the crisis came, it became obvious that some of the men's judgments were clouded. A number of them headed for the largest wooden building in town, the company boardinghouse, instead of running for the river. Women and children who also tried to find refuge in the three-story building could be excused for the mistake. But an experienced woodsman should have known that the place was a firetrap. No one was sure how many died in the boardinghouse. The estimates ranged from forty to two hundred. But it is likely that some who holed up there had been staggering along the splintered board sidewalks of Peshtigo not long before, seeking a place to sleep off the weekend. It took only a few minutes for the building to burn. Nothing was left of its human cargo but "a heap of indistinguishable calcined bones and charred flesh," a survivor reported.

Some of those endangered by the fire were caught alone in the woods. A landlooker, Anders Holm, was timber cruising for the Sargent and Bromfield Company south of Peshtigo when he saw the flames approaching. He ran to a clearing belonging to a young bachelor, Sven Carlsten, who was using a grubbing hoe to dig a trench around his cabin. Holm advised him to run for it. Sven said no. Then a nearby stump burst into flame, as if from spontaneous combustion. The wooden shingles on the cabin roof began to smoke.

"Come on," Holm yelled. "You can't fight this one."

"All right. But first I got to get some things."

Sven dashed into the cabin. He grabbed up his rifle, an empty water bucket and a red petticoat he kept hanging on the wall to remind him that there was more to life than a lonely cabin in the woods. Then the two men ran for the tote road that led toward Peshtigo. Along the way, Sven dropped his pail, then his rifle, and finally the petticoat. They got to town as the board sidewalks were bursting into flame. Without slowing up, they reached the river.

When Carlsten went back to his clearing after the fire, the cabin was gone. On the way, he looked for the red petticoat. Not even a singed remnant remained. It was a disappointment to him. A man could build another cabin with a few days' work. He could save up and buy another rifle, another water bucket. But there wasn't another red petticoat available for miles.

After wiping out Peshtigo, the fire roared north toward the twin lumber towns of Marinette, Wisconsin, and Menominee, Michigan, separated by the Menominee River. Marinette and its neighboring community of Menekaune—now a part of Marinette—were in the greatest danger. Luckily, three steamers were in port when the fire approached. Women and children, along with a few men who decided to flee instead of fight, hurried aboard. Then the ships headed out into the bay.

At a Menekaune shipyard was a small schooner, the *Stella,* tied up awaiting repairs. Several dozen people scrambled to her deck and started to cut her loose. The shipyard owner, S. V. D. Philbrook, picked up a handspike.

"The first man to cut them lines gets this across his head," he yelled.

It was not until a full cargo of refugees was on the little sailing ship and the ropes were smoldering between her and the pier that Philbrook gave the order to cut the lines. Pushed by the same wind that was fanning the fire, the *Stella* drifted out into the river and grounded on a sandbar, safe.

At Marinette, such lumber barons as Ike Stephenson, later the financial angel of the Wisconsin Progressive movement, took charge of saving the little city. Holding the loss in that community to fourteen buildings was more a result of the fact that Marinette was not in the main pathway of the fire than to the human effort, however. The flames jumped the river and headed on north along the bay, killing the last twenty-two victims at the Upper Michigan settlement of Birch Creek. Rain came on October 9 and extinguished the fire.

Those lumberjacks who survived organized search parties to look for companions who had been caught in the woods. They might need food, a doctor or a decent burial. One of the bodies discovered was that of a young logging camp foreman. As the search party passed by, his corpse crashed to the ground from the burned-out remnants of a tall pine. He had been roasted there, clinging to a branch. His body, found six days after the fire, was among the last to be identified. After a week, it was felt that anyone unable to escape the fire would be beyond help. Besides, some of the partially burned timber could be saved. It was time to shoulder axes and take up saws and go back to work.

Thirty years later, the body of a presumed Peshtigo fire victim was found in a swamp near the Peshtigo River. It was well preserved, but no one recognized the man. An enterprising promoter hauled the body around to county fairs and charged admission to view it, but business was poor. By then, there had been plenty of other forest fires. The memory of the worst one in American history had already grown dim.

The Chicago fire and the Peshtigo fire were not the only ones to take place in the Lake States on October 8, 1871. A series of forest fires on Michigan's lower peninsula ruined several lumber towns and killed several hundred persons. As in Wisconsin, these large fires grew from smaller ones that had been burning for weeks without anyone worrying much about them.

The first outbreak came at Holland, Michigan, a Dutch settlement across Lake Michigan from Milwaukee, with the blazing forest setting fire to houses in midafternoon of that disastrous Sunday. Some of the Hollanders were members of a religious sect that felt Sunday work was unholy, even in an emergency. They refused to join other residents in trying to fight the fire and about two thirds of the city of three thousand persons was wiped out, although the loss of life was small.

A hundred fifty miles to the north, Manistee lumberjacks interrupted their Sunday drinking to fight a fire that menaced not only the homes but, a more serious matter, the saloons. With nothing but shovels and buckets of water, they managed to save part of the village.

Lansing, the state capital, was threatened by another forest fire that day, being saved mostly by efforts of students from the State College of Agriculture.

At a backwoods settlement in central Michigan's Gratiot County, a bearded Englishman, Jacob Laird, took charge of saving the Case & Turner sawmill, staying behind to fight the blaze with water and dirt after all the other workmen fled. He paused only long enough to curse the fire and defy it to kill him. His beard, most of his hair and his shirt were burned off. But he was helped by a lucky shift of the wind and the mill was saved. Its owners not only doubled his wages but bought him a brand-new suit.

The Reverend E. J. Goodspeed, who hurried into print with an account of the Michigan fires, described the conversion to religion of a sawmill operator in the western Michigan woods. According to the preacher, the fellow was a wicked man but brave. When the fire approached, he and his two brothers tried to save their mill, but it was soon plain they were losing the fight. The blasphemous one loosed a tirade, climaxed by a challenge: "God can do as he damned well pleases!"

By what Goodspeed considered a minor miracle—a lumberjack would have said it was a stroke of luck—it began to rain. The shower changed to a downpour. The sinner threw himself to his knees in the mud and tried to give thanks. But he'd forgotten how to pray.

"Oh, to hell with it," he said finally, climbing to his feet. He began waving his hat and shouting: "Hooray for God! Hooray for God!"

The rain that the reverend's favorite sinner called down from heaven failed to arrive elsewhere, at least in time to save such lumber towns as Forester, Richmondville, White Rock, Forestville, Sand Beach and Huron City. A committee appointed by the governor later reported that fourteen thousand square miles of Michigan was blackened by fires that were among the most destructive of timber resources ever recorded.

After the 1871 fires, a man in Port Huron, Michigan, walked for more than a mile on trunks of fallen trees, never once touching the ground. Loggers salvaged some of these pines. Settlers burned others to clear the land for crops.

Ten years after the 1871 fires had burned out, such clearing was still being done even though the summer of 1881 was unusually hot, arid and dangerous. The Bay City *Daily Morning Call* said that the Thumb region of Michigan, mostly cutover land covered by huge piles of slashings, was "as dry as a man after eating salt mackerel." So the time was ripe for another disaster.

On September 5, a southwest wind strong enough to blow down trees fired several small fires into a wall of flames that reminded veteran lumberjacks of 1871. A husband, wife and son who tried to outrun the fire in a wagon were overtaken and killed. A mail carrier, Ira Humphrey, who turned down advice not to continue toward Bad Axe, was burned to death in his buggy north of

Marlette. Most of the buildings at Port Hope were destroyed, along with a half million board feet of lumber. In the Forester vicinity, only fifteen of three hundred buildings survived. Four hundred refugees saved themselves in the Bad Axe courthouse, which was new and made of brick, but only by organizing a bucket brigade and pouring water on its roof. By the time rains extinguished the fires two days later, fifteen thousand Michigan residents were homeless, close to thirty-five hundred buildings had been destroyed, nearly three hundred people were dead.

To house the homeless, Saginaw lumbermen offered green lumber—not free, but at wholesale prices. A Port Huron relief committee took advantage of this modified generosity to buy enough boards to give twenty-two hundred families materials to build temporary shanties before winter came.

A footnote to the 1881 Michigan fires was the role of Clara Barton, who had organized the American Red Cross in her rooms in Washington the previous May. At the time of the disaster there was only a single chapter of the organization. Two more were organized in New York State to help the fire victims. The agency's work in the Michigan pinery helped secure its official recognition as a disaster relief organization.

Another Michigan fire worth noting destroyed the lumber town of Ontonagon on the Upper Peninsula in 1896. The Diamond Match Company's mills burned, along with extensive piles of planks waiting to be splintered into matchsticks. The company decided to pull out, taking those logs that escaped the fire with it. There was great bitterness in the region against the outside owners who had decreed that the chief source of local employment would vanish. Many fire victims were living in tents, with the bitter winter weather nearly at hand. Local officials pleaded with the match firm to reconsider. But the decision was made. Logs that had been in the river when the fire came were loaded on a train and the locomotive started hauling its burden out of the valley. The engineer felt a massive hand on his shoulder.

"Back 'er down to the station, brother," Sheriff O'Rourke ordered.

The engineer backed her down. But the mills remained closed and the white pine era around Ontonagon was over.

It might be assumed that such disasters would have made the

lumberjacks and settlers more careful, but this was seldom the case. Pasture-maker fires continued to be set. Piles of slashings as much as forty feet high continued to be left behind by loggers. With every dry season came more fires, some of them large ones. In the twenty years after the Peshtigo fire set a record for death in the pineries, major fires were recorded around such Wisconsin lumber towns as Phillips, Marshfield, Fifield, Medford and even the rebuilt little city of Peshtigo. As loggers penetrated farther into Minnesota, it was that state's turn. In the late summer of 1894, for instance, there was so much smoke from burning forests around Sandstone, Kettle River and Mission Creek that a man could hardly see to swing his axe. In Pine County that August, the Great Northern trains were held up for three days because of the smoke. Then, on September 1, came the Hinckley fire, which killed four hundred eighteen persons in and around that lumber center of east-central Minnesota.

Hinckley had about twelve hundred residents, three churches, five saloons, two railroad stations and a sawmill owned by the Brennan Lumber Company. Like other pinery towns, its streets were mostly sawdust and its sidewalks and buildings were made of wood.

Live coals had started falling when the St. Paul & Duluth station agent got a telegraph message saying Pokegama (now Brook Park) had been virtually wiped out with great loss of life. That community was only nine miles away and the agent gave the alarm. Volunteers headed for the edge of Hinckley to try to save their homes.

When the flames appeared, they were borne on a sixty-mile-an-hour gale. The amateur firemen ran for their lives. Mothers snatched up babies. Men grabbed older children. But Hinckley was in the middle of the forest and there was no safe place to run.

At the Eastern Minnesota Railroad depot, a train of six wooden cars was standing. On a nearby siding was a freight train of four boxcars and a caboose. While one of the engineers held down on his locomotive whistle and kept it screaming, the crews fastened the two trains together.

Ed Barry and William Best, the engineers, were men of courage. They held their combined train at the station until several hundred persons climbed aboard. Paint on the passenger cars was beginning to blister before they steamed north toward Sandstone, stopping there only long enough to yell a warning. A few minutes after the train left, Sandstone was destroyed and forty-five of its residents killed.

The train got across the Kettle River bridge moments before the fire ate through the wooden underpinnings. Then it chugged on north, outrunning the fire that was bringing devastation to hundreds of square miles of forest behind it.

Some Hinckley residents who missed the train found a safe refuge in the shallow water of a gravel pit. Another two hundred or so ran north on the tracks of the St. Paul and Duluth Railroad. The fire was catching up with them and thirty-three of the slower runners had burned to death when a southbound train came around a bend.

Its engineer was Jim Root, who had run trains for General William Tecumseh Sherman in Georgia during the Civil War. He skidded to a halt and the refugees climbed on board. Then he threw the machinery into reverse and opened the throttle wide. There was an explosion. A piece of metal shattered the window of the locomotive cab. Jagged glass cut the engineer's forehead and neck. He grabbed a rag, wiped away the blood so he could see and got the train underway, backing up the track. By now there were flames in the woods on both sides. Worse, the rear car had caught fire.

A swampy pond called Skunk Lake was six miles away. Root made up his mind he would get there, if he lived. The throttle was so hot by now that it blistered his hand. He could scarcely breathe. He passed out, releasing the controls. The steam pressure fell to ninety-five pounds and the train slowed almost to a stop. The fireman, who had taken cover in the engine's water tank, jumped out and threw a bucket of water on the engineer. Root staggered to his feet, grabbed the throttle again and pulled it wide open.

There was a parlor car on the train. It was in charge of the porter, John Blair. Not many of those aboard were keeping their heads, but the black man refused to panic. Paint was running down the sides of the car. Little tongues of flame were licking at the wood. Some of the windows had shattered from the heat. Blair stood calmly by the water cooler, passing out cups until it was gone, soothing children, joking with adults, encouraging everybody by his example. It seemed likely that they were all going to burn up. But until that happened, this parlor car was his responsibility and he intended to deal with it as best he could.

Meanwhile, Root was on the verge of fainting again. But he held on until he had backed the train across the Skunk Lake bridge. Then he jammed on the brakes and slid to the floor of the cab. The fireman leaped out and began dousing flaming doors of the coaches with water so the passengers could get out. They ran for the lake and waded out into the muck, crouching down until they could feel the water up to their necks. Someone remembered the engineer and dragged him from the locomotive and into the lake. Including those passengers who had been heading for St. Paul when the train picked up the Hinckley refugees, something over three hundred persons survived that exciting example of pinery railroading, living to tell about the fire that destroyed Hinckley, Pokegama, Sandstone, Mission Creek and Partridge, Minnesota.

The Hinckley fire burned about three hundred fifty thousand acres of white pine. This loss, along with the number of deaths, finally persuaded the politicians to listen to such resident conservationists as General Christopher C. Andrews. A forest commission was appointed, a chief fire warden hired, and a start made on methods to prevent forest fires and to fight them more effectively. Still, the record continued to be poor for years. It was not until after a 1908 fire, which burned two million dollars' worth of timber and destroyed Chisholm, Minnesota, that the forest commissioner was given authority to appoint local fire wardens and to hire forest rangers. And it took another fire two years later, which killed twenty-nine persons and destroyed a million dollars' worth of timber, before Minnesota's Legislature appropriated funds to pay the rangers.

As late as 1918, a generation beyond the state's days of greatest logging glory, a forest fire killed about four hundred persons and burned most of Cloquet, Minnesota. The Cloquet fire ruined several lumber companies and forced others to spend nearly two million dollars to lay railroad tracks into areas of the state formerly considered too remote to be worth logging.

According to some estimates, for every three pine trees in Michigan, Wisconsin and Minnesota that were turned into useful lumber, one tree was wasted. Cutting methods and transportation losses were responsible for part of this 25 per cent wastage. But the forest fires were equally prodigal of resources that were turning out to be something less than limitless, after all.

The penalty for ignoring old Increase Lapham's right of usufruct, it finally became plain even to loggers, could be figured in lives and cold, hard cash.

CHAPTER X

The Wild, Wild North

"IN THEM DAYS, you could hire a livery and drive out to the houses at the edge of town," an old lumberjack said. "The rig would wait an hour or two for you and bring you back, all for about a dollar. The houses had a bar. After you had a drink, you could hire a girl and go upstairs with her. You paid her two dollars. The girl got one dollar and the house got the other dollar, and that is the way they made their living."

What were known as sporting houses were an accepted part of both urban and smalltown life in the Lake States, as elsewhere, during the period when the white pine was cut. Most cities had well-defined red-light districts. Majority opinion held that it was better to keep all the prostitutes in one part of town so the police could keep an eye on them. It was also widely believed that the services of women who worked in houses that were not homes were necessary to keep respectable females safe from lustful men. In such places as Milwaukee, before a reform wave washed over its River Street district in 1911, visitors could buy a guidebook listing the facilities offered by various madams. In the lumber towns, word-of-mouth advertising was sufficient.

The clergy spoke out against the evil institution. Other reformers complained now and then, some of them claiming that many of the girls had been sold into a degrading form of bondage. Finally, in that high-minded year of 1911, the Wisconsin Legislature declared that white slavery was against the law. Then it appointed a committee to find out if there was any such thing.

State Senator Howard Teasdale headed the investigating group. He has been described as "a great, hulking man with a stringy mustache and a left eyelid that perpetually drooped." It was said that he looked like "a sinister city boss," but "his jaw was firm and his motives pure." He was best known around Madison for being in favor of thrift and against Demon Rum. He accepted the call to find out why girls were going wrong, particularly in the vicinity of north woods lumber camps.

Judging from arrest statistics involving commercialized sex, Wisconsin was the least sinful state in the Midwest. But there was reason to suspect that police and prosecutors weren't trying very hard to enforce such laws as one passed in 1890, which made it a crime to run a disorderly house. It was also suspected that some of the law enforcement people were collecting a portion of the profits. When Teasdale sent a questionnaire to county district attorneys, most didn't bother to answer his request for detailed information on sin. Some who did respond were less than candid. The prosecutor in the pinery county of Vilas, for instance, said he knew of only two whorehouses in his vicinity, adding that the women there were "old and practically harmless." Teasdale suspected the official could have learned about other red lights burning in Vilas County windows by checking with the nearest lumberjack.

The mayor of Algoma, in northeastern Wisconsin, complained that the committee was "attracting the attention of fanatics and the press to something that cannot be prevented by investigation or law." But Teasdale also got letters from citizens who wanted vice wiped out. An anonymous letter from Woodruff complained that a brothel was running full blast in Arbor Vitae, "almost in plain sight of the beautiful fish hatchery." While one was turning out fish, it added, the other "is turning out degenerates."

The committee chairman hired detectives, including at least one woman, instructing them to slink through saloons and fancy houses and report what they saw. At two dollars and fifty cents a day plus expenses, the sleuths proved expensive. Some even offended Teasdale's sense of thrift by buying drinks for the house.

But they came up with plenty of information that had apparently escaped local lawmen's attention.

Teasdale's committee held hearings in a number of cities. Saloonkeepers, madams, dance hall operators and public officials were required to testify on why girls went astray. One witness blamed the hootchy-kootchy shows at county fairs. A Hurley judge said the problem stemmed from "natural cussedness." A Milwaukee social worker felt that immodest dress was to blame—fashion now permitted women to show their ankles, resulting in an epidemic of lustful thoughts.

But much of the discussion revolved around economics. The committee was told that it cost a young woman nine dollars a week to pay for her room, board and other essentials, while the wages paid female workers in shops and factories ranged between three and six dollars a week. By contrast, a prostitute named Daisy Allen said she'd grossed $4,375 from 875 customers during the 1909–10 sporting season. True, Miss Allen had been required to give half of this to her employer and had paid the madam an additional $313.28 for such items as laundry, silk stockings, a tapestry, bath salts, beer, chop suey and visits to the manicurist, dentist and doctor. Even so, her net income figured out to $36.02 a week—triple the pay of a schoolteacher, and at least six times that of the average clerk or factory girl. Daisy said she would have done better if she hadn't taken a three-week vacation when she hadn't earned a dime.

The joint legislative committee was even more impressed by how much money could be made in the management field. One businesswoman said she never grossed less than ten thousand dollars a year from her "boarders." Another told Teasdale she wouldn't give bed space to a woman who couldn't earn ten to fifteen dollars a week, free and clear. A third admitted charging customers a dollar for a beer, an example of immoral extravagance that made the chairman shudder.

The committee found that the average Wisconsin whore was twenty-six years old, had entered the profession voluntarily when she was nineteen and was now netting from fifteen to forty dollars a week. She was apt to have a police record and a history of venereal disease. But so far as the committee could discover, she had no desire to leave her profession for a respectable job paying three dollars a week.

Some of the committee hearings were held in the pinery region, where testimony indicated that working conditions were often primitive. They were told of a brothel at Woodruff, for instance, that consisted of a log cabin with three girls, run by a madam who was married to an Indian.

The legislators heard few complaints from the women about the life they led, but one prostitute, Jane Darlington, had a word of criticism for men. She had found that they looked down on the women whose services they purchased.

"You can't be a fool and live in one of those places," Miss Darlington said. "That's a mistaken idea that a great many men have. They think sporting people know nothing, that they're idiots."

Another prostitute, Alice Mosher, was asked by Teasdale: "Do boys have anything to do with girls going wrong?"

"Certainly, or they couldn't go wrong. A girl couldn't make herself go wrong, could she?"

"I don't know."

"You've been a boy, haven't you?"

"I never happened to go that way."

Miss Mosher regarded the senator skeptically. "No?" she said.

Most of the prostitutes indicated they had entered the trade for the money, some out of hardship and some to better themselves financially. Not one claimed to have been drugged, bludgeoned or spirited away by a white slaver. A Woodruff prostitute said she'd thought of quitting, but after averaging ten dollars a week from the lumberjacks compared to the four dollars a week she'd earned as a seamstress, she didn't see how she could afford to make the change.

In Superior, the committee learned, property that would rent for fifteen dollars a month elsewhere in town brought as much as one hundred seventy-five a month in the segregated red-light district. In addition, each of twenty-one Superior brothels had to pay a monthly fine of fifty-three dollars. In return, the madams were not required even to draw their shades.

To the disappointment of the reformers, most of the young women in the ancient profession claimed to be quite well satisfied with their jobs. But Teasdale had been authorized to find a solution to why girls went astray and he was not a man to shirk responsibility.

"I may safely say," this Methodist teetotaler safely said, "that seventy-five to eighty per cent of all the causes of immorality come from the liquor traffic."

It was certainly true that the liquor traffic flourished in the north country during the time when pines were being converted into boards and sawdust. A lumberjack who had good reason to know recalled that during the last half of the nineteenth century every other building housed a saloon on Ludington Street in Escanaba, Michigan, for example.

"Here the lumberjacks squandered their money in drink which might be more or less strong, depending on his degree of intoxication," the old-timer said.

Walter R. Nursey, writing in 1890, noted that the bartender "regulated the quality of his stuff to suit the degree of obfuscation." The customer got genuine Montana Red-Eye when he first arrived. But as the evening rolled on, he was ready to drink anything and often did, including Bourbon heavily cut with branch water to increase the proprietor's profits.

It was a hard-drinking crowd that cut the pines. To stand out, a man had to develop a specialty. Dave Pecor, foreman of the Peshtigo Company, for example, gained a reputation by downing a full glass of whiskey and then eating the glass. Others were known for their prowess in saloon brawls. Among these were Mike Harrigan, who was compared admiringly to a gorilla, and Bulldog Anderson, whose Scandinavian temper was slow to arouse but made him virtually unstoppable under sufficient provocation.

Sam Christie, said to be the toughest logger around Grand Rapids, Minnesota, was proud of his scars, especially one that resulted when a cook named Kelly cut Christie's throat from ear to ear during a fight in Hay Landing. Despite his experience at cutting up beef, the cook missed Sam's jugular and he lived to brawl again.

Another 'jack, "Traveling Dudley," got his name because he'd walked all the way from Maine to Minnesota. Dudley could fight as well as he could walk. He demonstrated this one night when he offered to take on an entire section crew from the St. Paul and

Duluth Railway, one at a time. The toughest section hand waited until Traveling Dudley was tired from whipping all the others, then took his turn. But the Maine man was ready for the challenge. He got both of his opponent's thumbs in his mouth and clamped down so hard that the man's friends had to use a railroad spike to pry the lumberjack's jaws apart.

Pinery humor ran to practical jokes which were apt to get a bit rough, not to say dangerous. A woods worker who shared a hotel bed with a male friend after a weekend spree might rise early and set the blankets on fire to see his companion leap up. That was a fine joke, especially if the victim escaped with no worse than first-degree burns.

A more elaborate jest was perpetrated by Bill Butser, who lived in the Green Bay region in the 1850s. An unknown sailor had drowned, washed ashore and been buried at Eagle Harbor. After a busy night at his favorite saloon, Butser decided it was a shame to waste the stranger. He dug him up, salted and packed him and sent him to a friend in a barrel labeled "pork." Writing about the macabre joke some years later, a local historian, Bella French Swisher, put it down to "youthful exuberance."

Another incident that was discussed during evenings on the deacon seats was more of a swindle than a joke. But the victim was a saloonkeeper, so the lumberjacks found it amusing. A lumber raft crew was heading down the Wisconsin when the men got thirsty and tied up at Sauk City. No one had been paid, so their pockets were empty. The foreman grabbed a bundle of shingles being carried on the raft and led the group into the barroom.

"Will you give us drinks for these?"

"I will," the barkeep said. "Carry them out back and step up to the bar."

The bundle was stashed behind the saloon and there were drinks all around until the value of the shingles was used up. But the thirst persisted.

"How about another bottle for another bundle?"

"Let me see 'em."

Several crewmen left, returning with a bundle of shingles. The trade was made. As the day wore on, the crewmen kept bringing in one bundle after another and ordering more rounds. The saloonkeeper was kept too busy to examine the shingles being stored

behind the building until after the raftsmen had left. Then he
wiped his hands on his apron and walked out, expecting to see
enough shakes to roof a house. The yard was empty. It took him a
moment to realize he'd been sold the same batch of shingles
eleven times before the crew headed downstream, taking the original bundle with them.

The brawling lumber towns in the pinery's heyday were often as
brash as the lumberjacks who howled through their streets. The
secretary of the La Crosse Board of Trade, for example, listed a
number of unusual civic assets in encouraging settlement there in
1863, including "several marriageable girls and three gambling
rooms."

"La Crosse is a go-ahead town," the official booster went on.
"Smart as a whip, sandy as a red hog. If you want to fight, foot
race or fizzle out, to marry or do worse, to make friends or enemies, to grow rich or poor, to wear good clothes or shabby ones,
to meddle with what is none of your business or be meddled with,
to talk about others or to be talked about, to be praised to your
face or slandered to your back, to get in with some good fellows,
make money and be happy, we bet on La Crosse against the
whole world!"

"Hayward, Hurley and Hell" were claimed by residents of the
first two localities to be the three toughest burgs in the universe. A
lot of otherwise respectable citizens took a defiant pride in bragging about what a rough community they lived in. At Stevens
Point, the legend was that the place had originally been called
Stevens' Pint in honor of George Stevens, who sold unusually
large schooners of beer for a nickel. The lumber town of Mercer,
a little south of the Michigan-Wisconsin border, boasted of a
basement saloon that could be entered only by means of a smooth
and slippery board ramp. It was easy enough to slide down if a
man was reasonably steady on his feet, but almost impossible to
climb when he wasn't. Once the drunk's money was gone, the
kindly barkeep rolled him up the ramp to the sidewalk.

Cavour, Wisconsin, was another favorite rest and recreation
center in the days when a thousand lumberjacks were working in
its neighborhood. A dirt arena outside the local hotel was set aside
to settle barroom arguments without endangering the glassware.

After the logging era had begun sliding inexorably downhill, an old-timer named Albert Hess defended the rules of this sport:

"They'd fight with their fists. And sometimes, if the other man was down, they'd jump on him with their calked boots. But the fighting was fair."

The Cavour Hotel had fourteen rooms and figured its overnight capacity at forty guests, or roughly three per bed. The bar could hold considerably more. In the basement was what was called a snake room, a place where drunks could sleep it off. Such rooms were common. Some provided a relatively safe refuge for a man too far gone to defend himself. Others were a convenient place to relieve unconscious men of any money they had left.

The roistering lumberjacks of the Lake States were merely upholding a loggers' tradition that began in Maine and eastern Canada. An Englishman, E. A. Kendall, who visited Maine's pine forests in 1801 reported that the men followed a pattern of "alternate toil and indolence, hardship and debauch." Of course, there were numerous exceptions to this rule. If they survived their youth, some lumberjacks simmered down into staid respectability, using their hard-won pay to buy groceries for their families. But the typical lumberjack was unattached, content to spend his money when he had it and work hard to survive when he didn't.

Hurley, Wisconsin, located across the Michigan line from Ironwood, catered to both miners and lumberjacks, offering wide-open gambling, eighty saloons and other amenities. Many of the saloons had from three to a dozen women working out of them. They often lived with the saloonkeeper and his wife, ate with the family and enjoyed a domestic sort of life when they weren't working.

One of the best-attended social events in Hurley in 1890 was the funeral of a saloon boarder, Lottie Morgan. She was murdered in an alley behind Crocker's Saloon, her head crushed by two blows from an axe. No one ever found out who killed her. Some of her friends decided she deserved a memorable send-off. Handbills invited the entire town to her funeral, held at the Opera House with three Protestant ministers and a priest attending. Her casket was placed in the center of the stage. Her favorite hymn, "Ashamed of Jesus," was played. The Reverend C. C. Todd spoke of how Lottie had been ladylike and courteous to all, then launched an attack on her profession. Some people claimed that houses of ill fame were a necessary evil, he said, but "do you want dollars stamped with woman's honor, dollars stamped with woman's blood?"

There was criticism of the preacher afterward for spoiling the occasion by asking such questions. But otherwise, it was agreed, Lottie had thrown a fine party, just as she always had done when she was alive. A week later, there was a move to duplicate the occasion. Unfortunately, no human guest of honor was available just then, so the handbills invited everyone to the funeral of Curley, Jr., who happened to be a dog. After the ceremonies, it was specified, everyone was expected to drink a toast to poor Curley in a saloon.

Florence, Wisconsin, another lumber town near the Michigan border, was nearly as notorious as Hurley. The Mudge family members were leading residents. Mina Mudge ran a dance hall, saloon and bawdy house at the edge of town. Her mother ran another bordello nearby. And her father fiddled for local dances until cold weather, when he packed his bag and his Bible and headed south to preach the gospel until the spring log drive. Then he returned to Florence to play his violin for patrons of the family business establishments.

Unwary visitors to Florence were sometimes embarrassed. The most popular brothels were a short drive from the station, so it was the custom for lumberjacks who arrived by train to hire a carriage and head directly from the depot to visit a member of the town's unofficial reception committee. The livery stable horses learned the routine. As soon as they left the depot, they headed directly for a house with a red light in the window. Respectable visitors, including those who had brought their own wives, had to tug at the reins and speak sharply to the horse. Otherwise, they wound up at a whorehouse without really intending to go there.

Chase Osborn, a former Milwaukee newspaperman who ran the weekly at Florence, decided to clean up the town. Before long, the young editor had to carry a loaded Winchester across his arm when he ventured on the main street. He managed to get one of the most notorious establishments closed, but sin soon made a comeback. Osborn left for Michigan, where he made a fortune in lumbering and was elected governor, in that order.

The head pimp driven out of Florence by Osborn went to Ewen, Michigan, which had the reputation of being especially hospitable to men in his line of work. Ewen was a favorite stopping place for the most famous brawler of his time, Silver Jack Driscoll. Stories about Silver Jack's ability to fell an ox with his fist or bend a Percheron's shoe with his bare hands may be slightly exaggerated. They may, in fact, be downright lies. But there's not a doubt that Driscoll was a tough cookie.

Silver Jack was not always available to his public, spending fourteen years in three separate hitches at the Michigan State Prison at Jackson. But when he wasn't engaged in armed robbery or paying the penalty for getting caught, he was a prominent member of the lumberjack drinking set. In every saloon, there were usually several customers who claimed to be able to lick any man in the house. But when Driscoll was around, they issued no such challenge.

The only fighter in the Michigan lumber region who was considered in the same class was another Canadian, Joe Fournier. Joe's first name was really Fabian, but a man had to be very foolish or very drunk to call him that. He was said to have an unusually thick cranium, a considerable asset in a brawl. He liked to demonstrate that his jaw muscles were equally strong by biting a chunk out of the bar.

There was a lot of country and a lot of saloons in the Michigan pinery. For years, the two barroom champions never met. Everyone understood that when they did there would be a showdown. It finally came when their paths crossed at the Red Keg Saloon in Averill.

Fournier opened the match by grabbing Silver Jack by the throat. The two crashed to the floor. Driscoll's eyes started bugging out. By a mighty effort, he loosened Joe's grip enough to breathe. But Silver Jack couldn't get free. According to some witnesses, the two lay that way for an hour, with Driscoll too short of breath to break loose but too strong to let Joe strangle him.

Now and then, Fournier would butt Driscoll with his head to keep him from wriggling, but he didn't loosen his grip. Even when the two struggled to their feet, he kept his fingers firmly around Silver Jack's throat. Then Fournier made a mistake. To increase his leverage, he put one foot on the brass rail. Driscoll drove his spiked heel into Joe's other foot, penetrating to the bone. Fournier gave a bellow of pain. He let go of Jack's throat. He backed up to get a running start, put down his head and charged. Driscoll skipped nimbly aside. The French-Canadian smashed into the oak bar, splintering it, and Driscoll drove his fist into Fournier's belly. Joe collapsed, gasping.

"Put the hoots to him, Jack," an onlooker yelled.

But Driscoll was satisfied. He stepped over his fallen opponent and ordered drinks for the house. In a final gesture that became part of his legend, Silver Jack bought a double for Fournier as soon as Joe was able to drink it.

Driscoll died a few years later in a hotel in L'Anse, Michigan, leaving behind a Bowie knife, eighty-five dollars in cash and a note suggesting the money be used to bury him. Fournier's end was more spectacular. He was killed in Bay City, Michigan, when he was hit on the head by a steel mallet wielded by Blinky Robinson. It was claimed the blow drove Joe's feet six inches into the ground, which isn't as unlikely as it sounds in a community that consisted mostly of hard-packed sawdust. Joe's head, everyone agreed, was hard. Blinky's mallet proved harder.

Bay City and the nearby community of Saginaw turned out as much as a billion board feet of logs in a single year in their prime, helping Michigan produce the gigantic total of one hundred sixty billion board feet of pine in a half century, enough boards to build ten million six-room houses or, for that matter, to construct a solid plank floor over the entire state, with a few square miles of flooring left over. With a combined population of forty-five thousand during their heyday as lumber towns, Bay City and Saginaw had no less than ninety-eight resident millionaires.

The two communities' civic assets also included a remarkable variety of places designed to relieve lumberjacks and sawmill workers of their pay. One of the most notorious was the Catacombs, located near Bay City's Third Street bridge. Few doubted that the proprietor robbed customers when he got the chance, but there was some question whether it was true that he avoided complaints by dropping his victims through a trapdoor into the river.

As in most lumber towns, before railroad travel became a practical method of getting to the saloons on a Saturday night, the winter season was slack in the Saginaw River establishments. One enterprising madam decided to take her business closer to the customers, moving thirty girls into an old log barn near a large lumber camp in the vicinity of Meredith, Michigan. A bar was improvised by putting planks across two barrels. Dirty mattresses were placed on the earthen floor. The wind soon ripped the tarpaper off the building, making working conditions difficult when the temperature hit thirty below. Still, business was brisk. The lumberjacks didn't object to snow swirling between the logs and hardly noticed the chill breezes. The madam's employees weren't used to such hardships, however. After one season, the experiment was not repeated.

Stewart H. Holbrook, whose *Holy Old Mackinaw* is a mother lode of tales about phases of lumberjack life ignored by more formal historians, is also the source of an account of another peripatetic enterprise. This one was run by Ma Smith, who normally was in charge of a two-dollar house on Water Street where Saginaw's City Council sometimes held informal meetings. Ma treated the aldermen kindly and vice versa.

Sometimes, however, the hot breath of reform was felt even in wicked Saginaw and on one occasion Ma was forced to close. She packed up her girls and equipment and moved to Crowe Island in the middle of the river, doing a fine business there until the enthusiasm for virtue waned on the mainland. Then she moved back to Water Street. She'd made more money on the island, she said, but her girls objected to being awakened at dawn by the boat whistles.

Saginaw was large enough to support theaters and variety halls as well as the more rudimentary forms of lumberjack amusement. Charles Harris, best known among musicologists for writing a tearjerker ballad called "After the Ball," got his start there. So did Lelia Koeber, who changed her name to Marie Dressler before becoming a stage and movie star. In another field, George Lavigne became lightweight champion of the world as the Saginaw Kid.

There was a touch of elegance in some of the less respectable places of amusement. Belle Stevens' place didn't rival the Chicago mansion of the Everleigh Sisters, but she ran a five-dollar house that stressed good taste even in the advertising cards handed to strangers at the depot: "Come Down and See Belle When in

Town." Cassie Hawkins ran a comparably ritzy joint in Bay City. Her admirers claimed she looked like Lillian Russell after you'd had a few drinks. A few drinks more, of course, and everybody in the place looked like Miss Russell, including those built more like Diamond Jim Brady.

Merchants of other varieties of soft goods also catered to the lumberjack trade, notably "Little Jake" Seligman. When the street outside his clothing store was crowded with newly paid men, Jake would appear in a second-floor window and start throwing out vests, announcing that any man who brought one inside could have a free coat and pants to go with it.

There was always a great scramble. When the free-for-all was over, the battered winners would limp into Jake's store, bearing a handful of tatters that had once been a vest. Seligman was as good as his word. He'd supply the victor with the free coat and pants, then sell him a new vest for twelve dollars. By a coincidence, twelve dollars was Jake's usual price for an entire suit.

Lumberjacks liked to brag that they drank only "squirrel whiskey," strong enough to make a man frisk up and down an oak looking for acorns. The competition to outdo others at the bar had an international flavor. As was noted by William H. Ellis, who grew up in Saginaw before moving to Oscoda, Michigan, everybody "was trying to beat everybody else," and this held true whether the contest involved work, a fight, or a reputation for being able to hold the most liquor.

In Oscoda, there were only eight saloons to accommodate a drinking population of three thousand, so the bars stayed open twenty-four hours a day. Ellis said that those mingling in the saloons were from all over the world—"Finns, Swedes, Irish, Scotch, Canucks, Italians, Chinese, Negroes, 'most every race on earth. And most of them knew how to up-end a drink."

The lumberjacks were not used to niceties and didn't worry unduly about cleanliness, but there were times when they drew the line. Ellis and a friend were heading for Black Bill O'Bryan's camp during a snowstorm one night when they decided to stay at a stopping place owned by Rory Frazer. Rory was sleeping off a drunk in the barn, but the woman who lived with him rented them a bed. In the morning, the young men came downstairs, drawn by the delicious aroma of pancakes and frying pork.

They watched as the woman greased the griddle with a piece of old shirt so dirty it took the edge off their appetites. Then they heard something drop on the griddle and spatter. In a moment there was another sizzle, then a third. Ellis nudged his friend.

"Look up in the rafters."

Roosting above the griddle was a flock of chickens. Flapjacks and guano was too rich a combination even for hungry lumberjacks. They left, skipping breakfast.

In discussing Michigan's contributions to the cultural side of lumberjack life, it would be unfair to omit Muskegon, once a lumber center with nearly half a hundred sawmills. It was claimed that a thirsty man could smell Muskegon's saloons fifty miles up the Muskegon River and the perfume from its Sawdust Flats nearly that far. The Flats got its name honestly. It was built on a swamp that had been filled in with sawdust. It included six city blocks of what a minister called "unspeakable whoredom." A lumberjack claimed the reverend was wrong.

"Hell," he said, "they always speak to me."

Some of the Flats' sisterhood were known throughout the region. Spanish Lou, for instance, was particularly popular with teamsters because she could swear in eight languages and often did. The teamsters figured they got double value for their money, buying not only a few minutes of Lou's time but a chance to pick up new words to try on their oxen or horses.

Big Delia was the most notable madam, a six-footer who chewed a pack of tobacco per day because her teeth bothered her. She demanded decorum. One logger who refused to take off his calked boots before walking into the parlor learned that she meant what she said.

"They scratch up the floor and tear the bed sheets, God damn it," she explained as she broke his jaw.

Delia headed the entertainment committee when the Flats decided to do its patriotic part in celebrating Independence Day of 1887. A delegation called on city officials, asking for permission to hold a dance for loggers. It was hard to say no to Big Delia. Besides, as an alderman observed, the girls were over twenty-one and free—or, at least, fairly inexpensive. So permission was granted. Carpenters began hammering together a large wooden pavilion. A party of pimps went to the woods to cut evergreen boughs to use on the roof instead of shingles. An American flag was nailed behind the bandstand.

Someone suggested that the three hundred Muskegon women might not be enough to go around, so others were recruited from as far as Chicago. All the local musicians planned to march in the city's Fourth of July parade, so Delia had to send across the lake for a band from Milwaukee. There was a mixup. Not one band but two arrived on the morning of the Fourth.

"What we going to do with two bands from Milwaukee?" the vice chairman asked.

"Fill 'em up with beer," Delia ordered, proving she knew her geography.

The instructions were followed with enthusiasm. By noon, when an estimated one thousand lumberjacks, river pigs and sawmill workers were waiting impatiently for the dancing to begin, members of one of the bands had passed out cold. But the spare musicians were able to find the bandstand, and if some wrong notes were hit, who cared?

The highlight of the afternoon was a fight between women known as Black Jap and John L. Jap was waltzing gaily with a handsome logger when John L. cut in by hitting her on the jaw. Instead of stepping politely aside, as etiquette required, Jap counterpunched. The scrap lasted for half an hour, ending in an exhausted draw. Dancing resumed, lasting until late evening.

Not all Muskegon's residents were amused by what was called the Western Michigan Whores' Benevolent Association Convention. The aldermen sent word to Delia that once was enough.

"It never used to be when you were younger, honey," she replied, but the patriotic gathering was not repeated.

Minneapolis, which got its start as a sawmill center, provided the usual amenities. "Swede Annie," for instance, ran a place that was particularly popular with her fellow Scandinavians. In neighboring St. Paul, a district called "Under the Hill" was famous. At Stillwater, Minnesota's first major center of lumbering, there was plenty of local talent, but with the Twin Cities only twenty miles away the competition for the lumberjacks' dollars was rough.

Duluth had to compete with neighboring Superior and its municipally approved whorehouses, but it managed to draw a good crowd from as far away as Cloquet. Later in the white pine era, Bemidji, Brainerd, Hibbing and even chilly International Falls did their best to uphold north woods standards in entertainment. Hibbing, for example, had sixty saloons and two hundred professional women, according to one estimate.

In Houghton and Hurley, in Minneapolis and Stillwater, in Ashland and Saginaw and hundreds of other communities large and small in the pineries, sin of several kinds was an accepted enterprise. But if a lumberjack wanted to impress the crowd when he walked into a strange saloon, all he had to say was, "I'm from Seney." That was a signal for the timid to leave and the hardy to edge away.

Nowadays, Seney is a sleepy four-corners in the tourist country of Michigan's Upper Peninsula, its name known mainly because of a federal wildlife refuge nearby. There was plenty of wild life there in the old days, too, but it seldom wore feathers.

Seney was named for one of the contractors who built a railroad that later became part of the Duluth, South Shore and Atlantic. In the early 1880s, it went from a small collection of log huts to a considerable settlement. By the end of that decade, it had perhaps three thousand permanent residents.

The Alger, Smith Company began logging the region along the Fox River, a tributary of the Manistique River, and established its headquarters at Seney. By the early 1890s, half a dozen other lumber companies had offices there. The town had ten hotels, nine of which included bars, and a dozen other saloons.

Seney was connected to Manistique on the lake shore by a tote road that went by way of Germfask, then known as The Dump. Its eminence as the toughest town in the pinery lasted only about fifteen years. Most of the lumber camps in the area pulled out around 1894, having cut all the pine.

During its heyday as a hellhole, it attracted riffraff of both sexes. Besides a number of smaller bordellos, it boasted two of the largest in the state. These "hoodlums," as the houses were called, contained some of the toughest women in the woods. In Muskegon, a madam who chewed tobacco was worthy of comment. In Seney, so many of the girls indulged in Peerless Cut Plug that no one paid any attention. A waltz with one of these lovelies with brown teeth often ended near the door, where her friends were waiting to grab her partner, knock him out and steal his money.

One visitor compared Seney to "an ugly and poisonous toad-stool" that had grown up at the terminus of a logging railroad. So many loggers and railroad workers converged on the town in its early months that many had to sleep on the ground. Seney's first saloons had no walls or roofs, consisting of a makeshift bar formed by a timber laid across two stumps. Four enterprising pimps soon arrived to cash in on this gathering of customers, bringing thirty women. The girls refused to work in the open air, so their backers confiscated a warehouse belonging to the railroad. The station clerk ordered them to leave. They threw him out and opened for business, which was so brisk the warehouse stayed open twenty-four hours a day.

The railroad wanted its building back and was willing to spend a hundred dollars to get it. It hired a gang of toughs headed by "Pig-Foot" Macdonald to act as an eviction committee. They opened the discussion by throwing the four pimps through a window. Then they smashed everything breakable except the bottles, which they confiscated, and went off to collect their pay. Macdonald said it hardly seemed honest to take money for something that had been so much fun, but he took it anyway.

The organizers of that pioneer bordello left town, but others soon arrived. For a time, a group of enterprising women showed up each morning on the train from Marquette, did a thriving business in stalls of the livery stable, then left on the midnight train.

The two principal stores in Seney were Hargraves' and one called Morse & Schneider's. Both not only offered a wide variety of merchandise but collected the lumberjacks' mail and accepted cash deposits, paying 6 per cent. One young woman deposited the impressive sum of fifteen hundred dollars. A clerk asked how she'd managed to save that much in a month. She got most of it, she explained demurely, from pockets of pants that were not being worn at the time. Shortly afterward, she drew out her savings and left for Benton Harbor to get married.

"Me and my fiancé separated to make a stake," she told friends. "I guess I beat him to it."

Another professional woman bought a hundred dollars' worth of expensive women's clothes each Christmas and sent them to Houghton, Michigan. This habit aroused some curiosity, but she refused to explain. Finally a drunken lumberjack got so angry when she brushed off his questions that he beat her up, leaving her in the snowy woods for dead. When she reappeared in town, bloody and naked, he thought she was a ghost and fled.

A few days later, a clerk in Hargraves' store sent a boy to tell her an out-of-town visitor was asking for her. She got dressed in her finery and reported for duty, expecting at least a railroad conductor. Instead she found her old mother, who had arrived to take her home to Houghton.

Brutality was more common in Seney than in most lumber towns, apparently. Another incident began when a local merchant was taking one of his women clerks to a lumber camp on an errand and saw a nude woman standing in a bordello doorway. He complained to the proprietor, who agreed to take steps. The boss pimp had a few drinks at Hughie Logan's saloon, then started interviewing his girls, moving from room to room. In each, he began the conversation by blackening an eye, then demanding a confession. When he finally found the culprit, he knocked her down, kicked her nearly unconscious, then threw her out of the second-story window into a snowbank, heaving her trunk out after her. She limped off to the depot and departed, a symbol of how standards of propriety must be upheld even in Seney.

Trains arriving there sometimes had lost every pane of glass in the passenger car windows, kicked out by lumberjacks getting in the mood for Saturday night. A traveler might find himself in trouble before he'd left the station. Two thugs known as Pump Handle Joe and Stubfoot O'Donnell lurked there, greeting newcomers by standing them on their heads to shake out loose change from their pockets.

This was considered a good test of whether a new arrival could take a joke, although Joe and Stubfoot got paid for their trouble by pocketing the money. Another favorite form of wit around Seney was nailing Old Light Heart's shoes to the wooden sidewalk.

Old Light Heart, whose favorite food was raw liver, had lost all his toes to frostbite, leaving an empty space at the front of his boots. When he got drunk and passed out, it was a simple matter to hammer in the nails and wait to see the fun when he tried to stand up. What happened was that he got sore enough to take on the whole town, but that was difficult to do while his shoes were nailed to the sidewalk.

The place was full of colorful characters with names to match. Roaring Jimmy Gleason, for instance. Teapot Kelly. Frying Pan Mag, Black Jack McDonald and Protestant Bob McGuire. Not to forget Stuttering Jim Gallagher, who left calk marks on the face of anyone who laughed at his handicap. Or P. K. Small, better known as Snap Jaw Small because of a parlor trick he developed to cadge free drinks. In return for a shot of whiskey, Snap Jaw was willing to bite off the head of a frog or a snake. This was considered amusing, but on one occasion Small went too far. He bit off the head of Frank O'Brien's pet owl. O'Brien responded by knocking him down with a cant hook.

Some months later, Snap Jaw was in a saloon brawl when his opponent bit off the end of Small's nose. A number of his admirers considered this poetic justice.

CHAPTER XI

Death by Hanging

TOWARD THE END of the white pine era in the Lake States, a logging town named Emerson was established near the southern shore of Lake Superior. What was unusual about it was that it had no saloon. According to Hugh R. Emerson, son of one of the founders, many lumberjacks who worked there "came to get away from the whiskey habit, at least for a while." The refusal of the Emerson Land Company to allow liquor in its town was remarkable, he added, "in an era and locality where drunkenness and lawlessness were common."

That liquor and trouble often went together was taken for granted. But considering the heavy drinking, the brawling and the frequent lack of effective law-enforcement machinery, it is also worth noting that major crime was uncommon in the pineries. Still, in the days when signing on to cut trees meant enforced celibacy from November until the spring thaw, most respectable women steered clear of the woods workers during their April festivities.

One young wife who failed to follow this rule caused trouble in a small lumber town in the early days of Wisconsin logging. She sashayed past a saloon, bustle bobbing. Several drunks were lounging in the door, watching the fights going on up and down the mud street. They gave her the eye, which annoyed her. Then one spoke to her, it was later reported, "in a manner not suited to her status of wife." She ran home to her husband and told him of the insult.

Grabbing a piece of timber, he headed for the saloon, hit the foul-mouthed fellow over the head and killed him. To keep up appearances, he was arrested. But the lumberjack jury quickly ruled it was a case of justifiable homicide.

Justice of a sort was apt to be sudden in the north country. There was, for example, the incident at the Klause brothers' saloon in Oconto, Wisconsin, where Sunday-night dances were held in the second-floor ballroom. Denny White, a New Brunswick man, was the ringleader of a gang of rowdies who liked to break up the dances. The Klauses countered by hiring a bouncer and buying him a revolver. The next time White and his friends showed up, the bouncer pulled the gun and fired.

Unfortunately, his aim was poor. The shot missed White and hit Joe Rule, a bystander, who died. The bouncer was jailed, but only briefly. Rule's friends smashed in the door with a log, dragged the prisoner across the river and hanged him to a tree on the future site of the county courthouse. There was some criticism of the lynching, particularly when it was reported that the mob had refused to let the bouncer say his final prayers. But majority opinion held that it was all for the best. A fellow who couldn't hit the man he was aiming at was a dangerous sort to have around.

In the nineteenth-century pineries, there were respectable citizens who felt that a lynching now and then was a useful sort of thing. Editor A. J. Turner of the Portage (Wisconsin) *Weekly Register,* for example, declared in 1869 that "the occasion may arise when it becomes necessary and proper for the people to dispense, for the time being, with the usual agencies they employ to punish crime." And even the Chicago *Tribune,* joining Turner in commenting on a couple of illegal Portage hangings, admitted that these lynchings "might be regarded as approaching as near real justice as ever occurs in such cases."

Pat Wildrick, an outlaw, and Attorney William H. Spain were the victims. Spain had been captain of a Civil War regiment. He had long been feuding with Barney Britt, who'd been one of his soldiers. The fact that Britt was Catholic and Spain was an Orangeman had something to do with the hard feelings between the two Irishmen. Exactly what caused the final quarrel between them is in doubt, but the result was that Spain shot and killed Britt on a Portage street. The marshal and a deputy sheriff arrested the lawyer. They started for the jail, but when a mob blocked their way the lawmen decided to hide their prisoner in the Wells Fargo office. Its door was soon battered down. Spain was dragged to a tree and strung up. This version of frontier justice required only twenty minutes between the murder and the lynching.

The hanging of Spain's client, Wildrick, was more deliberate. Wildrick had been arrested for robbing a resident of Kilbourn City. He had broken jail, been recaptured, then turned loose on bail. While out on bail, he'd robbed a farmer and been thrown into the Portage jail. By then, the public was grumbling about all the legal delays and maneuvering. But it was not until two of Wildrick's friends killed the Kilbourn City man to keep him from testifying that vigilante justice moved into action.

An estimated one hundred twenty-five masked men commandeered a train and rode it from Kilbourn City to Portage. They got off near the jail late at night, ordering the train to wait. They overpowered the sheriff and his deputy, dragged Wildrick outside and hanged him to an oak. It was all done so quietly that nearby residents did not awaken. The vigilantes got back on the train and went home. A grand jury later indicted eleven of them but none was brought to trial.

Legal executions had been ended some years earlier in Michigan and Wisconsin, the first two states to abolish the death penalty, but the illegal variety continued in those states and in Minnesota during the lumberjack era. One of the most notorious of the Michigan lynchings took place in 1881 in Menominee, which then claimed to be the largest lumber port in the world. The village had as many as thirty-two sawmills in the vicinity and thousands of lumberjacks in the nearby woods. Marinette, just across the Wisconsin border, was considered less law-abiding than Menominee, but there were some rough characters on the Michigan side of the line, too. Among them were Frank and John McDonald, who had come to Michigan from Ontario to work for the Ramsey and Jones Company. The McDonalds were cousins, but had been raised as brothers after one set of parents died.

During a weekend spree, they were thrown in jail for three days for being drunk and disorderly. That was a common hazard of going to town. Most lumberjacks would have shrugged it off. But the McDonalds decided they had a grudge against the Menominee authorities. Before taking jobs at a Girard Lumber Company camp, they bought dirks and waved the knives around, threatening that the next time they came to town there'd be trouble.

The camp was on the Pine River, a tributary of the Menominee, near a settlement called Quinnesec, Michigan. The McDonalds proved to be troublemakers there. Finally, Sheriff Julius Reprecht was called to the camp to deal with them. They had been hitting the bottle before he arrived and were in no mood to discuss the matter. Frank, the younger of the two, jumped Reprecht and beat him unconscious. The sheriff limped back to Menominee and deputized George Kittson, a two-hundred-pounder who had a reputation as a formidable scrapper. Kittson went to Quinnesec with a warrant, surprised the McDonalds, arrested them and brought them back for trial. They were given eighteen months each in the state prison for beating up the sheriff.

A few weeks after they got out, the McDonalds were back in Menominee looking for trouble. They toured the saloons, winding up at a combination bar and boardinghouse called the Montreal in Frenchtown, now part of Menominee's west side. Norman, one of George Kittson's brothers, was tending bar. The McDonalds started bragging about what they'd do to the deputy when they found him. After a few more drinks, they left for a nearby bordello, the Three Chimney House, where they found another Kittson brother, Billy, drinking whiskey with the women.

The McDonalds moved in on the party. Billy got sore when the girls began paying more attention to the cousins than to him. A fight started. Outnumbered two to one, Kittson grabbed a bottle and smashed it over Frank McDonald's head, then ran for the Montreal for reinforcements. The McDonalds caught him before he got there. John knocked him to his knees with a peavey, then stabbed him with a six-inch knife. Norman Kittson heard the commotion and hurried to his brother's aid. He got stabbed in the neck. As he fell to the ground, he pulled a revolver from his jacket and shot Frank McDonald in the leg. Meanwhile, Billy Kittson had been stabbed again. Deciding he'd had enough, he staggered to the bar of the Montreal and was about to order a medicinal shot of whiskey when he fell over, dead.

The Canadian cousins decided they'd better leave town. They stole a horse and buggy and drove to a doctor's office near the North Western depot to get patched up, then started for Cedar River, a day's drive to the north. But Sheriff David Barclay, who'd recently been elected, caught up with them and brought them back to stand trial.

Frank was then twenty-three and John McDonald was twenty-seven years old. Both were charged with Billy Kittson's murder. Half a dozen witnesses were thrown into the county jail to make sure they'd be around to testify.

At once, there was talk of a hanging party. Luther B. Noyes, who published the *Eagle* in Marinette, tried to head it off with an editorial declaring "it will be decidedly unhealthy for a mob that would attempt any lynching here." But at a meeting held in the local town hall, the sentiments were different.

The meeting had been called to hold memorial services for President James A. Garfield, who had died about a week earlier after being wounded by a disappointed job hunter. When word of Kittson's murder and the McDonalds' arrest reached the hall, the mood changed from one of mourning to anger. Threats were made to break into the jail and string the Canadians up. But there was a major stumbling block. Out of respect for the assassinated President and the solemnity of the occasion, most of the men were stone-cold sober. Lynchings and whiskey went together in the north country. The night passed without anything more serious than a lot of angry talk.

The next day, Coroner Henry Nason opened an inquest into the Kittson murder. But there was so much bad feeling in town that he quickly adjourned it and sent the prisoners back to the jail, where it would be easier to protect them. Meanwhile, a group of angry and thirsty men gathered at Max Forvilly's saloon to talk and drink.

Forvilly's hotel was the largest in Marinette and his saloon was well stocked. By evening, when everyone was satisfactorily drunk, a mob formed mainly of lumberjacks and river boom workers headed for the back door of the Menominee courthouse, the entrance to the jail.

Sheriff Barclay, a six-footer who took a back step for no man, wasn't there. He'd left shortly before to go to the livery stable he operated, leaving his brother Robert and another deputy, Jack Fryer, in charge. The sheriff's family, as was common in small towns, lived in the jail. Mrs. Barclay heard the commotion at the back door. She locked her two children in the living quarters. But the sheriff's daughter, Jane, peeked out the window in time to see a group of men pick up a pole and batter down the door, yelling and cursing.

The two deputies were quickly overpowered. The mob broke into the prisoners' cells. The McDonalds put up a fight but subsided when one of the cousins was hit over the head with an axe. Ropes were tied around their necks and they were dragged outside onto Ogden Avenue.

"For God's sake, boys," one cousin pleaded, "if you're going to hang us, at least get us a priest."

A bystander ran to St. John's Catholic Church and brought back Father Francious Heliard. He pushed his way to the front of the crowd and pleaded with the leaders to take the McDonalds back to jail for trial. Somebody pushed him down in the gutter. Others spit on him. The priest pulled himself to his feet and raised his hands high.

"Then I curse you all! May all who are responsible for this crime you are about to commit die with their boots on!"

There were a few, more timid or less drunk, who hesitated at this. The others laughed, shoved the priest aside and dragged the McDonalds to the back of a buggy, tied them to it and ordered the driver to whip up his horse. Ogden Avenue was lined with spectators now. Women screamed. Lumberjacks whooped and hollered. Mill whistles blew. Church bells rang. The noise inspired some of the drunks in the mob to new heights of action. They followed as the McDonalds were dragged down the street, now and then running forward to jump on the men with their calked boots. No suitable tree was handy, so it was decided to string up the cousins to a railway crossing sign that said LOOK OUT FOR THE CARS. By then, according to Editor Noyes's account, the McDonalds were already dead.

That should have ended the matter, but it didn't. Sam Peltier, who owned a large boardinghouse and saloon called the Lumberman's Home, came boiling out complaining about having two corpses dangling near his front door.

"They'll scare the women and children. They'll scare the horses."

"Yeah, Sam," somebody yelled, "and they won't be too good for your business, either, will they?"

Still, Peltier had a point. The bodies were hauled down and dragged back to the Three Chimney House. They were thrown onto a bed and several of the women who hadn't left before the mob got there were forced to snuggle up to the dead men. Then the drunks chased residents and customers of the brothel outside and set fire to the place, burning it to the ground. The McDonalds were hung a second time, swinging from a nearby jack pine.

By the time they sobered up, some of the lynchers began feeling ashamed of themselves. Such nonparticipants as Noyes were indignant. He wrote that he had "the most utter abhorrence and loathing for such barbaric deviltry."

Several members of the mob were arrested, but subsequently turned loose. Max Forvilly, who'd supplied the meeting place and sold the liquor, was brought to trial, but a jury found him not guilty. As was usual in such cases, no one went to jail for helping to lynch the McDonalds.

Louis Portvan (sometimes called Porter), who was rumored to have tied the noose around the neck of one of the McDonalds, was found dead some years later near Amasa, Michigan, sitting with his back against a tree. According to Jim Borski, who spent considerable time delving into the story of the McDonalds' lynching, Portvan may have been killed by a timber rattler. At any rate, he had his boots on.

One of the men who had been jailed briefly as a witness, Thomas Dunn, was cut in two by a saw in a mill. Frank Saucier, who may have supplied the pole to batter in the jailhouse door, dropped dead some years later, perhaps of a heart attack. Albert Lemieux, a timber cruiser who was part of the mob, died of a slashed throat. He was playing cards with Dunc Cruikshank at the time, Borski reported. There was some question about whether Lemieux killed himself or Cruikshank did it. Albert Beach, a river pig involved in the lynching, tipped over in a boat on the Menominee and was drowned.

Elsewhere, such deaths would have been accepted as part of the normal hazards of the north. But the priest's curse had made an impression. Those who felt guilty about their roles in the lynching kept anxious count. It seems likely that others who had been part of the mob died with their boots off, lying peacefully in a soft bed, surrounded by grieving relatives. But the deaths of the ones who had no time to strip off their footwear were the ones the lumberjacks spoke of, sitting on deacon seats in the pinery while the cold wind howled through the trees and the bunkhouse lamps cast long shadows.

Two months after the double lynching in Menominee, another illegal hanging took place in Wisconsin's Chippewa River Valley. Edward Maxwell, a Nebraskan who had served time in the Illinois penitentiary, was wanted for horse stealing when he and his brother, Alonzo, shot and killed two deputies who were trying to arrest them. Alonzo made good his escape. Edward was captured and brought to Durand. Deputies were taking him back to jail after a preliminary court hearing when one of the bystanders yelled, "Hang him!" The deputies were forced aside. Maxwell fought, a contemporary account said, "like a tiger." But someone brought a rope, someone fashioned a noose, someone got the noose around the prisoner's neck.

"Haul away," came the yell, and in a moment Maxwell was gasping for breath, the fight gone out of him. He was dragged to an oak east of the Pepin County courthouse and strung up, dangling thirty feet in the air with his handcuffs still on and shackles still on his feet.

It should not be supposed that hanging was the invariable fate of murderers. Another Durand slaying ended more happily for the killer, if not for the victim, Brad Wheeler. He lived along the Chippewa at a place known as Five Mile Bluff, making a living by supplying cordwood to steamboats. His wife, Mag, was twenty-three years old in 1866, seventeen years younger than her husband, and was described as a "well-developed woman, comely to look upon." Among those who looked upon her was Jim Carter, who lived with the Wheelers and helped Brad cut wood.

One Saturday night, the two men got to arguing over whether Wheeler cheated at cards. Mag chased them out of the house. As the argument continued, Brad grabbed a club and Carter picked up a gun barrel. Carter's weapon proved more effective. He hit his boss over the head, killing him.

The widow apparently didn't consider Wheeler much of a loss. She was persuaded by Carter to help him get rid of the body. They dumped it through a hole in the river ice, then backed Wheeler's horse and cutter into the stream nearby, making it appear that he'd been drowned accidentally. The authorities were suspicious and arrested Mag and her young boarder. But there was no body and no proof so they were turned loose. They continued to live cozily together until the ice melted and the body turned up. Wheeler's head was split open, so the two were arrested. Durand had no jail, so they were taken to Eau Claire, then to La Crosse, where the trial was held. After early testimony in which the prosecution tried to prove that Mag had killed her husband with a hatchet, Carter changed his plea to guilty. He said later—after he'd served five years in prison—that he'd agreed to take all the blame on condition that she wait for him and try to get him a pardon.

The jury found both Carter and Mrs. Wheeler guilty of first-degree murder, but her conviction was appealed and she was paroled, living at the sheriff's home in Eau Claire. A former boyfriend showed up and the two of them headed south to get married. It was presumed around the Chippewa that they lived happily ever after, for they never returned to the pinery region.

Meanwhile, Carter was complaining that he'd been had. The former Mrs. Wheeler hadn't kept her part of the bargain, he said, so he was withdrawing his confession. He now claimed she'd been the one who struck the fatal blow. Eventually, he persuaded the governor to pardon him. He got married, raised a family and supported them with a responsible job as foreman of a Chippewa Falls sawmill.

The lack of law and order in the pineries did not escape the attention of reformers, including a number of what the camp residents called sky pilots. One of those who traveled through the Minnesota woods was the Reverend Frank Higgins, who spent twenty years tramping through remote forest areas trying to get the men to mend their ways. Higgins was credited with temporarily cleaning up Bemidji, whose sixty-two saloons made it a popular place to spend a weekend. Another rough community, Deer River, also felt Higgins' influence.

Among the other traveling preachers was Holy Bill Poyseor,

who impressed the residents of lumber camps on Michigan's Upper Peninsula by traveling four hundred miles during the hard winter of 1894, his two dogs pulling a child's sled loaded with Bibles and other supplies.

Generally, superior force rather than a preacher's moral persuasion was the most effective way of dealing with lumberjacks who got out of line. The manager of a hotel on the west side of Fort Howard (now part of Green Bay) got a reputation for knowing how to deal with such annoyances. It was in 1870 when a man who worked at F. B. Gardner's sawmill in Pensaukee got drunk and went looking for a fight at the Fort Howard hotel. He announced that he'd come to clean up the place. The manager spoke up.

"Do you play poker?"

"Damned right I do."

"Well," the manager said, hitting him over the head with a poker, "I hold a royal flush."

That cooled off the drunk, at least until he'd regained consciousness. It also gained the hotel manager the respect of his customers. As one veteran lumberjack said, when he was an old man looking back at his youth, the Great Lakes pineries were "as tough and turbulent a frontier as this country has ever known," with the woods worker having little respect for any rules that were not enforced by a heavy fist.

The lumberjacks did their full share of sinning, but they were also sinned against, notably by the proprietors of some of the places established to take their money. Jack Brennan, for instance, paid a "bunco steerer" to meet trains that brought potential customers to Marinette. He urged the thirsty to head straight for Brennan's saloon, where Jack met them at the door wearing a spotless apron, giving them the glad hand and buying the first round of drinks. There was continuous music. There were women. There was all the hospitality a man could desire, until his money was gone. Then there was a bouncer to throw the penniless drunk into the gutter.

As has already been indicated, the favorite sport at the saloons, next to drinking, was fighting. Among numerous young men who made a reputation as brawlers were three brothers named Munroe, who worked in northeastern Wisconsin for their lumberman father in the 1870s. They usually operated as a team and were hard to beat. But one night in 1874, customers at a Green Bay saloon ganged up on the brothers and whipped them soundly. Nursing their bruises, they headed back to the woods.

A few days later, a muscular young fellow named John Carland showed up, looking for a job.

"Can you fight?" one brother asked.

"I can lick you, I guess."

"Let's see if you can."

The job applicant fought one Munroe and whipped him. Another brother tried, and Carland won again. The third brother stepped forward. Carland knocked him down.

"You're hired," Carland was told. "And you'll get two dollars a day instead of the usual thirty dollars a month, provided—"

"Provided what?"

"That you go to town with us Saturday night."

Carland agreed. When the Saturday workday was over, the three Munroes and their new ally headed for Green Bay. They cleaned out every dive on the East Side, then crossed the Fox River and challenged the resident bullies in Fort Howard. They wound up in jail, but not before leaving a trail of bruised and battered victims. The father bailed them out, spending all of his ready cash on fines and court costs. But the lads turned out just fine. A few years later, the brothers took options on pine land that turned out to be full of iron ore. They became wealthy and supported their father in style for the rest of his life.

The name of Seney must be brought up again in any discussion of the violence that lay close to the surface in lumberjack life. Among that community's leading residents were Dan Dunne, who ran one saloon, and the Harcourt brothers, who operated another. Dunne had moved to Seney after collecting fire insurance on his bar in Roscommon, Michigan. He'd paid a lumberjack fifty dollars to burn it down. When the arsonist showed up in Seney, demanding a larger share of the insurance money, Dunne took him to an island in a nearby river to discuss the matter. The lumberjack was never seen alive again. Some years later, his skeleton was found on the island along with that of a druggist who made the mistake of asking Dunne to pay back some money he'd borrowed.

It was in 1893 when Steve Harcourt walked into Dunne's saloon and took a shot at Dan. He missed. The bullet hit a large beveled mirror that was the pride of the establishment. Dunne retaliated by shooting Harcourt in the mouth and, as he staggered toward the door, sent another bullet into his belly. Harcourt was carried home. Dunne was required to go to Manistique to post a bond attesting that he would keep the peace. When Steve died, his brother Jim walked into a saloon at Trout Lake where Dunne was having a drink. Dan reached for his pocket and Harcourt shot him. Dunne died. Jim served time in prison for manslaughter, then returned to Seney and was elected town clerk.

Another resident who managed to stand out in a rough crowd was Tim Kaine, who once carried a grudge for four years. He'd asked his camp boss, Jim Dugan, for time off. Dugan responded by knocking him down with a cant hook. Dugan then went home to Canada, staying away from Seney for forty-eight months. When he returned, Kaine was waiting. He greeted his old boss by knocking him down. Dugan scrambled to his feet and the fight was on. It lasted for more than an hour before Kaine knocked Dugan unconscious. He started to jump on him but his friends persuaded him to go to the saloon and celebrate his victory before Dugan was fatally injured.

By now, Kaine was a camp boss himself, charged with maintaining the rules. He docked the pay of a man named Isaac Stretcher when Ike quit before the day's work was over. Stretcher headed for Seney and started talking about what he'd do when he met Kaine. No man to avoid a fight, Kaine went looking for his disgruntled former employee that evening. As he was passing an alley, Stretcher leaped out and plunged a knife in his back. Kaine died. The killer would have been lynched if Sheriff Tom McCann hadn't kept the crowd back by waving a large revolver. Stretcher served seven and a half years in prison instead of getting hung.

While Seney was in a class by itself, there were a number of other places on the Upper Peninsula where a man could get in trouble without trying hard. Escanaba, for example, had no less than one hundred two saloons, along with a red-light district around Thomas Street where the houses were open for business day and night. One admiring visitor claimed Escanaba's tenderloin "contained a concentration of sin unsurpassed in the sawmill towns."

At Manistique, southwest of Seney, a lumberman named George Orr tried to establish an oasis of purity. Just before Manistique changed from a handful of log huts to a flourishing lumber center, Orr and his agents bought up most of the land and banned saloons and bordellos. But his operatives somehow overlooked a small section of ground in the west end of town. Dan Heffron saw his chance. He bought the parcel and opened a large saloon, with rooms for women overhead. Others took up holdings on Dan's real estate and soon Heffron's land, not Orr's, was the center of the rapidly growing business district.

Heffron (or Heffernan, as he's sometimes called) managed to get his young brother, Denis, elected county sheriff. Still, Dan eventually got in trouble with the law. He was permitted to wait outside the courthouse while a jury pondered a verdict on his various crimes and misdemeanors. He was a man with friends even in the jury room, however. When a guilty verdict was voted, a red bandana waved from the window. Heffron's sleigh was waiting. He ran to it, dived under a buffalo robe and told his driver to take off, escaping just ahead of another sleigh full of deputies.

The lawmen were gaining on him when he got lucky. At the edge of town, the road went across a railroad track. A long freight was approaching.

"We'll never make it," Dan's driver said, starting to pull back on the reins.

"The hell we won't. Keep a-whipping."

The sleigh skidded across the tracks inches ahead of the locomotive. The train cut off pursuit. Heffron never was captured. He wound up in Chicago, the Pacific Northwest or the Klondike, depending on which story you prefer to believe.

CHAPTER XII

Life Among the Lumber Barons

A TALL Swede left Ellis Island to catch a train west. A Salvation Army lassie stopped him. Shaking her tambourine, she asked: "Sir, will you work for Jesus?"

The immigrant deliberated for a moment, then shook his head.

"Ay tank ay rather work for Louie Sands," he said, and kept on walking.

Sands's success in the Michigan pineries had made him a hero in his native Scandinavia. He had become a millionaire by logging millions of feet of white pine around Clam Lake (now Cadillac) and Manistee. If there was a choice, he preferred to hire Swedes, Norwegians or Danes, which is why the area near his camps along the AuSable River became known as Little Denmark. Working for Louie was a way for Scandinavians to get a toehold in the New World.

Sands didn't dress like a millionaire and seldom acted like one. He appeared unannounced in his far-flung camps, looking like a laborer down on his luck, ready to swing an axe or take an end of a crosscut saw. Legends grew up around him, such as the one about the time he was driving his wagon on the trail to Clam Lake. Some miles from town, one of his two horses collapsed and died. The average millionaire, even in the pineries, would either have waited for help or have unhitched the other mare and ridden to town. Not Sands. He dragged the dead animal to one side, took off its harness, hitched himself to the wagon. Then he and the remaining horse pulled the wagon into Clam Lake. And why not? The wagon was his. Louie Sands was not a man to abandon anything of value that belonged to him.

The men labeled lumber barons by posterity were often a trifle eccentric. One, for example, lived in a great, wooden mansion near Watters, Michigan, that was surrounded by a solid wall built of mortar and champagne bottles. Empty ones, of course, and their owner had done most of the emptying. Then there was Al Powers, who made his fortune around Hibbing, Minnesota. That community had sixty saloons and two hundred whores but it drew the line at prizefights. As a general rule, no one paid much attention to the official ban on pugilism. But one year, a boxing match was called off because of a temporary attack of civic morality. Powers, who had been looking forward to watching the fight, went into action. He invited anyone who wanted to see the match to board a train made up of ninety logging cars attached to his locomotive. The train chugged over the line into Itasca County, out of reach of the bluenoses, and the fight was held there.

"My track ain't as long as the Great Northern's," Powers bragged. "But by God, it's just as wide."

The vast majority of the men who chopped down the white pine forests got nothing for their trouble but a scant living. Only a few —lucky or clever, and often both—got rich. Being a trifle unscrupulous helped, too.

One man who became wealthy as a pinery land speculator owed his success to a thought that struck him as he was traveling through the woods, working as a landlooker.

"I'm a considerable big damned fool," he told himself. "Why should I locate all this land for the company and none for myself?"

He made up his mind to be a fool no longer. He marked his platbook to indicate that a large section of choice pinery property was a worthless swamp. His employers, trusting his judgment, passed up the chance to claim that tract. The landlooker borrowed six hundred dollars and bought it himself. Before the year was out, he sold part of the acreage for seventy-five hundred dollars and cut nine million feet of timber from the rest.

"I didn't work for the company after that," he added in describing how he'd got a start toward wealthy respectability.

It was possible to start small and rise fast. John H. Knapp, for example, inherited a thousand dollars from his father and invested it in a small lumber company. He soon held the controlling interest in what became Wisconsin's largest such firm. Philetus Sawyer, who learned lumbering in New York State, arrived in Wisconsin with two thousand dollars, bought a small sawmill near Oshkosh and within four years was one of the state's richest men. Isaac Stephenson, who started his career as a fourteen-dollar-a-month lumberjack in Maine, became a power in the lumber industries of both Michigan and Wisconsin, accumulating something like twelve million dollars at a time when there was no income tax and a working man was expected to survive on a dollar a day. Along the way, Ike acquired such side benefits as a Milwaukee newspaper, the *Free Press*.

One of Stephenson's associates was Daniel Wells, Jr., who made a fortune in lumbering and land speculation and was proud to be pointed out as the richest man in Milwaukee. At one point he decided to make a killing by cornering the lard market so that any American who had a need for pig fat would have to pay his price. Instead, he dropped a million dollars on the deal. The next time he visited his Marinette sawmills, Stephenson said he had something to show him.

"Dan'l, come over and see what we've got behind the company boardinghouse. Finest bunch of hogs in town. They're getting fat on the scraps we throw them."

"Damn the hogs, Ike. I never want to look a hog in the face again as long as I live."

Stephenson and Sawyer were among a considerable number of wealthy lumbermen who went into politics. Philetus' political foes charged he'd bought his seat in the United States Senate, bribing the state legislature to give it to him in the days before direct election to the office. Sawyer denied he'd done anything wrong, but Ike Stephenson was more frank. His Senate seat, he told an interviewer, cost him one hundred thousand dollars, mostly in contributions to that Progressive reformer, Fighting Bob La Follette.

Loggers and lumbermen often felt that getting into politics was a necessity to protect their interests. To control such vital matters as taxation on timberlands, they ran for local or county office. State office was the next logical step, in view of the need to keep the Legislature friendly to their business. A few went on from there to Congress. Thaddeus C. Pound of Chippewa Falls and William Price of Black River Falls were other Wisconsin examples, along with Sawyer and Stephenson.

Among the Michigan representatives was J. W. Fordney, who got his start as a landlooker before becoming a leading Saginaw lumberman. He spent twenty years in Congress, serving as chairman of the Ways and Means Committee. At a time when Saginaw's population was thirty thousand, it had a dozen daily newspapers, mostly owned by lumber kings willing to subsidize a printing press to explain to neighbors why they should be elected to public office.

Across the state in Muskegon, the leading lumber baron was Charles H. Hackley. In 1856 he'd landed a job in a sawmill there at a dollar a day. Before his death forty-nine years later, he'd given more than a million dollars to his adopted city, and his will increased the total to six million. The money was earmarked for parks, schools, hospitals, a library and—most remarkable, considering his background—a collection of oil paintings.

Notable among the region's wealthy lumbermen was Joseph G. Thorp, who demonstrated that he not only knew how to make money but was no slouch at spending it. A founder of the Eau Claire Lumber Company, he prospered to the point where he could afford a mansion in his hometown and another in Madison, where he was a member of the state Senate. That home, later to become the governor's executive mansion, was Madison's showplace and the center of its social life.

Thorp demonstrated his liberality in 1870 by giving his wife a camel's hair shawl that cost him five thousand dollars as she was leaving for a European trip with their eighteen-year-old daughter, Sarah. They came back to Wisconsin with an even more valuable prize, the renowned Norwegian violinist Ole Bull.

Bull was then sixty years old. He was known not only as a musician but as the founder of Oleana, a rustic utopia he'd established in Pennsylvania. He had become angry at the tight-fisted residents of his hometown, Bergen, after he started a national theater there. When the authorities refused to chip in enough tax money to make it a success, Bull announced he would take his talents to America, where they'd be appreciated. Before leaving, he turned the theater over to a melancholy youth, Henrik Ibsen, who was also to make a name for himself.

Bull arrived in the United States in 1852 and bought twelve thousand acres in northern Pennsylvania. He established thirty Norwegian families there, raised the Norwegian flag and announced that he had founded New Norway. For several weeks, he laid aside his fiddle and superintended the construction of houses and a general store, stocking the latter with such useful items as tall silk hats.

The Oleana colony grew to a population of perhaps three hundred immigrants. But the site was mountainous, forested and not suitable for farming. Within a year, Bull realized Oleana was costing more money than he could earn with his violin and he withdrew his support. Most of the settlers soon left, generally for more suitable farming country in Wisconsin or Minnesota.

Bull remained in the United States, doing well on a series of concert tours. It was on one of these that he first met Sarah Thorp, the lumberman's daughter. A widower, he was smitten. But he was old enough to be her grandfather and he went back to Norway. When Mrs. Thorp showed up in Europe with Sarah and the five-thousand-dollar shawl, however, the romance moved rapidly forward.

"Other than human powers have decided my fate," Ole announced to his fans. "The sunbeams I shut out, but the sun itself I could not annihilate."

After the marriage, the couple headed for Thorp's Madison mansion. To show off his new son-in-law, the lumberman threw the biggest party Wisconsin had ever seen. An orchestra and a caterer were imported from Chicago. The caterer brought a thirty-thousand-dollar dinner set, so Thorp's friends ate from solid silver plates, dipping solid silver cups into a solid silver punch bowl. A thousand invitations were sent out. Among the guests was the bride's little brother, Joe, who later added a second celebrity to the family by marrying the daughter of the poet Henry Wadsworth Longfellow.

It was hard for other wealthy lumbermen to match Thorp's acquisition of such a famous son-in-law, but they made do by endowing libraries and music halls, running for Congress or building large and often spectacularly ugly houses. Others concentrated on piling up additional wealth, branching out into such fields as mining, flour milling and railroading. W. D. Washburn, for example, a lumberman who shifted his operations from Michigan to Minnesota in the 1880s, established the Minneapolis, St. Paul and Sault Ste. Marie Railway, the first to connect the pineries with the Atlantic without going through the Chicago bottleneck.

Duluth, which was hard hit by the Panic of 1873, got a new lease on the future nine years later when the federal government began selling two million acres of Minnesota pine land, much of it for a dollar and a quarter an acre. Lumbermen and other speculators from Wisconsin, Michigan, Maine and elsewhere converged on the Lake Superior port city, bearing money and wide ambitions.

Some wound up not only with pine acreage but valuable ore lands. Wellington Burt, who had worked for thirteen dollars a month in a lumber camp on Michigan's Pine River, was among the lucky ones. By now, he was rich and influential, able to buy heavily at the government land sale. What he was seeking was pine, and that proved profitable. But it was the iron ore under his land that made him a new fortune. One mine alone brought two hundred and fifty thousand dollars a year in royalties.

A landlooker, Marshall H. Alworth, advised two investors, Morton B. Hull and William Boeing, to invest twenty thousand dollars at the Duluth sale. They discovered later that they'd bought acreage containing ten million tons of iron ore. Alworth did well for himself, too. While working for a Michigan firm in Minnesota, he agreed to accept his pay in timberland, a common arrangement. Unknown to him, the trees he acquired were growing on top of ore so rich that the landlooker was soon able to retire to Duluth and lead the life of a millionaire.

Orrin Higgins, who operated a chain of groceries in New York and Pennsylvania, took a flier in Minnesota pine land with his son Frank, buying eleven thousand acres. When ore was found, much of this land soared in value from a dollar and a quarter to fifty thousand dollars an acre.

Such speculators owed a debt of gratitude to the sons of Lewis H. Merritt, a landlooker and sawmill operator who settled at Oneota, Minnesota, about 1860. Between hikes through the woods to look at trees, he found time to father seven sons. When they grew up, they became landlookers, too.

One of them, Leonidas, served as the model for a statue of a timber cruiser in front of the Capitol in St. Paul. With his brother, Alfred, he was looking for ore as well as pine when they found the Mesabi Range. It contained some of the world's richest iron ore, part of it close enough to the surface to be mined easily. The Merritt brothers bought considerable portions of the range and dreamed of becoming wealthy. But in the 1893 Panic they lost out to the Rockefellers, who knew little about surviving in the woods but much about survival in the financial markets. When Leonidas died in 1926, his estate amounted to less than twenty-five hundred dollars.

Among Minnesota lumbermen who cashed in on the ore found beneath their land was Len Day, who came from Maine to cut pine on the Rum River. He did well as a lumberman before the discovery of iron made him rich. He moved to Minneapolis, where he never ventured out in public without his plug hat.

The ability of a few lumbermen to become wealthy and put on such airs depended not only on the exploitation of the natural resources that existed in the region but on the willingness of tens of thousands of lumberjacks, mill workers and others to work long hours for small pay. There was surprisingly little grumbling about this, partly because a steady supply of cheap labor kept flowing to the Lake States from Europe. But now and then, a rebellion took place.

Such an incident in 1881 has been called the Sawdust War, although it was actually not much more than a skirmish. At 6 A.M. on July 11, several hundred employees of the Eau Claire Lumber Company quit, announcing they wouldn't come back until their workday was cut from twelve hours to ten. They formed into a ragged line of march and made the rounds of other mills to persuade fellow workers to join the strike.

Soon, only one sawmill in Eau Claire was operating. It was owned by two brothers, Arthur and John Sherman. They pointed out to the strikers that they'd already lowered the work schedule to ten hours. The leaders demanded that the Sherman mill close anyway, so the Shermans went to the brewery next door and bought a barrel of beer, trundled it back to the mill yard and told

the strikers to drink hearty. That soon convinced everyone that
Art and John were fine fellows. After the beer was gone, the
crowd weaved on.

Workmen who declined to join the walkout were persuaded,
generally by being knocked down. Brawls continued until all the
recalcitrant ones were convinced. For the next several days, bands
of workmen roamed the little lumber city with banners reading
TEN HOURS OR NO SAWDUST. The saloons did a fine business.

The mill owners, as might be expected, did not take this rebellion philosophically. With no logs being sawed, except by the
Shermans, the town's economy and the owners' profits were
threatened. A delegation went to Madison to have a talk with
Governor William E. Smith, who made an inspection tour of Eau
Claire, then called out the militia. Six companies totaling three
hundred seventy-five men arrived, establishing a camp in a west-
side park.

The strikers threw a dance and invited the soldiers, who had a
fine time. Negotiations were arranged. On July 29, an agreement
was reached. The militia confiscated the strikers' banners and the
men went back to work. They got a few concessions but not the
ten-hour day. The strike had been an interesting break in the summer's routine, but by now the men's money was gone, the bar-
tenders were no longer friendly, and it was time to saw more logs.

The same year as Eau Claire's Sawdust War, a similar strike for
shorter hours was held in Michigan. Workmen at the Muskegon
Booming Association walked off their jobs. Troops were called.
The men went back. The troops left. The strike began again. The
mill owners imported a new crew from Ontario. The strikers met
the Canadians at the depot, escorted them to a hall and made it
clear that anybody who chose to work would not stay healthy.
The Canadians got on the next train north. Pinkerton strike-
breakers were brought in and they were harder to scare away.
There were battles with clubs, neither side winning a clear-cut victory. But the detective agency employees knew little about making
pines into boards and after some weeks the owners decided the
only way they'd get the logs sorted and cut was to agree to a ten-
hour day.

That was the first major victory for sawmill workers, and word
spread through the industry. Other walkouts were held here and

there. Finally, in 1886, the unrest reached those brawling sawdust centers, Bay City and Saginaw. Once more the Pinkertons arrived, ready for battle. Once again, most owners eventually realized that a ten-hour day was the lesser of evils. But one man held out.

"I'm damned if I'm going to let a bunch of mill hands tell me how to saw logs," A. W. Wright declared.

The next morning, when he put on his plug hat and drove to his office, a neatly carved miniature coffin was tied to his door. Wright was a stubborn man but he could take a hint. He sold out and left town.

After the Saginaw Valley capitulated to the shorter schedule, other lumber cities followed. The ten-hour day became common for mill workers. In the woods, the hours continued to be regulated by the amount of daylight. On the rivers, of course, the hours remained indefinite. When the logs were running, a man was expected to keep working as long as he could see and sometimes longer.

Despite the success of some of the organized walkouts, the usual means of expressing dissatisfaction with pay, hours or working conditions was to quit the job and look for another. In the woods, a disgruntled worker often picked a fight with the boss before he left, if he thought he could lick him. Knocking a foreman down gave a fellow something pleasant to think about as he hiked to town, knowing he'd lost a fifth of the pay due him by quitting before his work contract was up.

Of all the lumbermen who made or lost fortunes in the Lake States, the most influential was Frederick Weyerhaeuser, who became to lumbering what John D. Rockefeller was to oil and Andrew Carnegie to steel. Born near the Rhine in 1834, Weyerhaeuser arrived in Erie, Pennsylvania, when he was eighteen, getting a job in a brewery there. He soon headed for Rock Island, Illinois, and worked in a sawmill owned by Mead, Smith and Marsh, which handled logs floated down the Mississippi from the Wisconsin pine country. By the time he was twenty-two, he had saved enough money to invest in the business. The following year, the firm failed. Frederick took over its yard at Coal Valley, Illinois, and in 1860 joined with his brother-in-law, F. C. A. Denkmann, to acquire the bankrupt company's mill in Rock Island. His initial investment on what became the start of an empire cost him five hundred dollars.

As his milling interests in Rock Island expanded, Weyerhaeuser branched out into land speculation, buying extensively in the Chippewa River pinery as early as 1864. From there, he and his associates expanded their holdings northward in Wisconsin and later in Minnesota. By 1887, Weyerhaeuser had sawmills in seven lumber towns in three states. Three years later, he headed the group that acquired the Northern Pacific's huge land grant in Minnesota.

Weyerhaeuser's formidable business talents included an ability to persuade competitors to co-operate instead of squabbling. The combine he formed never wholly succeeded in making tame fat cats out of all the prickly individualists who had established baronies in the woods, but he had more success along these lines than anyone else.

As befitted his enthusiasm for peace with profit, the German tried to keep a low profile. Most of those who rose to the top in lumbering and logging in those days swaggered a bit. Weyerhaeuser stood out because he spoke only when he had something important to say, threw his weight around only when necessary and put on no airs, particularly in places where lumberjacks were watching. Despite himself, he was the center of attention because of his power. It was no secret that he was a millionaire and the most influential figure in what had become the principal industry of three states. But he still dressed like a dollar-a-day shanty boy when he visited remote lumber towns. The lumberjacks also respected his ability to outwalk even a landlooker when he was rambling through the forest, inspecting pine. They regarded him with a touch of envy, no doubt. But there was a touch of amused superiority in their attitude, too. Why should a man work so hard and worry so much about getting more money when, as any sensible 'jack knew, the thing to do with cash was spend it?

A turning point in Weyerhaeuser's career came in 1880, the year when Eau Claire mill owners decided they couldn't lick his Mississippi Logging Company and joined it. From then on, Chippewa Valley logging, transportation and sawmills were largely controlled by a single company, which could regulate supplies and, to a considerable extent, prices.

The habit rich lumbermen like Weyerhaeuser had of showing up unexpectedly in portions of their far-flung dominions was understandable. Sometimes this was the only way they could discover what was going on.

Philetus Sawyer, before he was a senator but after he'd become a rich man with a reputation for shrewdness, took such a scouting trip to his northern pine lands. He was hiking through the woods when he came upon a neat house that looked out of place in this remote corner of Wisconsin. The woman who answered his knock didn't recognize him but she was willing to talk.

"A fine house you have, madam."

"Oh, this ain't a house, exactly. It's a school. And I'm the teacher."

Sawyer owned all the land for miles, except this forgotten forty acres. His suspicions mounted.

"Whose children do you teach, madam?"

"Why, my own."

"There are no neighbors who send children to your school?"

"We ain't got neighbors, mister. Nobody else lives in the district."

"Then how is the school supported?"

"Oh, my husband and the hired man and the trout fishers organized the school, levied a tax and the county treasurer collected it and we hired a teacher. That's me."

Sawyer got the picture. The woman didn't need to tell him who was paying the tax or why she and her family were able to live in such a fine house. He rounded up the husband.

"I guess it would be cheaper to buy your farm," he told him, "move you to Oshkosh and board you at a first-class hotel until all your children are grown."

"How's that? Who are you?"

"Never mind," Sawyer said, and stalked off, brooding about the ability of the poor to take unfair advantage of the rich.

The same year that Sawyer stumbled on the school he was supporting, a more serious tax problem arose in his Oshkosh headquarters. Generally, lumber barons did a competent job of bribing or browbeating local taxing authorities into keeping valuations of their properties low. But the Oshkosh Board of Review, in what a chronicler called "a spasm of civic virtue," raised the personal

property tax of the community's eighty richest men. Of the
$703,000 added to the assessments, Sawyer and his sons were
nicked for $100,000. There was a great uproar and you can be
sure Philetus' voice contributed its full share. But the board stood
its ground.

If lumber barons were sometimes considered fair game during
the height of their power and influence, they have fared considerably worse since then. Their operations left much of the former
pinery a wasteland Their methods of exploiting the nation's most
valuable stands of white pine seemed to posterity not only irre-
sponsible but downright foolish, even from a selfish viewpoint. But
the lumbermen were not as universally unscrupulous as some critics have painted them.

By the 1870s, it was plain enough that the trees in Michigan,
Wisconsin and Minnesota were being cut at a rate that would
eventually leave the land denuded of a marketable asset it had
taken nature several hundred years to create. Estimates of when
this would happen appeared in trade journals of the time. There
were debates between optimists and pessimists over when the pine
would run out, but no one doubted that the day would come.
There were those—mostly outside the lumber industry—who felt
that slashing through the pineries without giving thought to the future was downright immoral. There were others, including some
influential lumbermen, who regarded the prospect of running out
of pine with dismay.

But efforts to curtail production of logs proved futile. As settlers continued to push westward into a largely treeless region, the
demand for lumber seemed insatiable. The market was there. The
competition to supply it was keen.

One compelling reason for wasteful production was the inability
of the lumber companies to work out an arrangement among
themselves to curtail cutting. It was tried—not in the interests of
good forestry but as a means of keeping the market from periodic
glutting which sent down prices. But even such combines as the
one put together by Weyerhaeuser were unable to control an industry composed of hundreds of individualistic operators. A single
lumber company couldn't afford to behave more responsibly without losing out to its competitors. Many lumbermen understood
that, in the long run, it would be more sensible to hold back on

the forests' destruction. But they also understood that if they did, they'd go broke. An 1876 letter to the editor of the *Northwestern Lumberman* put the situation in perspective:

"You have scolded the lumbermen for cutting so much timber. Well, we have cut a great deal, but what can we do about it? Quit? Who will pay the debts or feed those who are now working for us? . . . When we are out of timber, then we will curtail. But until that day, never. So help us Moses!"

CHAPTER XIII

The Hodag, the Agropelter and the High-Behind

THE MEN WHO CUT the pine were proudly self-sufficient. But they lived in a place where the trees were giants, the weather was sometimes extreme, and the least sensitive of men must feel in his soul that he was a puny figure in contrast to nature's power. Perhaps because the men felt insignificant next to the doomed but awsome forests, the tales they told were defiantly tall.

As everyone must know by now, the principal legendary figure created in the yarning competitions around the deacon seats was Paul Bunyan. He has long since evolved into something of a literary figure, his fame spread by writers with soft hands who would have been useless in the big woods. But he was originally an authentic creation of the lumberjacks.

Bunyan led a shanty boy's life, according to the stories, but he had some advantages over the ordinary woods worker. He was larger, for one thing. One authority said he was exactly twelve feet and eleven inches tall and weighed eight hundred eighty-eight pounds, without his socks. But his dimensions varied with the tale-teller. His ox, Babe, was eleven feet tall and measured forty-two axe handles and a plug of tobacco between the eyes.

Babe's color is usually given as blue, and so it was in later years. But the ox was originally white. The color change came during the Michigan Winter of the Blue Snow. Babe spent so

much time outdoors that he turned blue, too. That's not surprising
when you're told that this winter was so cold that flames in the
coal oil lamps froze solid. Even Paul couldn't blow them out. He
had to break them into chunks and toss them out the window.
When spring came, the flames thawed out, starting a forest fire
that burned the St. Mary's River in two. With dry land between
one end of the river and the other, the water backed up, causing
Lake Superior to rise alarmingly. Residents of Duluth sent an
urgent appeal to Bunyan. He grabbed his shovel and dug a ship
canal at the Soo, connecting the two ends of the St. Mary's again.
It was quite a job, even for Paul. In fact, it made him eighteen
minutes late for dinner.

According to one theory, the Bunyan stories go back to lumberjack camps in New Brunswick, where the mythical axeman was
called Paul Bonhomme. Maine loggers picked up the tales, changing the name to Bunyan. From there, the stories made the rounds
of camps in the Lake States. Some of the lore was handed down
from one yarn-spinner to another. Other stories were made up as
the tale-teller went along, limited only by his imagination.

Fantastic exaggeration was a staple of nineteenth-century
American humor. Its lumberjack offshoot not only helped while
away dull evenings but was used to impress greenhorns who were
still in awe of the woods and their companions, so could be persuaded to believe almost anything. The accepted technique in this
continuing game was to invent as outrageous a lie as possible, but
tell it so gravely and impressively that it was hard not to accept it
as truth. When one man's lie was finished, other old-timers would
nod their heads and agree that's exactly how it happened. Then
someone else would try to top the story.

The tale about the Winter of the Blue Snow, for instance, might
inspire a lumberjack to describe the year when it snowed so much
that it buried Bunyan's camp. Paul's cook, Big Joe, had to get up
early every morning and dig a hole in the snow so smoke from his
cookstove could escape. When spring came, there was a hole in
the air one hundred seventy-eight feet long above the chimney.

Bunyan and his crew—Johnny Inkslinger, Ole Olson and the
rest—have received most of the attention from outsiders, but
there were plenty of other characters in the deacon seat repertoire.
Joe Mufraw (or Mouffreau), for instance. He could kick so high he

left calk marks on an eight-foot ceiling. He performed such feats as hooking a logging chain to a crooked tote road and pulling it straight. Then there was another Canadian, Bluenose Brainerd. He arrived from Nova Scotia in a balloon, it was said, landing in the top of a tall Wisconsin (or Michigan or Minnesota) pine. He lived there, eating bird's eggs and pine cones. But when the tree was cut, Bluenose sailed through the air into a logging camp and decided, as long as he was there, he might as well grab one end of a crosscut saw.

The rafting crews had their own mythical strong man, who served them in place of Paul Bunyan. Whiskey Jack wasn't as big, being a mere seven feet tall, but he could lick any man on the river. Many of the tales told about Whiskey Jack have to do with the unbounded thirst he and his men had for liquor, putting the stories in the category of imaginative expansions on reality rather than total fantasy.

There was a thin line between the tall tales and the rough practical jokes that were another staple of life in the big woods. Gene Shepard, a timber cruiser, combined the two in his creation of the Hodag, a mythical beast still mentioned around Shepard's hometown of Rhinelander, Wisconsin.

Impressing the greenhorns, Shepard told how he was in the woods when the ground began to tremble and fierce growls were heard. He investigated, the landlooker said, and discovered an animal that was a cross between a dinosaur and a bulldog. It had two large horns, sharp spines along its back, a spearlike tail and glowing green eyes. With the help of friends, Shephard said, he dug a huge pit, covered the trap with branches and lured the Hodag into it.

The Hodag began as just another bunkhouse story, but Shepard carried it a step further. With the help of a skilled woodcarver, he created an animal out of wood and leather that resembled his description of the beast. In a dim light and with a willing suspension of disbelief, it looked as if it had been alive. Shepard made a tidy profit exhibiting the Hodag at county fairs and finally aroused the puzzled attention of the Smithsonian Institution. When the museum sent investigators to look at this rare prehistoric monster, Shepard decided he'd gone far enough and admitted the hoax. And a most successful one, from the lumberjacks' standpoint. It had not only fooled the greenhorns in lumber camps, it had fooled the rubes at county fairs.

Shepard's Hodag was a variation of the Hugag, one of the mythical denizens of the big woods used to frighten tenderfeet. On nights when the snow lay ten feet deep and the mercury stood a foot below zero, apprentice tree-choppers were warned to beware of this beast. The Hugag was as large as a moose, had no joints in its legs, no hair on its head or neck. It claimed its victims by sneaking up and falling on them.

The High-Behind was another bugaboo for those naïve enough to believe a lumberjack. Its rear quarters were taller than its front and it could destroy an unwary intruder by running backward over him. Newcomers to the woods were also warned to watch out for the Agropelter, which lived in hollow trees and dropped dead limbs on passersby.

The only man to be attacked by an Agropelter and live, it was agreed, was Ole Kittelson. Cruising for timber along the St. Croix, he came too close to the mythical beast's lair. Down came a widowmaker, a dead branch heavy enough to destroy an ox. But Ole was lucky. It hit him on the head. Being Scandinavian, his skull was so hard that the limb splintered into harmless sawdust.

Greenhorns also heard of such strange beasts as the Axe-Handle Hound, which prowled through camps when everyone was asleep and ate axe handles; the Tote-Road Shagamaw, a shy creature with bear claws in front and moose hooves behind, which ate mackinaws and mittens that had been left on stumps; the hoop snake, which rolled merrily through the woods with its tail in its mouth, and the gilly grouse. This bird was said to live only along the Onion River. Its specialty was laying square eggs.

An outsider might suppose that men who worked in temperatures that sometimes hit fifty below would prefer stories about life in a hot climate, or that they'd choose a symbol of lumberjack prowess who had escaped from the hardships of the woods. But Paul Bunyan was conceived as an extension of themselves. His powers were carried to absurd extremes. But if no mere human could equal his feats, there was a lively awareness by the taletellers that when loggers were viewed collectively they were accomplishing seemingly impossible tasks themselves.

Their forerunners had stood on the coast of Maine and looked west at a continent full of trees. By the 1880s, when the old stories about Bunyan and his crew became a staple of bunkhouse conversation in the Lake States, such men had chopped and sawed their way beyond the Mississippi and were already eyeing the even more formidable forests of the Pacific Northwest.

This was an accomplishment worthy of pride. An individual woods worker might be low-paid, lice-ridden, regarded by whores and saloonkeepers as fair game. But he and his fellows had tackled a job too big for them and accomplished it. If they left ruined acreage behind, so be it. They had provided the raw material for housing a nation, and there was something to be said for that.

Paul Bunyan could tie his axe to a rope and cut forty acres with a single swing. An exaggeration, of course. But a crew of lumberjacks could chop down a forty of prime pine pretty fast, too.

Bunyan, the stories said, cleared the Dakotas of trees. And if the tenderfoot was skeptical, the tale-teller had an answer: "Go to the Dakotas, kid. Take a look. You won't find a single pine."

Bunyan's road sprinkler sprang a leak in Minnesota and before it could be plugged had created a river. "You don't believe me? Take a look. The Mississippi is there to prove it."

Denuding the Dakotas or creating the Mississippi could not be credited to lumberjack crews except in myth. But in truth, the men in colorful mackinaws had wiped out the original timber growth in areas as large as North and South Dakota. And in the spring they could convert a brook into a stream big enough to carry sixteen-foot logs to the mills.

The lumberjacks constituted a great fraternity of males who called each other by such names as Tanbark Bill, Paddy the Pig, Blowhard Ike, Maneater Cunyan, Pumphandle Joe, Slabwood Johnson, Cedar Root Charlie. Acceptance in the club required a willingness to undergo primitive living conditions and the presence of danger, both at work and at play. To gain respect, a man had to be able to beat his companions by felling a tree more skillfully, riding a log more daringly, drinking bad whiskey more willingly, spending his pay more wastefully. He had to be able to stand up for his rights with his fists, boots and teeth. And if he could tell a bigger lie with a straighter face in the bunkhouse bull sessions, so much the better.

Games favored by lumberjacks bore a remarkable resemblance

to fraternity initiations, including the emphasis on punishing the victim on the least dignified portion of his anatomy. Hotass, shuffle the brogan, buy my sheep—the point of all these bunkhouse sports was that someone got kicked or swatted and must accept his humiliation with good grace in the hope that his turn would come and he'd get to do the kicking or swatting.

The height of the lumberjack period came at a time when there was an accepted double standard in the use of language. Decent women were not supposed to know certain words, let alone say them. Decent men did not use such words when women were listening. These rules were not universally followed, but one advantage of getting away from mixed company was that a man could demonstrate his ability to speak Anglo-Saxon. Short but powerful verbs and nouns demonstrated his masculinity. Sailors, soldiers, lumberjacks and other all-male groups—including small boys, out of earshot of mothers—could triumph over feminine repressions by turning the air blue, a custom that continued until recently. Then women demanded and got the right to demonstrate their ability to use the not-very-secret language, spoiling its chief reason for existence.

It seems clear enough that one reason why some men returned, winter after miserable winter, to the life in the woods was the chance to get away from women and family responsibilities. There were many other reasons, including the fact that those who cut trees were caught up in a system that left them little choice of occupations. But for many of the men, there was a persistent attraction in an environment wholly male, the nineteenth-century logging camp.

A considerable number of those who worked in the woods eventually married and some were quickly tamed. But for those husbands who continued to make a living part of each year by cutting pines, the life they led in the woods was a bachelor's life. Their recreations were a bachelor's recreations. The prevailing attitude toward money and toward the future were bachelor's attitudes.

The weekend sprees, the stag socials, the games played in the bunkhouse—these were the things that stood out in the memories of nineteenth-century lumberjacks, judging from tales they told when they had grown too old to swing an axe. But the truth is, most of the time in the pine forests was spent in hard labor under tough bosses. The bosses, in turn, were subject to nagging demands from employers whose success depended on getting the most pine for the least pay. Except on Saturday, a lumberjack was normally asleep early, too weary to care that his bunk was shared by graybacks, bedbugs and a male companion as tired and unwashed as he.

There were Sundays when a 'jack might have a chance to drown his troubles or nurse his hangover. But generally, even this one day of leisure each week was given over to chores—patching clothes, replacing buttons, boiling apparel in a large lard can over an open fire as part of the unending and futile war against body lice.

The life led in the pineries attracted a wide variety of humanity, ranging from immigrants seeking to make a start in a new land to outlaws looking for a hiding place. Almost anybody might show up in the woods, and if a hand was needed few questions were asked. At a single camp near Traverse City, Michigan, for instance, the crew one year included an escaped mental patient, a former West Point cadet, and a cookee who had traveled with a minstrel show.

The days when lumberjacks were subject to few laws except those laid down by the lumber companies gradually ended as the nineteenth century wore on. The time came when there were even attempts to enforce regulations against shooting deer the year round, a rule that old-timers considered as absurd as passing a law setting down specified times for swatting a mosquito.

In Michigan's north country, a conscientious game warden nabbed an old logger named Erickson for laying in a supply of venison. Brought before a justice of the peace, Erickson demanded a jury. Six men were picked. An Irishman, Barney Morgan, was elected foreman. Erickson was put on the stand and admitted the warden had caught him skinning a deer.

"And did you shoot that deer, Mr. Erickson?"

"I shot him."

"Were you aware that it was not deer season?"

"I guess. I didn't pay no attention to such foolishness."

That seemed to settle the matter. The six men soon filed back in with a verdict. Morgan said they'd decided the defendant was not guilty.

"Not guilty!" The justice rose from his bench and glared down at the Irishman. "How the hell can you stand there and say he's not guilty? You heard him admit he shot the deer out of season. How can you come up with a verdict like that?"

"Easy as pie, Judge. Erickson is such a damned liar, we didn't believe him."

The times might be changing, but in the lumber towns there were still allowances for eccentricity. In Escanaba, Michigan, for instance, one of the best-known weekend visitors from the lumber camps was Horse-and-Buggy Ritchie. He wasn't satisfied to be one of the crowd at the saloons or in the houses of the red-light district on Thomas Street (now First Avenue). After a few drinks to get in the proper mood, he'd put on a pair of women's high-top shoes, roll his pants above his knobby knees and rent a buggy at a livery stable. He'd get between the shafts and go prancing along, pulling the buggy, pretending he was a horse. If a piece of paper blew across his path, he'd shy like a skittish filly.

His friends considered Ritchie a trifle odd, but harmless. He was invariably polite when he was pulling his buggy, they pointed out in his defense. When he'd meet another horse on the street he'd always whinny, friendly-like.

Escanaba took some pride in having a lumberjack who thought he was a horse. Residents considered him in the same class as Popcorn Charlie, who introduced popcorn vending to the community about 1870. The lumberjacks were careful not to stand too close when they kidded Ritchie—he was apt to kick. But Charlie was a five-footer and fair game.

"Hey, Popcorn, you ought to sue the city. They built the sidewalk too close to your ass."

Such remarks and even more personal ones passed for wit around Escanaba then, but such language would not have pleased Mrs. Kidd if she'd overheard. She lived next door to the jail, where many of the 'jacks wound up before the weekend was over. She cooked for the prisoners in her home kitchen, regarding the job as a challenge and an opportunity.

"I can out-bake, out-broil and out-fry any man in any lumber camp in Michigan," she bragged.

Many a lumberjack with a hangover could swear she told the simple truth. But there was one drawback to Mrs. Kidd's cooking. A visitor got a chance to enjoy it for only one day, and usually a day when his appetite was not of the best. The next morning, it was off to the justice of the peace, who would inquire about the state of the prisoner's finances and tailor his fine accordingly. Relieved of the last of his pay, the lumberjack was of no further use and the justice would tell him, "Go back to the woods."

As a general rule, the lumberjacks paid little attention to anything that was happening outside the pineries. But when Chicago presented its Columbian Exposition of 1893, word of what was going on there prompted lively discussions around the camps' deacon seats. Some men vowed to hang onto their pay long enough to finance a trip to see Little Egypt, but others scoffed at this ambition.

"Hell's fire, boys, I can see things like that in Saginaw or Hurley. But I'll tell you what I would like to see at the World's Fair. I'd like to see that load of logs they got there."

The fair's promoters had asked lumbermen to provide an exhibit of loggers' skills and the Nestor Estate Logging Company, cutting pine near the Ontonagon River in northern Michigan, agreed to furnish the timber if its crew would do the cutting and stacking on a Sunday, so there'd be no interference with the regular six-day work week.

The challenge was to send to Chicago the biggest load of logs ever hauled on a single sleigh. The Michigan crew, recognizing that every lumberjack in the woods would be judging their efforts, did itself proud.

Before that Sunday was over, they had loaded enough eighteen-foot pine logs on a sled to make a pile eighteen feet tall and totaling more than thirty-six thousand board feet. It was February. The iced road was in prime condition. Two horses were able to haul this record-sized burden to the shipping point. Then it required nine railroad flat cars to transport the sleigh and logs to Chicago.

Paul Bunyan and his blue ox might have done better. But thirty-six thousand board feet of pine on a single sled was impressive enough to make the city folks marvel, and to give the lumberjacks a chance to do some bragging in the saloons.

CHAPTER XIV

Michigan's Glory Days

FROM THE 1870s to the 1890s, when Wisconsin moved ahead, Michigan led all other states in lumber production. In the last half of the nineteenth century, the value of its pineries' output surpassed by a billion dollars the gold panned or mined on the West Coast during the sixty years after the rush for California riches that began in 1849.

The Titabawassee River Boom Company, which operated at the confluence of that stream with the Saginaw River, sorted over ten billion board feet of timber in the thirty years ending in 1894. And the logs that floated down the eight hundred and sixty-four miles of tributaries to the Saginaw were only a portion of those that were converted into boards in the Michigan lumber towns.

The Saginaw's peak year was 1882. By then, some of the sawmill operators had boardinghouses and barracks for their men, along with stores and repair shops. Wellington Burt's mill near Zilwaukee, Michigan, even had a schoolhouse and a library, but other lumbermen preferred to have the taxpayers finance such frills.

Once the logs were cut and the boards seasoned at the mills and lumberyards of Saginaw and Bay City, the lumber was loaded on "hookers," the name for any of several varieties of shallow-draft lake ships. These schooners, steamers and barges, many of them owned by the lumber companies, delivered the boards to eastern markets by means of the Great Lakes or carried them to Chicago for shipment west. A statistician with time on his hands figured out that during a single month 2,679 vessels of various kinds passed beneath the Third Street Bridge in Bay City.

Something like one hundred fifteen million trees were cut in the Saginaw watershed between 1851 and 1897. They produced nearly twenty-three billion board feet of lumber, not counting more than five billion shingles and other lesser products.

Except for its Upper Peninsula, Michigan's pine was pretty well gone by the early 1880s. Lesser trees were harvested to keep the mills busy and Saginaw's three hundred six saloons prosperous. Toward the end, some mills imported logs all the way from Georgian Bay in Canada, nearly two hundred forty miles away as a hooker sailed. When Ontario ruled in 1898 that all logs cut on Crown lands must be processed in Canada, such international log rafting came to an end overnight. Most of the remaining mills along the Saginaw whined to a stop. By then, loggers and lumbermen who had become rich in the vicinity had generally moved on to northern Michigan, Wisconsin, Minnesota or the Pacific Northwest. So had many of the men who worked for them.

Toward the end of the Saginaw region's heyday, when it was furnishing more than a third of the pine being harvested in the Lake States, there was increased attention to reducing waste. The pines were disappearing at an alarming rate, and a number of mill owners dipped into their profits to replace circular saws with band saws. The former converted one board in each four to sawdust. The band saws, with a narrower kerf, wasted only one board in eight. Farther west, where logs were still plentiful, the old methods continued. Band saws were not common in Minnesota before the 1890s.

During the period when the Shiawassee, Cass, Flint and Titibawassee rivers carried vast quantities of pine to the Saginaw River each spring, there were eight hundred camps and something like twenty-five thousand loggers at work in the woods in that wilderness region. Night and day, the lake ships and rafts moved down the river, traveling in a scum of sawdust that floated far out into Saginaw Bay.

The Saginaw Valley had been first to feel the Michigan lumber boom, and it was the first to recognize its decline. As the pine began to play out, the industry moved north along the shore of

Lake Huron. By 1889 it had passed the AuSable and Black rivers and had made a new, if smaller, Saginaw of the little hamlet of Alpena on Thunder Bay River. The white sails of the lumber fleet began dotting Thunder Bay.

Alpena's moment in the spotlight was relatively brief, but for a time the Thunder Bay River was solid with pine logs from Alpena to the Long Rapids Bridge, and such characters as the Roaring Lion of Thunder Bay stalked the streets, forcing lesser men to give him room. The Lion's real name was Paulette Cicero. It is not clear whether being named Paulette forced him to develop his muscles as a lad, but by the time he was grown he was strong enough to lift an ox from the ground. Cicero was gentle enough when sober. Full of squirrel whiskey, he was a good man to avoid.

Cheboygan was another Michigan town that had its turn as a lumber center. It reached its peak in 1890, when eight large mills cut lumber to load aboard lake ships. For years after those days were nearly forgotten, a twelve-acre hill of sawdust near the city's State Street Bridge remained for tourists to gawk at.

Michigan's Lake Huron lumber towns were chiefly responsible for the fact that in 1890 Buffalo, New York, had one hundred thirty-two lumber dealers and sawmills, while another New York community, Tonawanda, was the greatest lumber-receiving port in the world.

Other Michigan towns marketed their lumber by way of Lake Michigan, sharing in the state's lumber boom. Escanaba, for instance, where lumberjacks mingled with miners and railway workers, attracted the attention of such lumber barons as Bill Bonifas.

Bonifas was not a baron when he arrived in the area. In fact, this immigrant from Luxembourg had hardly a dime in his jeans. But he had a strong back and a shrewd eye for the main chance. He got a job cutting cedar railroad ties in a swamp, carrying them out on his shoulders for a few pennies apiece. Still, the more ties he cut and carried, the more money he made. Bill was a worker. He saved enough cash to buy a horse, making the job go faster. Then he saved more money and brought his brothers and sisters from home to help him. The time came when he had enough capital to start a small lumber camp. The sisters cooked, the brothers chopped, and Bill worked harder than anybody. The small camp became a big one. Bonifas bought wisely in the competition for prime timberland. He got rich. But those who knew his background were generally willing to admit that he'd earned it.

Muskegon, Menominee, Manistee and Manistique were other Michigan towns that sent pine boards to Chicago, making it for a time the largest center of lumber wholesaling. Some Michigan pine stayed nearer home, serving as the raw material for the world's largest furniture factories in Grand Rapids, the manufacture of railway cars in Saginaw, wagon making in Pontiac, shipbuilding in Bay City, Port Huron and Grand Haven.

The need to get pine logs and lumber from one place to another encouraged the building of Michigan's railroads, including lines that penetrated the Upper Peninsula. With lumber companies no longer entirely dependent on access to water and with some camps operating the year round, the next logical step was taken in 1876.

A Michigan lumberman named Scott Gerish visited the Centennial Exposition in Philadelphia and saw a narrow-gauge locomotive on display. The engine and cars were light and cheap. Gerish decided that by laying temporary tracks to a stand of pine he owned in Clare County he could snake his logs out to the Muskegon River by rail.

The following winter was so mild that there was too little snow or ice for traditional logging methods. A number of the smaller companies went broke. But Gerish got his logs out on his narrow-gauge tracks, prospering to the point where other loggers were impressed. Within six years, there were forty-nine of the pint-sized railroads in Michigan, opening up regions that had been too far from streams to be worth cutting.

R. G. Peters of Manistee devised another method of moving timber. He cut off the tops of tall trees and ran taut cables between them, with skidding tongs attached to wheels that dangled underneath. With this contraption, a log could be carried through the air to where it was supposed to go. The device never really caught on in the Lake States, but when lumbering moved to the Pacific Northwest, variations of Peters' invention were widely used.

With better methods of getting logs to market and faster means of slicing them into boards, the destruction of the forests became swifter. As daylight penetrated more and more swamps, the swamps dried up. Massive efforts to encourage settlers to farm the cutover were undertaken. Some railroads sent agents to Europe to encourage immigration, seeking to sell acreage in the lines' huge land grants and encouraging farming so freight trains would have grain to carry to market.

In the days when Michigan lumber was cheap and plentiful, carriage building had become a specialty in places like Detroit and Flint. The requirements of sawmill operators had encouraged the rise of machine shops and foundries. When the automobile industry took its first hesitant steps, such facilities proved useful. And so, in some measure, Michigan's prominence in building horseless carriages followed naturally from its lumbering days. Some of the men who got rich in pine put their money to use in the highly speculative automotive field at a time when building cars seemed like a long-shot gamble.

Michigan's Upper Peninsula was opened to large-scale lumbering after much of the pine had been cut in the rest of the state. Along the Ontonagon River, for example, significant logging operations did not begin until 1881, the year when H. H. Rich and other Chicagoans organized the Ontonagon Lumber Company. The firm bought thirteen thousand acres of pinery, built a sawmill and began to ship two hundred thousand feet of lumber a day to Chicago. A larger mill was built nearby the following year by a Grand Rapids outfit, Sisson & Lilley. Then, in 1883, the Diamond Match Company began to buy up most of the holdings in the vicinity. By 1890, there were two match-making mills in Ontonagon, capable of using two million board feet of lumber per day.

Six years later, the match company mills burned and the town of Ontonagon was wiped out by fire. There were still millions of feet of logs in the vicinity, but for all practical purposes the pine episode there had ended. The lumberjacks who had harvested the crop for the absentee owners left.

Among the men who departed were five members of a camp crew on the Nett River. They hiked to Ontonagon to collect their pay, then stopped in a saloon to while away the time until they could catch a train out of town. One drink led to another. By the time they headed for the depot, the train had gone. This was a Saturday night and the next train would not arrive until Monday.

They decided to walk to Amasa, eighteen miles away. Amasa also had a saloon. After spending considerable time there, the five headed down the tracks toward Channing. It had been a long and tiring weekend. Somewhere between Amasa and Channing, the lumberjacks decided to take a nap, resting their heads on the rails. They were confident that no train would come along—they'd been hunting for one for nearly two days. And if it did come, surely they would hear it in plenty of time. But they didn't. A freight killed them all.

When the Upper Michigan lumber boom began, more than 80 per cent of the peninsula was covered with timber, much of it white pine. Within fifteen years, most of the trees worth cutting were gone. The rapidity of the tall timber's disappearance was a reflection of the more efficient logging methods being used. It came as a shock to those who depended on the pine for a living.

Even the least foresighted were beginning to realize that the claim by a lumber spokesman that "the supply of pine seems to be practically illimitable" was inaccurate. Equally wrong was his prediction that "the present generation of lumbermen will bequeath to their successors a long battle with the tall, strong trees that bear such a splendid harvest of dollars."

Millions of these dollars had been harvested. But the legacy for another generation of lumberjacks was rapidly running dry in Michigan.

CHAPTER XV

Big Business Takes Control

BY THE TIME Wisconsin wrested the lead in lumber production from Michigan around 1890, nearly one hundred twelve thousand men were employed in the three Lake States in cutting trees or sawing them up. Also living off the profits from the pineries were thousands of others—saloonkeepers, machinery manufacturers, prostitutes, lobbyists, farmers who supplied food for logging camps and lumber towns, land speculators, even such specialists as the glassmakers who sold replacements for windows kicked out on a Saturday night.

Many camps were large now and better organized. A cook might have a whole crew of assistants to help turn out food on a wood-fired range. Such luxuries as canned milk, fruit, fresh meat and vegetables were becoming routine in the better camps. Improvements had also been made in the equipment, right down to the tin horn used to call the men to supper. Some of these horns were as much as eight feet long and could frighten a bull moose a half mile away.

Fred Maynard, the cook at a Michigan camp, went his rivals one better by fitting the mouthpiece of a bugle into his dinner horn or "gaberel," as a patriotic gesture shortly after the war with Spain began. The first evening, when he sounded mess call, it sounded so military that the rumor spread that the Spanish fleet had landed men on the shores of Lake Huron. Some of the lumberjacks hid out, missing dinner. They weren't prepared to tackle the invading army with their axes without giving the matter some careful thought.

The efforts by railroads and others to sell cutover lands in the pinery to Europeans and city folks was well underway. The J. L. Gates Lumber Company, financed by Milwaukee's Pfister family, for example, sent agents to Chicago, New York and elsewhere to encourage urban dwellers to farm the cutover. The European agent of the Wisconsin Central Railroad persuaded five thousand Germans to settle near the railway's right-of-way between Stevens Point and Ashland. Most of these new settlers were from forested regions in Bavaria and many took jobs in the woods to raise a stake. They were generally either family men or planned to be. They violated established custom by hanging onto their pay or investing it in land, instead of blowing it on a few days of high living at the end of the season.

At some camps, the pay was directly related to the amount of work done. It was found that men with families would often turn out more logs than the carefree bachelor types. Albert Heidemann, who worked in Michigan and Wisconsin before heading west to cut more trees, bragged of a day when he and his brother sawed two hundred logs between daylight and dark. They were paid twenty cents per log, giving them the astonishing total of twenty dollars apiece for a day's work.

"The counter checked it twice," Heidemann said. "He didn't believe it either."

Albert worked seven days a week and as long as there was daylight, for he had a family to support. It kept growing. After one especially busy winter, he arrived home to find he was the father of a two-month-old baby he hadn't known for certain was on its way.

Some immigrants had come to America to raise money so they could send for their families. Not all succeeded. Louie Blanchard told of a Norwegian who drowned on a log drive on the Clam River. He had been saving his pay so his wife and children could join him. That death stood out in Blanchard's memory because it was the only one he recalled where there was a formal funeral along the river. A coffin was made out of split logs, and a preacher was brought from Grantsburg, Wisconsin. After the sermon, the Scandinavian was buried beneath a large Norway pine, which seemed appropriate. A collection was taken and sent to his family.

The work crews might be taking on an even more international air than in the old days, but the Easterners were still making most of the money. In 1898, someone compiled a list of the fourteen leading lumbermen along the Chippewa River. Three were from Maine, five from New York, two from Massachusetts, another from Pennsylvania. There was one Canadian on the list, but the only European immigrant was Frederick Weyerhaeuser.

His holdings and influence surpassed all the others. By now, he had put together combinations of mill owners at Chippewa Falls, Eau Claire, Menomonie and La Crosse in Wisconsin, Winona in Minnesota and various other river towns on the upper Mississippi. He was the leading spirit in the burgeoning operations of the Mississippi River Logging Company and the Chippewa Logging Company.

Whenever another lumberman found himself in financial difficulties, he was likely to sell out to the Weyerhaeuser group. For example, the Union Lumber Company, which had one of the largest sawmills in the world on the Chippewa and was considered a million-dollar operation, ran into trouble when its ready supply of cheap lumber ran out. Unlike the more successful companies, it had failed to buy up pinery land at a dollar and a quarter an acre. By the 1880s, some such property was selling for as much as forty-five dollars an acre. In 1881, Union sold out to the Weyerhaeuser interests.

On the Red Cedar, a Chippewa tributary, the firm of Knapp, Stout & Company stayed independent and forced other loggers on that stream to sell to its big mill in Menomonie. Small operators found it too costly to separate their logs from those marked with the Knapp, Stout brand, so they sold their pine to the company for as much as seventy-five cents less per thousand board feet, compared to prices for similar timber elsewhere.

By 1877, Knapp, Stout had twelve hundred employees. Within five years, it had more than doubled this impressive total. It kept thirty thousand acres of crop and pastureland to provide food for men and horses. As a six-million-dollar operation, it was surpassed in the vicinity only by the Weyerhaeuser holding companies, which bought logs cut by members of the combine and otherwise brought order out of what had been chaotic competition in the Chippewa Valley.

The Weyerhaeuser group spent more than five million dollars between 1881 and 1887 acquiring rival sawmills. By the end of that time, it owned more pine land and controlled more sawmill capacity than anyone else in the Lake States. It reportedly offered Knapp, Stout seven and a half million dollars to sell out, but was turned down.

As early as 1872, when Weyerhaeuser was elected president of the Mississippi River Logging Company, that firm was the principal financial power on the upper portion of the Mississippi. Four years later, it bought fifty thousand acres of Cornell University timberland. By the 1890s it owned such a large portion of the pinery region of western Wisconsin and eastern Minnesota that it could pretty well call the tune.

In 1879 the Chippewa River lumbermen who had been fighting Weyerhaeuser called a truce. The two groups pooled their resources, with the Mississippi River group getting 65 per cent of the profits. At first, the Chippewa logs were sorted in Beef Slough. When a sandbar built up there, the operations were moved to the Minnesota bank of the Mississippi at West Newton.

A federally owned dam was in the way, so the company blew it up. The Wisconsin Legislature, which objected to having Chippewa logs processed in Minnesota, protested this highhandedness to Congress. But Washington did not choose to tackle the Weyerhaeuser combine, and the Army Corps of Engineers ignored the loss of its dam.

By controlling the Chippewa, along with the upper Mississippi and the St. Croix, the combine was in a good position to set prices and to prosper. Before the cutting began, the Chippewa Valley held one sixth of all the white pine west of the Appalachians. In 1883 it turned out lumber at an annual rate of a billion board feet. Trees cut along the river provided raw material for houses as far away as Colorado and Texas.

In some towns there were attempts to organize unions of sawmill workers. Employers made a few gestures toward better working conditions. But in general, the pattern remained the same as before, with the working stiff at the mercy of the boss.

Sawmill accidents were common, ranging from amputated

fingers to the sudden bloody horror of death under a spinning circular saw. In 1885, for instance, the Menominee River Hospital at Marinette treated thirty-five serious mill-accident cases, and the Ashland hospital had twenty-one.

If an employee was injured, the law provided that his employer was liable for damages—but only if the claimant could prove the accident had not been the result of his own carelessness or that of a "fellow servant." This provision offered a wide loophole for the company. Most men who got hurt accepted a token settlement instead of going to court. Now and then, however, a stubborn employee persisted and might collect heavy damages. Some mills finally took out liability insurance against such injury claims, one owner grumbling that he was "somewhat weary of having our employees look to us in case of accident." It had been better in the old days, when if a man had a leg sawed off it was assumed to be his own tough luck. Despite the occasional payment to an injured man, sawmills lagged behind in taking safety measures. It was not until state inspectors forced installation of such an elemental precaution as safety guards on circular saws that most of the mills acquired them.

The pay in the woods and the mills remained nearly as low as it had been twenty years before. In 1897 the average annual wage in the Wisconsin lumber industry was $386—and that included foremen as well as cookees. Common workers got as little as $15 a month, with skilled employees earning $30 to $50.

Lumberjacks were often paid off in due bills, which could be traded for cash only after the logs were sold. The company store would accept these due bills for tobacco, mackinaws and other merchandise. But a workman who wanted to buy a round at the saloon had to exchange them for real money, generally at a 10 per cent discount. At some camps the men had to sign an agreement to buy only at the wanigan. Some of these company stores charged considerably more than private merchants.

A workman who was considered a troublemaker could be blacklisted and driven out of the industry. Sixty men who struck a La Crosse mill in 1873, seeking a ten-hour day, suffered this penalty. Disgruntled workers sometimes fought back by driving a large spike into a log. When the log was run through the mill, the spike could wreck an expensive saw and, incidentally, endanger anyone in the vicinity. At the request of mill owners, a bill was introduced in the Wisconsin Legislature making spiking a log a crime punishable by five years in prison.

Logging and lumber companies also ran into trouble from shipping interests. In 1868 the Wisconsin Supreme Court ruled that any stream capable of floating a log was a public highway and must be kept open for navigation. Nine years later, the U. S. Department of Justice filed a complaint that the Beef Slough boom operators had obstructed the Chippewa River, driving logs in such numbers that steamboats, ferries and lumber rafts were kept from using it. But a federal court ruled that the state had jurisdiction and the state court refused to act. The lumber industry had more clout in state capitals than the riverboat operators. Besides, as the years went by, the lumbermen owned most of the ships.

Congress got around to passing a law in 1899 forbidding the floating of loose logs where they would obstruct navigation. Lumber lobbyists had a word with the politicians. The following year, the bill was amended to exempt any stream where the floating of loose logs and rafts was the principal form of traffic.

Such problems with legislation were the concern of the owners, not the lumberjacks. Their responsibility was to get the trees cut and the logs to the mill, just as it had been in the white pine era's early days when operations were smaller. Tote roads had to be built, camps supplied and the maximum profit made for the owners in the shortest possible time. Once an area had been opened up to logging, the pines disappeared at an amazing rate, including such giants as one cut by a crew of the Yakey-Alexander Lumber Company near Schofield, Wisconsin. It measured more than sixteen feet around at the base. That tree was unusual enough, so a lumberjack counted its rings. It had been a seedling in 1511, just nineteen years after Christopher Columbus discovered there was a considerable body of land in the way of a westward voyage from Spain to the Indies.

The rapidity of the pine harvest can be illustrated by what happened around the Upper Namekagon River region in northwestern Wisconsin. Some small-scale logging was done there before the Civil War, but the cutting did not begin in earnest until the winter of 1882–83, when A. J. Hayward and R. L. McCormick built a sawmill in a jackpine flat that became the roaring lumber town of Hayward.

A railroad had been built in the river valley, making it possible to send boards and logs to market. Within a year, Hayward's population went from zero to one thousand, with three hundred men working in the sawmill and several hundred others spending part of each year in camps near such places as Phipps, Cable and Mosquito Brook. Winter logging roads were built through the woods, with sleds hauled over iced ruts to the creeks and rivers. Some of the logs were driven past the local sawmills to seek a better price, eventually floating as far as St. Louis.

Eldon Marple, who worked in lumber camps as a lad and later spent many hours studying the history of logging around Hayward, noted that the men who harvested pine had to be resourceful innovators, ready to "fit their operations to the conditions they found on the job they had to do. If a dam was needed to float their logs to market, it was built from materials at hand. A railroad or a tote road miles back into the hills was no more of a problem."

And so, when John O'Brien contracted with the North Wisconsin Lumber Company to deliver logs from the flats west of Round Lake to the mill at Hayward, it was up to him to figure out what to do about a steep hill that lay between. A rude highway, the Spider Lake Road, had been completed to the top of the hill from Hayward, so O'Brien and his men hauled the logs to a storage yard there and waited for the heavy snows to come so the timber could be taken down the precipitous slope toward the mill. O'Brien decided, on the basis of long experience in Minnesota's Stillwater country, that the usual methods wouldn't do.

Ordinarily, when logs had to be taken down a hill, a second pair of horses, the "pole team," was hitched to the back of the load, pulling back so the sled and its cargo wouldn't run over the team ahead of the sleigh. On particularly bad grades, a teamster fastened loops of chain around the sled runners. Sand and hay were routinely thrown on the iced roadway to slow the descent.

But even with all these traditional methods, the hill on Spider Lake Road proved a killer. After several bad accidents, with men and horses dead and logs scattered, O'Brien decided he had better try something else. He discussed the matter with his foreman,

Louis Mishler, who suggested that the sleds be sent down without the horses.

So far as O'Brien knew, that had never been tried. But he said, "Go ahead." When the next sled was loaded, Mishler ordered the team unhitched at the top of the hill. The pole was tied up off the ground. The grade was sanded heavily by the road monkey. Hay was sprinkled on the ice. Then the heavily loaded sleigh was shoved over the brink to find its own way down the hill.

The method was an improvement in one respect—nobody got killed. But the sleds tended to go too fast and to tip over. So Mishler got a volunteer who rode atop the load and threw hay under the runners when the sled picked up too much speed. It was a dangerous job. But with luck, the sled, its load and its rider all reached the bottom of what was now called O'Brien's Hill in one piece.

Among the owners of the Hayward sawmill was a family named Laird. A younger son worked for O'Brien under an assumed name, trying to prove himself without taking advantage of his family connections. Young Laird frequently rode the sleds, throwing hay as he went and trying to keep from falling off.

O'Brien had a daughter, Nellie. One afternoon, she decided to drive her sleigh up the hill to visit her father. As she was partway up, a loaded sled started down. The snow was banked high on either side of the narrow road. There was no place to turn off.

Laird was riding atop the careening logging sled. He saw the girl. Clambering swiftly down from the top of the load, he unfastened the pole and dropped it. The heavy timber splintered, scattering the logs, wrecking the sled and sending the young man flying. But he survived and Nellie was saved. Laird, who was now a hero around Hayward, revealed his identity as a prince of a sawmill empire. Before long, he and John O'Brien's daughter were married. No doubt they lived as happily ever after as is considered proper outside of a bedtime story.

The fate of the white pine forest in the vicinity of Hayward was not as happy. Within fifteen years after the community was founded, most of the big trees were gone.

CHAPTER XVI

West to Minnesota

BEFORE LOGGING BEGAN there, Minnesota's forests were estimated to be 10 per cent larger than those in Michigan and 30 per cent more extensive than Wisconsin's. But Michigan pine grew thicker and Wisconsin pine was more accessible. It was not until the 1880s that the lumber barons focused their full attention on the westernmost of the three states.

By then, white pine was getting scarce in Michigan, except for its Upper Peninsula. Lumber production was still rising in Wisconsin, but it was becoming obvious that the pineries there would not last forever, after all. The loggers needed new stands of virgin trees to supply a demand that continued to grow as the nation pushed west. Plains settlers in their sod houses wanted boards and had finally raised enough wheat to pay for them. The need for housing also expanded in the cities. In 1882 alone, three quarters of a million immigrants arrived from Europe.

To meet an unprecedented demand for pine, the annual cut in the three states rose year by year—3.5 billion board feet in 1877, 5.6 billion in 1880, 7.5 billion in 1882. Minnesota's portion of the Mississippi Valley produced nearly one seventh of this astonishing output. Between 1880 and 1890, the number of Minnesotans in the logging and lumbering industries rose from 2,854 to 16,170.

As the Michigan trees grew scarcer, some of those who had made fortunes there from lumbering skipped Wisconsin entirely and headed straight for Minnesota. Among Michiganders turned Minnesotans was a Vermonter, H. C. Akeley, who had left New England to become rich in Grand Haven and Muskegon. Now he established a sawmill at Minneapolis and sent crews to the Itasca region to supply it with logs.

"H.C. don't say nothing," an admirer noted, "but he saws wood."

The Cross Lake Logging Company—for a time, the largest pine-cutting outfit in Minnesota—was owned in part by Arthur Hill, who had made his money in Saginaw. Another big operation, the Swan River Logging Company, belonged to Michigan men named Wright and Davis, who had bought large sections of pinery between Hibbing, Minnesota, and the Mississippi.

Other transplanted barons from Michigan helped turn the area around the small lumber settlement of St. Anthony Falls into a city called Minneapolis. The St. Paul & Pacific reached that community in 1862, before other centers had the advantage of being able to ship lumber by train. Soon what became the Twin Cities of Minneapolis and St. Paul were outdistancing their rivals on the strength of their strategic location as railway centers. Long freights carried lumber west and brought back wheat.

By the time St. Anthony Falls was absorbed into the eastern limits of Minneapolis in 1872, sawmills and lumber piles stretched almost solidly along a two-and-a-half mile portion of the Mississippi. In the 1880s, a decade when its population rose from 46,-887 to 164,738, Minneapolis became not only the nation's leading lumber center but the world's primary wheat market and America's chief flour producer. Its growth and prosperity were based on an original foundation of white pine trees.

The Nicollett Hotel became the principal hangout for the state's lumbermen, and a logger who needed a job could usually find one in Minneapolis. Al Powers was rounding up a crew to drive logs on a tributary of the Prairie River when a stranger asked for work. Powers looked him up and down. He was clean, well-dressed and gentlemanly, so Al was naturally suspicious.

"You sure as hell don't look like a river pig. You ever driven before?"

"Mr. Powers, you ever hear tell of Christ walking on the waters?"

"Yes."

"Well, I was right behind him. On a log."

The fellow might not look like a river pig, but he surely could brag like one. That was good enough for Al Powers, who hired him at once.

Minneapolis' role as a sawmill center began to decline after 1876, when mill owners were notified that their leases to use power at the river dams would not be renewed. The sawmills gradually moved to upstream points, closer to the source of logs, and within ten years only one was left at St. Anthony Falls. But Minneapolis continued to be a major marketing center for lumber.

In that city's early days as a lumber town, its leading rival was Stillwater. A high percentage of the lumberjacks sending pine down to Stillwater's mills by way of the St. Croix were French-Canadians. For some reason, they preferred to do their drinking in the saloons at the small community of Somerset.

Located across the Wisconsin border, Somerset took pride in its sinful ways. It offended visitors from Hayward and Hurley, as well as lovers of alliteration, by claiming that the number of toughest places in the universe had grown to four—Hayward, Hurley, Hell and Somerset.

In most logging communities, an old-timer recalled fondly, you had to insult a man to make him fight.

"But in Somerset, just say 'bonjour, mon vieux,' which means 'hello, old pal,' and you were in the most beautiful scrap this side of the Revolutionary War."

The whiskey served at Somerset saloons was said to be so powerful a man could get drunk two miles away just thinking about it. But drinking was not the only sport for the Canadian Frenchmen on a spree. Bending hitching posts was another. So was heaving a friend through a plate-glass window.

Even the clergy had to be tough in Somerset, or at least athletic. According to local legend, a missionary priest who failed to attract a single lumberjack to his services finally issued a challenge. He would take on the best axeman in town in a contest to see who could chop through a log first.

"If he beats me, you don't go to church. If I beat him, you go to church."

The woods dwellers were used to life being one competition

after another, and a contest for a chance to save their immortal souls seemed like an interesting sporting event. The missionary won. The lumberjacks kept their part of the bargain, although some claimed the good father had cheated. Before he started chopping, he'd said a prayer, giving him an unfair advantage. And the Lord had listened. The part of the log where the priestly one used his axe turned out to be hollow.

Another center of the Minnesota lumber trade was St. Cloud, located near the dividing line between prairie and pinery. Its lumber sold in the Dakotas and as far away as Winnipeg.

As had happened earlier in Wisconsin and Michigan, the lumber and logging booms in Minnesota encouraged the rise of factories specializing in wooden products ranging from carriages and furniture to barrels and boats. Such places as Winona and Stillwater kept a considerable share of their sawmills' product at home to turn into finished goods.

This was a period of rampant boosterism, with every little burg hoping to become a big one and each little city claiming pre-eminence in one field or another. Crookston, a community that specialized in wheat as well as lumber, claimed to be "The Queen City of the Red River Valley." Duluth called itself "The Zenith City of the Unsalted Seas," although it's unlikely that many lumberjacks who converged on it for weekend recreation thought of it in quite that way.

Construction of the Watab Branch of the St. Paul & Pacific was a boon to business at Anoka, a place that for a time claimed to be northern Minnesota's largest lumber town. Located at the junction of the Rum and Mississippi rivers, Anoka sent most of its lumber west to the Dakotas rather than to the traditional markets in the East or South.

Duluth's role as a lumbering center began in earnest in 1870, when completion of the Lake Superior & Mississippi Railroad from St. Paul gave it easy access to the Twin Cities. The rails went through the St. Croix Valley, encouraging construction of sawmills at such places as Pine City, North Branch and Hinckley. It was in Hinckley, incidentally, where Minnesota lumberjacks later beat the record load of logs sent to the Columbian Exposition by piling 36,600 board feet on a sled, creating a stack of pine that was twenty-six feet high, twenty-one feet wide and eighteen feet long.

As a gateway to Minnesota's Arrowhead country, Duluth had major advantages in the competition to surpass its rival towns, but its early history was one of wide swings from optimism to gloom. It began with a period of rapid growth, then ran into a combination of hard times and a scarlet fever epidemic that killed some residents and prompted others to pack up and leave. By the end of the Civil War, Duluth had declined to only two occupied houses, according to one authority.

Then the city's luck swung back. Gold was discovered nearby, at Lake Vermillion. Prospectors converged on Duluth and soon it was booming again. E. H. Eames, the state geologist, was among those who jumped to the conclusion that Minnesota would become a new California. A few years earlier, he and his brother Richard had found iron ore as much as sixty feet thick near the mouth of a stream called Two Rivers in the Vermillion Range. Some of those in Eames's party suggested that the iron ore might have some value. The geologist cut them short.

"To hell with iron," he said. "It's gold we're after."

Christian Wieland, a civil engineer who accompanied the Eames brothers on the 1865 expedition, disagreed. He took samples of the iron ore to Ontonagon, Michigan, where he found financial backing. He built a road from Beaver Bay to the future site of a St. Louis County community named Babbitt and began to haul in supplies to open an iron mine. But his Michigan backer died, the funds dried up and the project was abandoned.

Another Ontonagon resident, Peter Mitchell, also understood there was money to be made in iron ore. Several years later, he began explorations of Wieland's discovery and forwarded ore samples to a Philadelphia financier, Charlemagne Tower. The result was that in 1882 the Minnesota Iron Mining Company was organized. Two years later, the first shipment of iron ore from the region was made from a mine near a community named Tower.

For the remainder of the nineteenth century and into the twentieth, lumbering and mining became the twin industries of portions of the north country. With both fields expanding at once, such communities as Virginia, Minnesota, grew into flourishing towns almost overnight.

That village, which soon called itself "The Queen City of the Range," got its start in 1892 when ore was discovered there. It was named for the home state of Alfred Humphrey, president of the Virginia Improvement Company that laid out the town and sold the first lots at auction in Duluth. Small business sites went for four hundred dollars to merchants who had never seen that portion of the Mesabi Range. Log and rough board buildings were thrown together. Lumbermen, lumberjacks, landlookers, speculators and businessmen converged on the place, along with the usual quota of gamblers, saloonkeepers and madams.

A preacher showed up, too. The Reverend E. N. Raymond announced he was ready to hold Presbyterian services. Hardly anyone showed up. The minister decided that if the sinners wouldn't seek him out, he'd go looking for them. He found his full quota among players and onlookers at a high-stakes poker game. Raymond spent the rest of Sunday watching the card players. Toward evening, he made a suggestion.

"Men, I've watched your play all day. Now I think it's fair that you come along and watch mine."

The winners were willing and the losers were persuaded. Eighty poker players and kibitzers attended the evening service. As one man who had lost heavily pointed out, listening to the preacher could do no harm and it might be just the thing he needed to change his luck.

After a spur line of the Duluth, Missabe and Northern Railroad reached Virginia in 1893, the population rose from 181 to 5,000. Late that year, the new city was practically wiped out by a forest fire. This setback was followed by a slump in ore sales, along with a decline in lumber prices. Many residents left, but others stayed to rebuild the town. It burned a second time when a fire in the Finlayson Mill got out of control. When the buildings were replaced a second time, Virginia made sure its principal structures were not made of wood.

The Missabe Mountain Mine of the Mesabi Range, located at Virginia, was said to be the largest single iron mine in the world, but lumbering continued to hold its own in the vicinity. Such large sawmills as the one opened by the Rainy Lake Lumber Company made Virginia one of Minnesota's leading lumber centers during the early years of the twentieth century.

Development of the Mesabi Range might have begun twenty years earlier if such early prospectors as E. H. Eames had not believed that only gold was worth digging. The gold fever of the 1860s had hardly died around its principal center, Duluth, when railroad fever arrived to take its place.

The principal carrier of this ailment was Jay Cooke, an Ohioan who had become a Philadelphia banker and made a national reputation by selling the astonishing total of one billion dollars' worth of federal securities to support the Union government during the Civil War.

Cooke was a principal mover in plans to connect the Great Lakes with the Pacific by running the Northern Pacific Railway from Duluth to Tacoma, Washington. Cooke undertook to finance the road by selling bonds. But investors had been stung so often in buying expensive pieces of paper from railroads that they had developed a healthy dose of skepticism. The bonds not only failed to sell in sufficient quantity but Jay Cooke & Company went bankrupt, a principal cause of the Panic of 1873.

Cooke's railway empire collapsed. So did Duluth. Its population declined from 5,000 to 1,300 within a few months. But both Cooke and the city on Lake Superior recovered. By 1880 the financier had made himself another fortune in silver mines and Duluth was well on the way to prosperity, thanks to increased activity in the nearby pineries.

Duluth and Superior, just across St. Louis Bay in Wisconsin, served as supply centers for loggers. A single firm, Alger-Smith Company, bought $250,000 worth of groceries there annually, for instance. Smaller logging operations also needed food, tools and other supplies. These sometimes included whiskey, which led to complications, occasionally fatal ones.

Bob Starr and two friends were in St. Louis County on a small logging job one winter when they got thirsty. Duluth was temptingly close, but they couldn't afford to take time away from work. They hired an Indian to carry a message to a druggist: "Send us a gallon of good alcohol." But the merchant misunderstood. The mistake was discovered when the bodies of Starr and his companions were found near a half-emptied jug that had held *wood* alcohol, not *good* alcohol.

Sawmills went up rapidly around Duluth in the 1880s, sawing pine from northwestern Wisconsin as well as Minnesota. The logs arrived by way of the St. Louis River or were towed along the shoreline from other streams that flow into Lake Superior.

Between 1880 and 1883, eleven sawmills were built in Duluth and Superior, marketing their output mostly in the Dakotas by way of the Northern Pacific. But the most active period of Duluth lumbering did not arrive until the 1890s, after the demand for boards slackened to the west. The slack was taken up by such markets as Tonawanda, New York, at the eastern end of Lake Erie. More than seven hundred million board feet of lumber passed through the canal at Sault Ste. Marie from Lake Superior ports in 1894, and the Duluth region accounted for a large share.

Minnesota's Arrowhead country, the region north and east of Duluth and as far west as Bemidji, was later crisscrossed by logging railroads, but toward the end of the nineteenth century rafts towed by steam tugs were the usual method of getting timber from there to the sawmills.

It was Duluth's role as a supply center and shipping point as well as its flourishing sawmills which enabled it to snap back when Jay Cooke's plans for the Northern Pacific collapsed. Helping pick up the pieces dropped by the Philadelphia financier was a familiar figure, Frederick Weyerhaeuser. He and his associates bought the railroad's huge land grant in Minnesota, moving their headquarters to St. Paul. The German immigrant who had become the Rockefeller of lumbering built a handsome mansion on Summit Avenue. His next-door neighbor was James J. Hill, a Scotch-Irish Canadian who had become a leading railroad promoter and financier.

As might be expected, Weyerhaeuser was one of the first to recognize that lands where pine had been cut were still potentially profitable. After the C. N. Nelson Lumber Company had logged all the pine from one large tract in Minnesota, Weyerhaeuser paid one million dollars for the property. Lumberjacks assumed that old Frederick had flipped his lid at last. But the Weyerhaeuser combine made millions from logging what Nelson had left behind. Railways used tamarack for ties. Paper mills wanted spruce. Farmers on the treeless plains needed cedar fenceposts. The assumption that only white pine was worth cutting died hard, but it finally died.

By the turn of the century, Minnesota had an estimated twenty thousand men working in its forests, mostly in St. Louis, Itasca and Beltrami counties. Between 1880 and 1890, the state's output of lumber more than doubled, reaching more than one billion board feet a year. That was enough, a logger bragged, to build a board sidewalk nine feet wide around the earth at the equator.

The state's last boom town was Bemidji. Named for an Indian chief, it was located at the headwaters of the Mississippi. In 1895, tamarack still grew where its streets would be laid out. A few years later, it had fourteen mills cutting a million board feet of lumber a day and leaders of its lumber industry gathered to swap lies at the Remore Hotel, entering the building under crossed pike poles that marked its front door.

Bemidji's glory as a lumber capital lasted less than twenty years, but until the pine ran short it was a lively place. It had several hotels, forty-two saloons running night and day, and a theater, the Variety, that was pointed out proudly to visitors as the place where a man named Russ Whipple had been shot. The sporting houses were on a hill near the downtown section, opening for business each afternoon at five to catch the before-dinner trade.

One combination hotel and saloon was run by Spider Gagnon, known in the Arrowhead pinery as a man able to steal a man's wallet through a locked door. When a lumberjack went to his room, Gagnon warned him to lock up. If the man was too drunk to find the keyhole, Spider ceremoniously locked him in, then threw the key through the open transom. When the snoring began, he'd return with a fishpole, shove it through the transom, snag the guest's pants, take out most of the money, then carefully return the pants to the chair where the drunk had tossed them. When the lumberjack came roaring downstairs the next morning, complaining that he'd been robbed, Spider had an alibi.

"Robbed? Wasn't your door locked?"

"Yeah, but—"

"It still locked this morning?"

"Yeah. But when I hit the bunk last night I had forty or fifty bucks and now I got two and change."

"You must've blown it last night, friend. Nobody walks through a locked door. The transom's too small. The window's too high. So how could you have been robbed?"

When Euclid J. Bourgeois arrived there on a fall day in 1898,

Bemidji's claim to be the wildest town in the land except for Butte, Montana, was still a few years ahead of it, but it was growing rapidly. A pine tree still grew in the middle of Third Street. A duck pond was located on the future site of the Union Depot. But a school and a city hall had been built, two sawmills were operating, and the Great Northern had reached the city the previous July, with the Northern Minnesota's first train due in December.

Bourgeois found the town in an uproar, making ready to defend itself against the Chippewas. The militia had been called out. Guards were posted on every road. An Indian who ventured into Bemidji had to explain his intentions very carefully before he was allowed to pass.

Actually, the band of warriors led by Chief Bugonegeshig had no intention of attacking Bemidji. "Old Bug," as the lumberjacks called him, was waiting in ambush at Bear Island, about thirty miles from Walker. Troops from Fort Snelling, led by Brigadier General John M. Bacon, were moving cautiously to the attack.

The Pillager band of Chippewas had been getting increasingly restless for months before the outbreak. Timber cruisers were sneaking around their reservation, checking out the pine in the expectation that their employers could buy it cheap when it came on the market. Other whites were stealing "dead and down" reservation timber which, by federal rule, only a Chippewa was allowed to sell.

What triggered the revolt was the decision of a deputy marshal, Bob Morrison, to arrest Bugonegeshig for being drunk. The chief yelled for help. His friends came running. Having defied the authorities by rescuing Old Bug, the Pillagers decided they might as well hold an uprising.

The news that a band of Minnesota Indians was on the warpath alarmed the state. Old-timers recalled the Sioux troubles of 1862 when something like six hundred whites were killed and several towns, including New Ulm, were wiped out. Twenty counties had been virtually depopulated before soldiers turned their attention away from fighting Confederates long enough to regain control of Minnesota.

Bugonegeshig's revolt was not in the same league as the one of thirty-six years earlier, and the danger to lumber towns in the region was minimal. Most Indians remained peacefully on their reservations, preferring not to get shot. Old Bug's followers apparently numbered about fifty young men, although from the hysterical accounts in Minnesota and Wisconsin newspapers of the day it sounded as if they were a mighty army. One federal official on the scene sent an urgent plea to Washington to rush another five thousand soldiers to the north woods to keep Minnesota from going back to the Indians.

General Bacon had fought Indians before and did not share in the panic. With eighty men, he headed for Bear Island to bring Old Bug to heel. The plan was to sneak up on the Pillagers, but as the soldiers approached, one of them thought he saw a redskin in the underbrush and fired his gun. That was ample warning and the Chippewas were waiting.

There was a gun battle. For a time the word around Walker, particularly among newspaper correspondents, was that the eighty had been wiped out to a man and Bacon had become a second Custer. Two newsmen were with the soldiers and it was supposed that they had either been shot or captured. A Milwaukee *Journal* correspondent chartered a boat and sailed around the shores of the island, yelling the names of his colleagues. When no one answered, that confirmed his belief that the entire party was dead.

It took several days to get the situation in perspective. In the fight with the Chippewas, Major Melville Wilkinson, a veteran of the Civil War, and five other soldiers were killed. The Indians claimed no Chippewa was so much as scratched, although this is open to doubt.

At any rate, both sides were ready for peace. Two whites and a chief named Guynewonaush went to Bear Island to work out terms of surrender. Meanwhile, an enterprising western newspaperman interviewed Geronimo, an Apache who had done some notable fighting against the white men in his time. The old chief said the Minnesota Indians were "making a great mistake and are fools"—not for holding an uprising but for rebelling at a time when there were too many white men around to make the project feasible.

The Pillager band went back to its reservation and the excitement ended. But Chief Guynewonaush had something to say about the cause of the trouble. It wasn't whiskey, he said. It was "the manner in which Indian pine lands are being stolen by lumbermen." After several years of fruitless appeals to Washington, he added, Bugonegeshig and his followers had decided to take matters into their own hands.

Although peace was restored, hard feelings remained. The Chippewas continued to believe that the lumber interests were out to cheat them. It's plain that they were quite correct.

In 1896, for example, a portion of the Red Lake Reservation land was offered for sale. The Indians requested federal help in estimating the amount of timber on various tracts, so land prices could be set accordingly. Washington, in turn, asked lumbermen for suggestions. They advised hiring their own landlookers, men who knew the business.

The timber cruisers also knew who was paying their wages. They made honest but secret estimates for their employers and much lower estimates for the government and the Indians. One tract on the Blackduck River, for example, was said to have sixty-five thousand board feet of timber—hardly enough to be worth cutting. When it was logged, the total turned out to be nine hundred thousand board feet.

At the Crookston auction, the lumber companies began bidding against each other and on the first day the land went for close to its actual worth. That would never do, so the usual agreement to avoid competitive bidding was worked out. Weyerhaeuser was assigned one area, C. A. Smith another, Pat and Jim Meehan's Thief River Falls Lumber Company a third, and so on.

But for once, the barons overstepped themselves. The precipitous decline in prices was so obvious that even a government agent could tell what was happening. The auction was stopped. The Department of Interior discharged all the company landlookers. In their place, it sent out a fellow named J. George Wright, who was said by an admirer to be "afraid of neither God nor the devil" and so tough "he could spit ice." Wright reported that the lumber companies had been trying to pull a fast one. The remainder of the reservation land was withdrawn from sale. Logging stopped there for several years. Then the land was sold through sealed bids, with a minimum price of five dollars per thousand for pine.

One way for Indians to make sure they weren't being cheated was to do the logging themselves. Among the successful efforts along this line was a logging operation run by a chief named Shogogeshig, whose crew cut two million board feet of logs around Little Cut Foot Sioux Lake, floated them down to the Mississippi and sold the timber to a dealer at Grand Rapids, Minnesota, just east of the Leech Lake Reservation. Shogogeshig was also successful in keeping Jim Hill's railroad from crossing Indian land until the chief was murdered at Deer River. With him out of the way, the big loggers as well as the railroad were able to move onto the preserve.

Near another Indian reservation was the village of Red Lake, a jumping-off place for settlers heading into the countryside to take up claims. To file a claim, a man had to pay a fee of fourteen dollars and fifty cents, in addition to the one dollar and a quarter an acre the land would cost if his claim was approved. According to one old-timer, the government "was betting each homesteader a hundred sixty acres of land against fourteen dollars and fifty cents that he would starve to death before he could prove up his land."

Out-of-work lumberjacks descended on Red Lake in the summer. Sometimes they formed what was called a "boo gang," taking over an abandoned building—or one they could throw the occupant out of, which amounted to the same thing. By pooling their resources, cadging food and drinks and doing odd jobs of work that came their way, they could survive until fall when work would be plentiful again.

Among Red Lake's prominent residents was an Indian with the distinctive name of Chief Moosedung. He ran a store in a shanty set into a hillside. His son, Moosedung the Younger, was later involved in a court fight over land sought by the Thief River Falls Lumber Company. Moosedung the Younger agreed to sell the acreage at Thief River Falls for forty-three hundred dollars. But his relatives rallied around for a piece of the action and, when he refused to split the proceeds, five of them took him to the white man's court. Moosedung the Younger finally won, but the legal difficulties tied up the real estate deal for years.

The Thief River folks didn't mind. The only reason they'd wanted the land was to keep a rival outfit from building a sawmill there.

CHAPTER XVII

Some Colorful Characters

PAT MEEHAN, who arrived in Minnesota from Stevens Point, Wisconsin, with his brother Jim, was a three-hundred-pounder, making him one of the biggest lumbermen in the state in more ways than one. The Meehans got their start buying logs from homesteaders and off Indian reservations. But they soon prospered to the point where they owned a fleet of steamboats to haul logs and supplies. Their men cut a considerable share of the pine around such rivers as the Blackduck.

There was nothing Pat liked more than to lean back, his long-stemmed meerschaum in hand, and brag about how the Meehans had bought timber for forty-five cents a thousand board feet from people who didn't know it was worth twice that. He also enjoyed telling how he pulled a fast one on the village of Red Lake. That community had offered a cash bonus to anyone who'd build a sawmill and put it in operation above the Marshall Dam on the Red Lake River. Pat and Jim built the mill, sawed one log, collected the money and pulled out.

Another Minnesota man who stood out in the crowd was Al Nason, who cut pine around Lake Pokegama. Witnesses swore they'd seen him lift a 330-pound barrel of salt pork onto his shoulder and walk off with it without so much as a grunt.

W. W. Hale, a Pennsylvanian who ran a logging operation near Grand Rapids, Minnesota, in the 1870s got himself talked about, too. He violated an unwritten rule among loggers that nothing must interfere with the main business at hand—cutting logs. Because of religious scruples, he permitted his crews to knock off work early enough on Saturday to get their week's clothes-washing and other chores done. He permitted no work on Sundays, the lumberjacks' usual washday.

Conversation was the loggers' principal recreation for much of the year and stories were passed along from one man to another, such as the one told by John Koop about the night he took a room at the hotel in a town he had founded, Lake Port, which later changed its name to LaPorte, Minnesota. Koop said he lit the kerosene lamp and got into bed to read himself to sleep. But the light kept growing dimmer and dimmer. When it went out, Koop jumped up to investigate.

"I lit a match. The lamp chimney was so full of bedbugs they'd choked out the light. I walked all the way to Walker in the rain. I couldn't stay there any more."

LaPorte was known to some lumberjacks as Robber's Roost. It was said to be the wildest town between Brainerd and Bemidji, Minnesota, not as modest a distinction then as it sounds now. The postmaster was a widower, Nelson Daughters, whose cabin was across from the depot. Selling liquor to Indians was illegal. When a delegation of thirsty Chippewas asked Daughters to buy some for them, he refused. In revenge, they noised it about that the postmaster had given them whiskey. He was arrested and taken to Walker for trial.

When he saw how many false witnesses were waiting to testify, he jumped bail and hid out near home. A deputy ambushed him, shooting him in the head, then throwing the wounded man aboard a train. He died before he reached Walker. There was talk around LaPorte about lynching the deputy. But the officer had gone back to the county seat and it was decided that going so far just to hang a man was too much trouble.

Although LaPorte was small, it supplied even smaller communities in the area with such necessities as liquor. One saloonkeeper who had his supplies hauled in by wagon suspected that the teamsters helped themselves liberally during the trip. Toward the end of the journey, they would stop at a creek and fill up the barrel with water. Luckily, the stream was named Alcohol Creek, so if a customer complained that the whiskey tasted weak the bartender could take a solemn oath that there was plenty of alcohol in it.

Getting watered whiskey was not unusual in the backwoods saloons, but selling bottles of the diluted stuff could be dangerous when the temperature was thirty below, as a Minnesota saloonkeeper discovered. A lumberjack was carrying a bottle in his back pocket when it froze, broke and cut his leg. After the customer healed, he came back to complain. The barkeep said he was sorry, it was all a mistake.

"That was the summer strength whiskey I sold you," he explained. "I meant to give you the winter kind."

Walker, located a few miles southeast of LaPorte, consisted mostly of a dozen saloons in those days. As a result, Thomas B. Walker, president of a Minneapolis bank and one of the nation's largest owners of pinery lands, turned down an invitation to build a sawmill there, even though the town had been named in his honor. He was a teetotaler and he decided to found a community that would be free from the hazards of strong drink. The new community of Akeley on Upper Crow Wing Lake, named for Walker's partner, H. C. Akeley, soon grew as big as the village of Walker, even though a provision against liquor was written into the deeds when lots were sold. Another town was started nearby to give Akeley residents a place to get a drink. Walker, who had influence with the county board, prevented Shingobee from being platted, but the saloons there prospered anyway.

There were big eaters as well as heavy drinkers in Minnesota. Hungry Mike Sullivan, for instance. A six-footer who weighed two hundred twenty-five pounds, he could eat a dozen eggs and a double order of pancakes for breakfast and be ready for another oversized meal at 10 A.M. When he wanted a sandwich to tide him over until lunch, he'd slice a large loaf of bread lengthways and fill it with meat. Mike was a Canadian with a red mustache, a big voice and an ability to get along with the men in the camps he ran, providing they weren't caught smoking cigarettes. Lighting up anything except a cigar or a pipe could get a man fired. In fact, it could get two men fired. Sullivan always discharged the culprit's partner, too, so he wouldn't have to take the long walk back to town alone.

Charles L. Wight recalled a day when Hungry Mike caught

three members of his crew trading supplies. One had the matches, another the tobacco, the third supplied the cigarette papers. Sullivan took immediate action.

"Makings, you hit the trail. Matches, you go with him. Tobacco, you go along so they won't get lonesome on the road."

No one could deny that Hungry Mike lived up to his nickname, as did Hurry Up Jimmy Sullivan, who kept his men jumping from sunup to dark, and a foreman who worked for him. The foreman was known as Moonlight Eric because he turned out his crews as early as 3 A.M., making sure they'd be ready to cut trees when it got light enough to see.

Danny McDowell was also mentioned in discussions of eccentric residents of the region, mostly because of a transaction he entered into with Red Mitchell, who had a cabin a few miles south of Lothrop, Minnesota, on Ten Mile Lake. For a year or so, Lothrop was the terminus of the Brainerd and Northern Railroad, consisting mostly of a railroad camp, a single store, numerous saloons, and a hotel operated by Mary Bain where it was not necessary for male guests to sleep alone unless they'd spent their pay.

When the railroad completed another stretch of roadbed and its camp moved on, Lothrop all but disappeared. Mary opened an establishment called the Golden West at Blackduck, taking her women with her. But one, a veteran at the business named Lizzie, decided to stay behind. She married Red Mitchell and moved into his cabin.

After a while, Mitchell decided he was getting too old for such an active life there in the woods. He sold his place to McDowell, who had been a brakeman on the railroad. With the cabin and land went all of Mitchell's personal property, which was carefully inventoried. The inventory was filed at the courthouse at Walker. It included Red's bed, stove, chair, axe and, at the bottom of the list, "one woman named Liz."

The Minnesota lumber boom attracted its share of professional gamblers. Charlie Miles, for instance, ran a large saloon and gambling house in Bemidji. Minneapolis also got its share of the action. Everett Farley once won twenty-six thousand dollars on a single trip to that city, but he's best remembered for a gamble he took with Weeping Willey Blakely. The two men were partners in a Cass Lake logging operation. They established a new town there and shook dice to see which one would have the honor of getting the place named for him. Willie lost. Farley, Minnesota, stayed on the map longer than his other winnings stayed in Farley's pocket.

In 1892, when he was keeping books for Price Brothers while they were logging the Prairie River, he made a bet that they couldn't find five hundred dollars of their money that he'd taken. An auditor was hired to go through the doctored records, but the shortage was hidden so well that, as Farley had predicted, he couldn't discover it.

Farley's hobbies were cards, women and wine, and he wore a sealskin coat that was the envy of Bemidji. But his old friends heard that after he moved farther west his final years were spent in a poorhouse.

Sometimes the lumberjacks' tales were about the work they had done rather than the fights they had had or the saloons they had visited. Wild Bill Metcalf, for example, once told me what it had been like to drive a steam hauler near Hayward.

William Hanson had brought one of these monsters with its caterpillar treads to the banks of Namekagon Lake in 1888 and other loggers in the vicinity had adopted this replacement for horses, impressed by the machine's ability to use steam power to haul a string of loaded sleighs.

Metcalf did not start his woods career on a hauler. When he was fifteen, he got work as a teamster near Spider Lake, arriving at the loading site before daybreak and wrestling with the logs by the light of an improvised torch made from a galvanized can with a spout on each side and wicks sticking out of the sprouts.

For driving a team from before daylight until after dark, Metcalf was paid a dollar a day. So when he got a chance to move to the steam hauler for twenty-five cents an hour, he jumped at it. By working twenty hours a day, he could make five dollars.

"I was the brakeman at first," Bill said. "But one day the steersman got in a fight at a water hole and got fired. So that left the engineer and me and I acted as brakeman and steersman both. We'd haul an average of eight sleighs at a time. Thirteen was the most we ever hauled, four thousand to six thousand feet to the load.

"The twenty-hour days didn't bother me until along toward

spring, when the sun got to shining down. I'd go to sleep steering the hauler. The engineer'd toot his whistle and I'd jump a foot."

Metcalf told of going into the woods in September and never getting out again until spring. Then he'd head for Hayward.

"I had a good time for three days, 'till the money was gone. We used to have barehanded knockdowns for the drinks. I come into Red Ole's saloon one time and nobody'd take me on. Then Johnny Schwartz, who weighed around two hundred pounds, he said he would. We bet drinks for the house.

"I hit him and he went down. So he walked back of the bar and set 'em up. After we'd finished the drinks he says, 'you can't do that again.' I says, 'I can try.' He went down again. We tried to get him to come to with water. But he was out cold. Somebody called the doctor. We'd just got Johnny on his pins again when in walked Red Ole.

"'Any more of that,' he says, 'and I'll have a hand in it.' 'You're next,' I says, and he backed off. Later, I was in another saloon and offering to fight. I was standing next to Fred Clark, the sheriff. He reached around and picked me up and threw me over the bar. 'That good for a drink?' he says. I had to admit it was."

Metcalf said the fights weren't usually serious, but sometimes they got out of hand, especially when the river pigs were in town in their "corked" boots.

"That's how the blacksmith got killed," Bill said.

"How?"

"Got kicked to death in the street."

Some years later, when the tall pines were gone and Metcalf was helping cut smaller trees, he decided to run for town chairman. He did most of his campaigning in the Hayward bars, buying drinks, avoiding fights, putting his best foot forward. When the results were announced, he headed straight for his favorite saloon.

"I won," he yelled, bursting through the door. "Before, I had to kiss your ass. Now you can all kiss mine."

Metcalf's early start as a lumberjack was not unusual. When a boy was big enough, he was considered old enough. Joe Boss, who was later in charge of a camp in the Hayward area, also started his lumberjack career when he was fifteen. Within three years, he was bossing a camp along the Flambeau River.

He told of a year when hands were short and he had to "put in an order with the mancatcher at Superior." After buying enough rounds at the saloon to lower resistance, this recruiting agent signed up a crew and sent them to Joe.

"The poor buggers had never seen the woods. One of them got killed. I saw how he was sawing and I told him he better go back to camp, but he wouldn't go. He and his partner were working on a leaning maple. The tree split and hit him in the back.

"I couldn't get along with those city buggers at all. I finally had to let them go."

Joe Parent, whose father was a Quebec Frenchman and whose mother was part Chippewa, was eight years old when the white pine was cut on the Lac Court Oreilles Reservation in northwestern Wisconsin. When those trees were gone, some of the Indians got jobs as lumberjacks elsewhere. Joe remembers watching the men coming home on a Saturday night.

"They had an Indian trail to the camp. It wasn't very far to walk. Maybe ten miles."

Parent started work around Birchwood, Wisconsin, in 1899, when the only building there was a log hut for the camp boss. His first job was to handle the chain used to load logs on a contraption called a go-devil. One end of the log being dragged rested on a crosspiece nailed across the wide end of the chopped-off tree fork, the other bumping along on the ground. Lumberjacks also called the device a crazy drag, a snow snake or a travois.

There were still pines four feet across in the woods when Joe started lumberjacking. The crew would get three sixteen-to-eighteen-footers out of one tree, even though they seldom used any part of a pine above the first branch. The rest was slashings, to be discarded.

"Sometimes we'd cut boom sticks sixty to eighty feet long out of a pine and use four yoke of oxen to haul them to the river," Parent told me. "Oxen were slower than horses, but strong. You'd drive them with a goad stick.

"It was a good life. I liked it, even if I never did see daylight in that camp only on Sundays—we went out early and came back late. We had two long tables for meals, with two cookees and a second cook who'd make pastries. Everybody had his tin dish. There was a big coffee pot at each end. You'd help yourself. We ate mostly beef and pork. And beans. We used to have lots of beans in camp, with sowbelly. They'd stick by you.

"Sundays, some would play poker. Saturday nights, we'd have music. Somebody'd play a fiddle, an accordion or a mouth organ. Others'd sit around, with everybody smoking Peerless or Adam's Standard in their corncob pipes. A lot would chew snuff or snoose. Some made their own snoose. They'd put tobacco in a glass jar and add alcohol and salt to make it strong enough. We could get five plugs of Spearhead tobacco for fifty cents in the wanigan.

"When I was at Birchwood, it was forty-five below zero for three weeks running. That's pretty chilly. But we all wore woolen clothes, from underwear to mackinaws, and the wool would absorb the sweat so you wouldn't get cold.

"Them lumberjacks'd have a great time in the saloons. Getting in fights. Doing some bragging about how many trees they'd cut in a day and such things. Most of 'em went to town to see the girls. You know. The houses with the women."

Hayward had thirteen saloons and five sporting houses in those days. Best remembered among the latter were Dirty Anne's and Old Lady Schutte's, which was across the river from town. Old-timers claim that lumberjacks would swim the river to get to Old Lady Schutte's, but that seems to be an exaggeration. Records indicate that a bridge was built before the house where her girls entertained. It's likely that now and then a drunk fell off the bridge and had to swim, but that wasn't the usual way across. The building, now a respectable private dwelling, still has calk marks in the upstairs rooms from the boots of customers who didn't pause to take off their shoes.

Fifield was another lively town in Wisconsin's northwest. Some years ago, when he was ninety, Big Hank Henrickson reminisced about what a fine place Fifield was to spend a weekend when he was young.

"Fights? Let me tell you. At Fifield, you could walk outside and look up and down the street and see half a dozen fights going on, all at the same time. Fifield was a great town."

Henrickson told me of a log jam so high that "if a man fell off it, he'd die before he hit the water." But when he was walking boss along the Flambeau, he said, he had such a good crew that they could handle anything.

"We didn't need much water. You could pour a bottle of beer on the street and my boys would drive a million feet of pine down it."

The year he was in charge of the last big drive on the Flambeau, the old man said, there was a big snowstorm in May. Or was it June? Anyway, the wood got all wet and the cook quit. After trying their own cooking for a few days, a volunteer "hoofed it out in the snow and brought another cook. But by that time, some of the men had quit."

Another drive that lingered in Henrickson's memory was on the Thornapple River.

"We had to take 'em out with a cutaway drive. That's where you block up the river to hold the water, and when the water builds up you bust that dam and build another farther down.

"Another time, when we were driving on the Flambeau, a fellow done the impossible and I went ahead and done it after him. That fellow wanted to commit suicide, so he rode over Beaver Dam on a log. He didn't manage to kill himself. Somehow, he made it. The next year we were working near Beaver Dam again and I was helping with the drive. I said to Steel Spring Kenny, 'I'll take it on alone.' I was getting close to the dam but the water roared and I didn't hear 'em yell to warn me. Then I saw the fix I was in.

"It was too late to get out, so I waited until a thirty-two-footer come along and I jumped on that son of a bitch. I went over the dam. Damned if I didn't live through it. Landed on an island. I was lucky. I knew lots of fellows who died in that part of the river.

"Another time, I was working upstream from there and I drifted off on a log, going through Cedar Rapids. They had to chase me four miles in a bateau. They ran the prow of that boat right between my legs and I got in. They was madder than hell at me. Had to pole all the way back up the river, with the logs running. Took us half a day. If they hadn't picked me up, I'd of gone over Beaver Dam again. I'd never made it twice. I'd used up all my luck the first time I went over and lived."

The bateaux used on the rivers might be as much as forty feet long. Alex LeTourneau, who started work in the woods as a thirteen-year-old, told me of the time when such a boat rammed into floating logs and flipped over, sending its thirteen-man crew into the water.

"Only two come out alive. The others went under the logs."

One of LeTourneau's duties as a youth was to drive a sleigh to the nearest town to get the mail, every now and then. It was a twenty-two-mile trip. If a man had been injured in the woods, he was bundled into the sleigh and taken to the doctor.

"I remember one fellow got hit on the side of the head and if he laid flat the blood went into his throat and he choked. So I got two fellows to hold him, one on each side. He rode all the way, standing up. He made it, too. He was back working in the woods before long."

Another old lumberjack, Clyde Hamblin, said that in those days men aged fast in the woods.

"A man who was fifty years old looked like an old man. A lot of them died young. They bruised themselves up so bad when they'd go to town.

"I remember one fellow came back to camp after a drunk. He was awful sick. Looked like he was going to die sure. Somebody asked him if he'd learned his lesson. He looked up and he says, sort of feeble like: 'If I ever get over this, I'm going to try 'er again.'"

Big Hank Henrickson brought up the name of Skunk Frank. He lived near Beaver Dam, getting his name because he was a trapper.

"The time he died, he was going up the river to get water and he fell stone dead. A fisherman fellow took Skunk Frank on his last ride, down the river. He was dead then, you know."

Nicknames were common in the woods, often referring to a man's habits or appearance. Clay Pipe Jimmy Redmond, an Eau Claire man, for instance. He was called that, Big Hank said, "because he'd eat up one clay pipe after another, chewing on them."

The lumberjack wasn't sure how Whitewater Ole got his name, but he remembered what happened to him.

"He drownded. Went over the falls. Several days later, he comes floating up and lands on the gravel right next to his house in Chippewa Falls."

Then there was Whiskey Sam Olson, who died young from the drink. And Pat Nelson, a foreman of logging camps, who couldn't write his own name. He was called Pat the Cinnamon.

"Once they was going to camp and all of them got drunk," Hamblin explained, "and Pat put on an old buffalo skin coat. He was running around and somebody said he looked just like a cinnamon bear. So that's how he got called Pat the Cinnamon. Or you take Curly Pete. He had curly hair, tight to his head. He'd never spend any money. He'd bum quarters enough to stay drunk all summer, till it was time to go back to the woods. In a fight, he'd grab a man and bump with his head like a buck sheep."

Fred Eytcheson, who came to the Hayward region in 1891, held out his left arm and explained how it got broken in five places, long ago in the big woods.

"I was going to put in a grouser and—"

"A grouser?"

"That's a piece of wood or a rock or something you use be-tween two logs when you're loading. So I reached in with the grouser and the fellow operating the jammer dropped a log. A jammer's a kind of derrick to load logs. So he dropped that big log and you could hear my bones crunch. A man will get hurt once in a while. But I've been lucky. I'm still all here."

When talking with outsiders, the old lumberjacks have to pause now and then to translate what comes close to being a foreign lan-guage, the jargon of the big woods. L. G. Sorden, who has been gathering and defining lumberjack terms for many years, recalls the story of a woods worker who was hospitalized and tried to tell his nurse what had happened.

"The ground loader threw the beads around a pine log. He claimed he had called for a St. Croix but he gave me a Saginaw. She gunned, broke three of my slats and one of my stilts and also a very fine skid."

"I don't understand," the nurse told him.

"I don't either," the lumberjack said. "He must have been yaps."

A man could go yaps (crazy) from cabin fever, but the usual cause was bottled to be sold in saloons. Not every lumberjack drank too much—some didn't drink at all. But the usual attitude was that it was better to take it when you could get it because who could tell when the chance would come again.

Big Hank Henrickson told of the time his boss gave him fifty dollars to buy food for a crew he was taking to camp.

"Boys," he told the men, "I'll flip this here fifty-cent piece. If it comes down heads, we won't waste that fifty bucks on grub. If it comes down tails, we'll take it out in whiskey."

Hank said that before the day was over, several of the men had to be carried to camp. But that was all right.

"I saved two or three quarts so we could have a drink around in the morning. But we went to work anyway.

"That was the winter we was working near Shaw Dam. Shaw Dam's the first place I ever ate sucker head soup. They shut down the dam and got the fish from the low water, then cut off the heads and threw the fish away. They put the sucker heads in a lard can, added fat pork, boiled 'em and there you were. Sucker head soup. It sort of put you in mind of oyster stew."

The old-timers agreed that Hayward had been quite a place when they and the town were young.

"Sand in the street so deep you couldn't back a wagon. Had to go around the block. The sewer run wide open. A fight on every corner. Those lumberjacks or river pigs—they'd get up on a bar with their corked shoes and the bartender didn't dare say nothing about it. He'd get under something and hide when those boys cut loose. Good old Hayward. You know the saying: 'Hayward, Hurley and Hell.'"

Neither Hayward nor Hurley nor possibly Hell ever had a free-for-all like the one that took place on Wisconsin's Elk River in 1888, however. Two rival companies were trying to get their logs to the mill at the same time and, as often happened, a fracas broke out. Usually such fights were confined to a few hotheads from each crew, but this one spread. Dozens of men—some say as many as a hundred on each side—were soon whaling away at each other with peaveys. With its hook and its spiked end, a peavey can be a serious weapon. Something in the neighborhood of eighty victims of that fight wound up in a Chippewa Falls hospital.

Lumberjacks talked about that gang battle for years, and those who missed it regretted it, or said they did. As one man explained

to me: "Back then, a good man would walk fifty miles to beat another good man. And then the one he knocked down would get up
and they'd go get drunk together." And another old-timer put it
this way: "In those days, about all there was to do was talk or
fight. And you got tired of talking."

CHAPTER XVIII

The White Pine Era Ends

The white pine phase of the lumberjack saga ended at different times in different places in Minnesota, Michigan and Wisconsin. When a Maine man, Daniel Shaw, sent the last raft of lumber down the Chippewa from Shawtown on the outskirts of Eau Claire on June 28, 1901, that was one turning point. When the Weyerhaeuser interests asked for expert advice from the federal Forestry Bureau on how to replant the cutover in 1903, that was another. When production of lumber started to decline after 1902 in Duluth, another straw had been tossed in the wind.

In some parts of the pinery, the era did not wind completely down until the 1920s. It was in 1926 that the last log drive floated down Minnesota's St. Louis River, for example. The ten-million-dollar sawmill complex of the Virginia and Rainy Lake Company in Virginia, Minnesota, kept operating until 1929. Then, on October 9, a long blast from the plant whistle sounded a requiem for the world's largest white-pine mill in the last of the white-pine states to be picked clean.

Elsewhere, the pine ran out earlier. It was in 1876 when the last logs were sent down the Wisconsin River. The Black River's finale was in 1897. The last pine passed through the St. Croix boom in 1914, following the watery trail of fifteen billion board feet of timber. By then, the days when Saginaw and Bay City, Muskegon and Oshkosh, Minneapolis and Eau Claire and hundreds of other communities in the three states had depended on white pine for their existence had become half-forgotten history.

The Lake States' domination of logging ended around the turn of the century. The lumber barons had seen the change coming well before then. They began buying choice forest land in the Pacific Northwest and along the Gulf of Mexico in the 1880s. So they were ready.

Weyerhaeuser, that shy and quiet fellow with no taste for booze, bawds or battle but plenty of moxie when it came to business, rode west with his railroad tycoon neighbor, Jim Hill. He made an initial purchase of nine hundred thousand acres, then added another million more in Washington, Oregon and Idaho. Those who emulated him were shocked at the inflated prices of western land, which ran as high as six dollars an acre. But the trees were even bigger than the pines of Wisconsin, Minnesota and Michigan, so perhaps they were worth the price.

Ghost towns had been common in the north woods for years as loggers or lumbermen abandoned once rowdy and flourishing villages when the trees in the region were gone. After 1900, the number of deserted settlements in the Lake States multiplied. Logging and lumbering remained the largest industry in the northern counties—at the turn of the century, 40 per cent of Wisconsin's manufacturing capital was invested in these allied fields, for example. But employment was decreasing. In 1895, something like forty thousand men were employed in cutting trees, transporting them or sawing them, in Wisconsin alone. Within ten years, employment had been cut nearly in half even though the eight-hour day—though not the five-day week—was becoming common in sawmill towns. The decline in the number of workers was even sharper in Michigan. In Minnesota, last of the three states to be exploited, the trend was also downward.

Lumberjacks were not given to worrying about the future much, but they understood the signs. A way of life was ending. Many had already run out of white pine to cut and were making do with lesser species. Some were forced into "piecework," cutting railroad ties and shaping them with a broadaxe or dealing with such kindling wood as cedar for fenceposts. Olaf Treland, a Norwegian who came to Minnesota's north country as a youth, could recall when he and two other men cut three hundred pines in a day and were pleased when the foreman—"a big, old rusty guy"—made his own count and admitted they weren't just bragging. But by now he was being paid a dime apiece for cutting and shaping railroad ties, paying his own board out of the average of two dollars a day the work brought him.

J. A. Reamer, who could remember walking through a virgin forest in "the days when they made men out of boys," participated in the wake for Flambeau River logging. It was called a celebration, but everyone understood it was not really that.

"I was at Ladysmith when the last drive came down," he wrote to a friend when he was an old man looking back. "Every saloon had all their whiskey bottles on the bars. Beer flowed like water that night. Some saloons set a barrel on the stove and everybody drank all he wanted. It seems like everybody—lumberjacks and the town people, too—got drunk, and you could take your pick of the fights. But nobody got hurt too much.

"The next day, the saloons got back their money. And in a couple of days, every lumberjack was broke. And no woods to go back to . . ."

In the 1890s, lumberjacks were still claiming defiantly that "we'll never get the pine cut if we log till hell freezes," but some saw the end approaching. Joe A. Moran, while in his teens, got a note from a friend, Fred Schweinhager, who was cooking for the Fred C. Leonard camp on the west fork of the Chippewa:

"Joe, if you care to see a real pine forest while it's still on the hoof, hook a tote team and come now. This is the last chance."

So Moran spent his 1896 vacation with the cook in the woods near Glidden, Wisconsin, close to Middle Clam Lake. He became a teacher and writer, but that last chance to see the pines before they were gone colored his later life.

Those who were young in the north country in the final days of its glory considered themselves lucky in their memories. Mrs. Chester W. Smith, for example, who lived in Winneconne, Wisconsin, from 1877 to 1890, wrote of "the shrieks of the saws, the whistles from mills, passenger boats and tugs" which made life in the village exciting. She was thankful that she had lived there in the days of sawmills, river rafts and tugboats, even though "I never want to see a slab again, for that wood was a trial in blacking pots and kettles and in burning out so quickly."

Population growth in pinery counties began to slow down in the 1890s, except in Minnesota. Wisconsin's Ashland County, for instance, had increased by 1,200 per cent in the 1880s. In the 1890s, population grew by a mere 9 per cent. Eau Claire County's population tripled in the 1860s and doubled in the 1870s, but by the 1890s it barely held its own.

With the growing scarcity of pine came new interest in conserving what was left. National and state governments began to consider setting aside forest lands while there were still such lands to set aside. More efficient cutting and distributing methods were encouraged.

But in many northern counties, hard-pressed to pay their expenses, government officials slapped heavy taxes on cutover land that might have been used for reforestation. Even those lumber companies that considered planting seedlings decided not to do so. Whether high taxes were the reason or an excuse, it was more businesslike to cut and get out, letting the empty acres go for taxes or selling the stump-filled fields to immigrants and city folks who had yet to learn that much of the cutover was suitable only for growing trees, not crops.

Much of the United States east of the Great Plains is cutover land. But in regions with better soil and longer growing seasons than the former pineries, chopping down the forests merely traded trees for an even more useful commodity, crop land. It was originally supposed this would hold true in the Lake States, and so it did in some places. But generally the regions which had been covered with pine were not suitable for farming, a fact that was discovered by painful experience on the part of settlers whose abandoned houses are gently rotting away in the north country.

One historian said that the loggers changed "the rich pineries into a shambles within a generation," adding that the basis of many a lumber fortune "was laid by cheating Uncle Sam." There is truth in such contentions as well as in this capsule summary of the Lake States' lumbering history: "Its rise was swift, its heyday short, its effects devastating, its decline precipitate."

Once the companies had cut and run, the problem of what to do with the cutover plagued state and local governments for several generations. A 1910 survey indicated that 80 per cent of the denuded pinery land in Wisconsin was not suited for farming. In

Minnesota, where more than a third of the state was left with a crop of stumps and slashings, tax delinquency and land abandonment were continuing problems. Three of the cutover counties in that state remained relatively prosperous because of iron mining. The others were in a bad way as soon as the loggers left. In two townships in St. Louis County, for instance, the assessed value of real estate dropped from $1,129,558 to $297,296 within a four-year period.

For most of the cutover, the obvious answer to the problem of what to do about the situation turned out to be right: Replant trees. First there had to be changes in the laws so that forest property would be taxed on a different basis than farmland, making it feasible to grow a crop that takes a generation to reach harvesting size. If the changes had come earlier, some lumbermen might have held onto their land instead of abandoning it to the tax man.

Still, reforestation has been successful in restoring large portions of the former pineries to a measure of usefulness and has even revived the logging industry to an extent. But the logs being cut there now are mostly pulpwood, weedy sticks that an old-time lumberjack would have considered an insult to his skills.

While many of the lumber companies were disengaging themselves from the Lake States in favor of investments in Arkansas, Louisiana and the Pacific Northwest, others tried to fight the trend by changing their methods. The Goodman Lumber Company, which owned seventy thousand acres of timberland in northeastern Wisconsin, is an example. It decided, as trees became scarcer, that it would be more efficient to move its mill to the forest instead of floating the logs to the mill.

In 1908, it established Goodman, Wisconsin, a company town owned and controlled by Robert Goodman. He built houses, stores and everything else needed for a village of a thousand persons in what was left of the big woods near the Menominee River. He encouraged married workers to settle there by offering low rents. Payroll deductions could be used to buy food, clothing, even furniture. Some families went for months without seeing a dollar in actual cash. As long as a worker did his job, his needs were taken care of. In exchange, Goodman ran the town to suit himself.

The owner's paternalism extended to his woods. He not only

chopped down trees, he planted them. As a result, the company survived long after cut-and-run operators had vanished. The company town continued until 1955, amid much grumbling from the residents about their nearly total dependence. Then it was sold to a Chicago company which, in turn, permitted occupants to buy the houses at prices ranging from one to four thousand dollars.

Earlier, when Goodman died and his enterprises shut down so that employees could attend his funeral, only fifteen residents of his model village bothered to go.

Goodman's attempt to extend the life of his forest was a rarity. The exodus of lumberjacks from the Lake States began even before production there reached its peak, with men heading west from restlessness or in hope of bettering themselves. One who made the trip was Gary Peavey, member of the Maine family that had given loggers one of their favorite means of dealing with recalcitrant lengths of pine. He had worked in Maine, then in Pennsylvania before helping take the first log drive down Minnesota's Rum River. In 1888 he headed for Puget Sound to tackle the big trees there. In the space of one lifetime, he demonstrated, a man could cut trees from the East Coast to the West Coast, leaving a trail of stumps to show where he'd been.

As the lumber barons acquired acreage along the Pacific, they offered experienced hands in the Lake States a free ticket if they'd help tackle the new timber territory. Entire trainloads of lumberjacks made the trip.

They were a revelation to Westerners. The West bragged that it was wild in those days. Its residents were accustomed to train robbers, drunken cowboys, gunfighters and other rough characters. But when those lumberjack specials rolled through town, it was the first time Westerners had seen a train with every window broken and most of the doors kicked off.

Once they got to where they were going and had sobered up, the Midwesterners made the bark fly. By 1905, the state of Washington was turning out four billion board feet of lumber in twelve months, as much as Wisconsin and Minnesota put together.

There was no sudden and dramatic climax to mark the close of the white-pine era along Lakes Michigan, Huron and Superior. It wound down gradually. It merged into lesser kinds of lumbering. It survived for a time after the region had been civilized to the point where a man could get in serious trouble merely for bashing a friend over the head with a cant hook. Remnants of that special age even continued into a more effete period when supplies were hauled to camp by truck and lumberjacks headed for saloons in Model T's.

Perhaps the story of the Defender of Cameron Dam is as good an example as any of how life changed in the north country. John Dietz, a settler in Wisconsin's Sawyer County, defied what he called "the largest company in the world" and, in the process, became the center of a nationwide controversy and the symbol of a revolt by the weak against the lumbering hierarchy.

By 1904, when Dietz picked up his rifle and stopped a log drive on the Thornapple River, even the Chippewa Lumber & Boom Company headed by Frederick Weyerhaeuser had to call on the sheriff and the courts to deal with him, instead of turning loose a crew of river pigs to persuade him to get out of the way. It was equally symbolic of new attitudes in the region that public sentiment generally favored Dietz.

Lumber barons were no longer in public favor in 1904. Hadn't they ruined large areas of three states with their wasteful cutting? Weren't they wrecking the economies of the north country by pulling out, often overnight? Hadn't they gypped thousands of poor and honest settlers by persuading them to buy land that wouldn't grow wheat? Dietz might be a hard-headed fellow. He might even be in the wrong, when it came to the fine print on documents drawn up by lawyers. But he was fighting the system that had prevailed for so long, and in many a saloon and parlor he was regarded as something of a hero.

Before Dietz, his wife and five children moved to one hundred sixty acres on the Thornapple, a tributary of the Chippewa, he had worked for Weyerhaeuser's company and he left with a profound dislike for the outfit which, he claimed, had not treated him fairly. He said it owed him several hundred dollars in back pay. He bought his farm in his wife's name and settled down to try to make a living.

The Thornapple was not much of a river, but it was large enough to float logs in the spring with the help of a series of dams. One of these was either partly on Dietz's property or adjoining it, a question that became a matter of considerable dispute.

The company claimed it had dam and flowage rights from the previous owner, the widow of Hugh Cameron. But in the spring of 1904, when its crew was driving logs on the Thornapple, Dietz stood at the dam with his rifle and demanded ten cents per thousand feet for letting the pine pass through.

The company said no. Letting a landowner charge a fee for such passage would set a dangerous and expensive precedent. Dietz put up NO TRESPASSING signs. The company countered with an injunction. When deputies tried to serve the papers, Dietz chased them off his property at gunpoint.

Newspapers got wind of what was going on in this remote region of the state, and soon reporters descended on the Defender of Cameron Dam. So many showed up, in fact, that Dietz said he had trouble killing enough deer out of season to keep his visitors supplied with venison.

Meanwhile, deputies kept creeping around in the underbrush, hoping to catch the settler without his rifle so they could serve the injunction papers. At first, both sides seemed to consider it something of an amusing game, but by 1906 it had turned ugly. Sheriff James Gylland and a six-man posse surprised Dietz and his two sons outside their cabin. There was a gun battle. One son, Clarence, was wounded. So was a member of the posse. The others fled, apparently not slowing down before they reached Ladysmith, thirty-five miles away.

The Dietz family claimed that the sheriff's helpers were "twenty-dollar-a-day thugs from Milwaukee, wearing stolen uniforms of the town militia." However that may be, they carried their wounded companion into the woods, took off his uniform and left him there. He crawled to a nearby house in his underwear. His hip wound was painful but not fatal. The bullet that hit Clarence Dietz had merely creased his skull.

The feud between the lumber company and Dietz dragged on. The governor tried to conciliate. The dam's defender turned him down, announcing to the press that the only way Weyerhaeuser and his men could use the Thornapple would be to kill him.

In 1910, Dietz ventured into Winter, Wisconsin, twelve miles from his farm, bringing along his rifle to keep process servers at bay. He got into an argument with a lumber company official and shot him. The wound was not fatal, but Sheriff Mike Madden decided the situation had gone far enough. He posted lookouts on the road Dietz had to use to drive to town for supplies. When word came that the family buggy was headed toward Winter, he laid an ambush.

As it happened, Dietz was not in the buggy. His eighteen-year-old daughter, Myra, was driving and two younger sons were along. The posse didn't take time to ask questions, however. It started shooting. Myra was wounded. One brother ran, dodging bullets, and told his father what had happened.

Dietz was being interviewed by Floyd Gibbons, a reporter for the Minneapolis *Tribune* who later became a war correspondent and radio personality. The farmer and the newsman jumped on horses and galloped off to town. They found Myra in a hotel room, waiting for the next train to Ashland so she could be sent to a hospital there. The train wasn't due for several days. Meanwhile, a deputy guarded the girl's door.

Gibbons rented the adjoining room, bored a hole in the wall and got his story. It made Myra a celebrity, and her shooting aroused further sympathy for Dietz's cause.

Finally, on October 6, 1910, more than six years after the dispute began, the sheriff and a posse of seventy-three men showed up at the Dietz cabin, accompanied by the state attorney general and the governor's secretary. Those two dignitaries marched to the door under a flag of truce and delivered a letter demanding the farmer's surrender and setting down terms. Dietz refused.

The next morning the posse returned and started firing. An estimated one thousand bullets hit the house. Dietz was slightly wounded in one hand. A deputy sheriff, Oscar Harp, was killed and two other attackers injured. Dietz finally surrendered—he said later that his wife talked him into it. He was convicted of murder, serving ten years in prison before being pardoned by the governor.

Ironically, by the time the feud ended, it no longer mattered very much to anybody whether the Cameron Dam could be used to drive logs down the Thornapple. Between the time when Dietz first chased off the logging crew and the gun battle that sent him to prison, the white-pine era had ended in Wisconsin. Only in Minnesota did it linger for a little longer, as lumberjacks fanned out into less accessible regions of that state. Then the pines were gone there, too.

Now the north country is a tame and settled place, its principal cash crop no longer tall pines but summer tourists. The days when it was full of hard-working brawlers in red shirts and mackinaws are still remembered there, but year by year there are fewer who can recall that time from experience rather than hearsay.

"The interminable forests of pine" which, a Lake States congressman once said, are "sufficient to supply all the wants of the citizens for all time to come" are gone—presumably forever.

Much of that inheritance was wasted by fire or greed or human stupidity. The cutting cost lives, either from the dangers of tackling a forest giant with an axe or those involved in celebrating payday. The pine harvest founded fortunes, but the vast majority of those who did the work got little of the pay.

And yet, what a grand experience it must have been. The old-timers who are still around, the ones who got in on the tag end of it before the pine was gone, are full of stories about the hardships, the camp lice, the drunken fights, the painted ladies, the close calls, the injuries and deaths. They sit around retirement homes or in a house owned by a middle-aged son or daughter and talk about how it was, telling the familiar stories they think the visitor wants to hear.

But before the talking ends, the old man who was once young and full of ginger often gets a faraway look in his eyes. With a half-embarrassed smile, he lets you know what he misses most. It isn't the springtime sprees nor the bunkhouse lies, not even the long board table full of food when a man had a boundless appetite to do the cook justice.

The pines, that's what he remembers best. The lordly pines.

Youth goes. Hungers go. Muscles, once like steel, grow flabby. But the memory of what it was like in the hush before dawn, with the branches blocking out the stars and the forest waiting for the axe, that remains.

PHOTO BY JAMES N. MEYER

Robert W. Wells, who retired as book editor of *The Milwaukee Journal* in June of 1984, is the author of 16 books and numerous short stories and articles for major magazines. His books include *Fire at Peshtigo,* an account of the deadliest forest fire in United States history; *Vince Lombardi: His Life and Times,* a biography of the legendary football coach; *Mean on Sunday,* the story of middle linebacker Ray Nitschke of the Green Bay Packers; and *This Is Milwaukee,* a humorous history of the city where Wells spent 37 of his 42 years in the newspaper business. He is also the author of a series of sports novels for teen-agers and a biography of General Anthony "Mad Anthony" Wayne.

Wells is a native of Ohio and, after graduating from Ohio State University in 1940, worked for three Ohio newspapers—the Columbus *Dispatch,* the Warren *Tribune-Chronicle,* and the Canton *Repository.* After two years in the Navy during World War II, where he was an ensign on a destroyer escort in the Pacific, he joined the staff of *The Milwaukee Journal.* He was a reporter, rewrite man, assistant city editor, New York correspondent, and columnist before taking over the book editor's post.

In his spare time, Wells has been a prolific writer for such magazines as *McCall's, Saturday Evening Post, Reader's Digest, Ladies Home Journal, Atlantic,* and *Harper's.* Several of his short stories have been adapted for radio and television, and a number are reprinted in anthologies.

Wells and his wife, Edith, now live in a 130-year-old stone house near Cedarburg, Wisconsin. They have three grown children, a daughter and two sons. Wells has a third son by a previous marriage.

Also from NORTHWORD INC

ALL-SEASON GUIDE TO WISCONSIN'S PARKS
Jim Umhoefer
"There are more than 70 state parks, forests, and trails in Wisconsin, and author Jim Umhoefer has visited them all. The guide is useful, informative, fun to read, and suited to all seasons, melding together commentary, maps, and photos. A browse through the book reveals the state's highest falls, best fishing holes—enjoyable regions to spend a few days. Bikers will find indispensable maps of the state's bike trails; hikers, campers, picnickers, vacationers, and anyone wanting to be outside will find this guide more than worth their money."—*Wisconsin Trails*
$9.95 • 8½ × 11, 80 pages, paper • ISBN 0-942802-00-4

ALL-SEASON GUIDE TO MINNESOTA'S PARKS
Jim Umhoefer
"To assemble this information-rich guidebook, Jim Umhoefer traveled 12,000 miles in Minnesota. He camped, hiked, biked, backpacked, swam, canoed, sledded, skied and snowmobiled in discovering his adopted state. His book captures that intimacy, revealing little details and recounting anecdotes that underscore the charm of Minnesota's lakes, streams and forests. In Itasca State Park, for example, he pinpoints the bison kill site, locates bald eagles' nesting spots, and shows sunset fanciers where to watch the sun disappear as the haunting melody of loons drifts across the lake."—*The Milwaukee Journal*
$9.95 • 8½ × 11, 104 pages, paper • ISBN 0-942802-06-3

CALKED BOOTS & CANT HOOKS
George Corrigan
Through Corrigan's eyes you can follow the evolution of the logging industry from horses to tractors and from cross-cuts to chain saws. Having worked dozens of woods' jobs, he describes the evolution with detail and accuracy as well as compassion. He loved the woods and the assortment of people who worked with him. With an ear for language, he has captured the character of the lumberjack.
$11.95 • 6 × 9, 288 pages, paper • ISBN 0-942802-14-4

FIRE & ICE
Don Davenport and Robert W. Wells
Combines two deadly disaster epics under one cover. "These are shocking tales of nature's fury: the 1958 killer storm that sent the big ore carrier *Carl D. Bradley* bubbling to the bottom of Lake Michigan, and the 1871 holocaust that charred bodies and blackened the landscape in Peshtigo, Wisconsin, the most disastrous fire in American history.

"*Shipwreck on Lake Michigan*, by Don Davenport, a Great Lakes scholar, is the kind of story a reader can't put down. Robert Wells tells the searing story of *Fire at Peshtigo* with the sure hand of a veteran newspaperman."—*The Milwaukee Journal*
$13.95 • 5½ × 8½, 450 pages, paper • ISBN 0-942802-04-7

LUMBERJACK LINGO
L.G. Sorden & Jacque Vallier
Over 4,000 terms and phrases fill this unusual dictionary. "*It's five a.m. and the gabriel blows. The bark eaters fall out of their muzzle loaders and head for the chuck house to bolt down a pile of stovelids with lots of blackstrap, some fried murphys or Johnny cake and maybe some logging berries.*" That's the colorful language of the lumberjack. Anyone with an interest in forestry or forest industries will enjoy reading this reference work, page by page.
$9.95 • 6 × 9, 288 pages, paper • ISBN 0-942802-12-8

UP COUNTRY
To the 17th century explorers, the great wilderness surrounding the Great Lakes was known simply as the "*Upper Country*". *Up Country*, a compilation of journals, letters, and memoirs is a book of firsthand experiences, offering pure impressions of primeval landscapes and of initial contacts between the European explorers and Native Americans. Edited by William Seno.
$11.95 • 6 × 9, 242 pages, paper • ISBN 0-933437-00-5

To receive our free color catalog or order any of these books call toll free 1-800-336-5666 (in Wisconsin 1-800-922-2460). NorthWord Inc., Box 128, Ashland, WI 54806.